Knowing
the Bible
101

Bruce BICKEL
&
Stan JANTZ

HARVEST HOUSE™ PUBLISHERS

EUGENE, OREGON

Cover design by Left Coast Design, Portland, Oregon

KNOWING THE BIBLE 101
Formerly titled *Bruce & Stan's® Guide to the Bible*
Copyright © 1998 by Bruce Bickel and Stan Jantz
Published by Harvest House Publishers
Eugene, Oregon 97402
www.harvesthousepublishers.com

Library of Congress Cataloging-in-Publication Data
Bickel, Bruce, 1952–
    Knowing the Bible 101 / Bruce Bickel and Stan Jantz.
        p. cm. — (Christianity 101®)
Includes bibliographical references and index.
    ISBN 978-0-7369-1261-7 (pbk.)
    1. Bible—Introduction. I. Title: Knowing the Bible one hundred one. II. Title: Knowing the Bible one hundred and one. III. Jantz, Stan, 1952–   IV. Title. V. Series.
    BS475.3.B53 2003
    220.6'1—dc21   2003004368

Printed in the United States of America

12   13   14   15   / BP-CF /   22   21   20   19

Contents

A Note from the Authors

After we wrote a book entitled *Bruce & Stan's Guide to God*, one reviewer said that we brought the subject of God "down from the monastery to the mall." We took that as a compliment. After all, it was our purpose to show that you can learn about God without being fluent in ancient Hebrew dialects and without a seminary degree. God isn't trying to hide Himself from you. Just the opposite. He can be easily found if you know where to look. Don't be intimidated. If two ordinary guys like us can explain these things, you can understand them.

We feel the same way about the Bible. It is a treasure waiting to be discovered, but many people are afraid to look into it. A 1996 survey by the Barna Group found that the average American owns, respects, and swears allegiance to the Bible, but doesn't read it. Eighty percent of the respondents said they consider the Bible to be the most influential book in human history. More than 90 percent of households surveyed owned a Bible (and 75 percent owned more than one), but nearly half said they never or only rarely read it. Why? Well, one so-called expert explained this disparity by explaining that the Bible is difficult to study. We disagree.

We wholeheartedly believe that the Bible is God's personal message to each and every one of us. God has preserved and protected His Word through the ages so that it is available and understandable to us. Not only is it in a language you can understand, but you can find it in the book racks at the grocery store, on the Internet, or in a recorded format.

With the able assistance of our editor, David Kopp, and with insights borrowed from Christian stalwarts (like Billy Graham, R. C. Sproul, Josh McDowell, Henrietta Mears, and others), we have written this book to show you that:

- The Bible is easily understood once you see the big picture and get past all of the "thees" and "thous" and bizarre names.

- The Bible contains eternal, universal truths which are relevant to you and the personal circumstances of your life.

- You can connect with God by reading the Bible.

Our motivation in writing this book is to encourage your personal exploration of God's message to you in the Bible. Our excitement for your spiritual journey is tempered with this one word of caution: You'll find a lot of great Christian books in the marketplace (including ours). These books can be a *supplement* to reading the Bible. But no book should be a *substitute* for reading the Bible.

We sincerely hope and pray that *Knowing the Bible 101* gets you excited about reading God's Word to see what He has to say to you.

Introduction

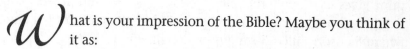hat is your impression of the Bible? Maybe you think of it as:

- An emotional antacid tablet—you read it only when your life has your stomach tied in knots.

- A sleeping tablet—you pull it out from the nightstand as a sure cure for insomnia.

- An "eternal life" insurance policy—you haven't read the fine print, but you are hoping that mere ownership of it protects you in the event of death. (Come to think of it, maybe you are relying on it more like eternal fire insurance.)

- A holy book reserved for monks and religious gurus.

- A storybook filled with fables and fairy tales (or whatever category fits angels and demons).

- Ancient wisdom literature pertinent to some bygone culture but irrelevant for today.

- God's holy words buried in a sacred text which can only be understood by a pastor or church leader.

- A book you know you should read, but...

Whatever your opinion of the Bible, we know that you are interested in finding out more about it (or else you would be reading some other book). We applaud your interest in the Bible, whether you approach the subject as a skeptic, a seeker, or a scholar. After all, the Bible is the bestselling book of all time (with about 6 billion copies printed, and that's not even counting those early editions in scrolls and stone tablets). You *should* know more about the Bible, which is why we've written this book: to help you know more.

What You'll Find Inside

Some of the books written about the Bible are more confusing than the Bible itself. We've read quite a few of them, and the tiny print gives us a headache. Our approach is a little different. We won't get hung up on minuscule details like the name of the city where Samson killed 30 men, or the size of a "homer," or the name of the guy who fell out a window when he went to sleep during a sermon (although we know this stuff: Ashkelon, about 90 gallons, and Eutychus). This isn't that kind of book. Instead, we'll focus on:

- *An Overview.* We'll show you how the whole Bible fits together. Although it consists of 66 books, written by about 40 different authors over 1500 years, all of the Bible stories and lessons fit together like a jigsaw puzzle. We'll help you fit the puzzle pieces together so you can see the big picture.

- *The Basics.* We'll keep it simple. There will be no fancy the-ological terminology thrown in to impress you. Oh, sure, every once in a while we'll use some technical jargon, but we will always explain it with words that we can spell. We'll give you the major themes, characters, stories, and lessons. But we stay away from the theological brain-teasers.

- *The Relevant.* If the Bible wasn't relevant, we wouldn't be writing this book (and we wouldn't expect you to be reading it). Its timeless truths are applicable in your relationships with your family, your friends, and your ene-mies. They apply in the classroom and the boardroom, in the backyard or the prison yard. We'll be sure to direct your attention to ways you can apply the Bible to your daily life.

- *The Personal.* We'll show you how the Bible was written by God *for* you and *to* you. The Bible has answers for your questions. It has solutions for your problems, your emo-tions, your hopes, your fears...you'll see why we say, "The Bible is all about you!"

Why You Need to Read This Book

The Bible claims to be the very words of God. It claims to teach us the truth about God. It claims that if you don't know God, you are doomed, but you can be rescued if you establish a personal rela-tionship with God. The Bible boldly promises hope and peace if you follow its teachings, and promises hardship and despair if you ignore its truth.

If you believe the claims of the Bible, then you will want to get serious about reading it. If you are skeptical, then you will want to read the Bible to determine for yourself whether its claims are true. Either way, it's a good idea to read and understand it.

We'll admit that we're prejudiced on this subject. We believe what the Bible says. We have found it true in history, science, logic, and most importantly, in our own lives. But we respect your ability to decide for yourself. So, we won't be doing any heavy-handed preaching. We'll point you to what the Bible says, and we'll let you be responsible for your own response.

This Book Is for You If...

- You have never read the Bible and don't know anything about it. But you are curious and interested in checking the whole thing out.

- You have had religion crammed down your throat by some Bible-thumpers. You want to investigate the Bible at your own speed and in your own manner without any hard sell.

- You have had some exposure to the stories of the Bible, but it seems that they were sweet stories for little kids. You are now interested in seeing whether (and how) the Bible relates to real life.

- You are struggling in your life. Maybe you're going through tough times with your parents, your kids, or your spouse. You might have health problems, trouble at school or on the job, or maybe you are struggling financially. You are getting desperate for help, but the answers you are getting seem shallow and useless. You want to turn to God for help and answers, and the Bible seems like the way to do it.

- You have recently had a life-changing encounter with God. You are serious about getting to know Him better. You know the Bible is the place to get started, but you don't know how to start.

- Your faith in God is strong, and you have a working knowledge of key verses and passages in the Bible. But you are still not sure how it all fits together, and you could use a review of the basics.

- You stand firm in your relationship with God, and you would like to explain the Bible to others. But you are having difficulty in figuring out how to present an overview of the Bible in plain, nontechnical language.

If you find yourself in any one of these categories, we think you'll benefit from *Knowing the Bible 101*.

How to Use This Book

We didn't write this book in one sitting, and we don't expect that you'll read it from page 1 to the end without a few breaks. In fact, you may not even want to read the chapters in order. No problem. Chapters 4 through 11 cover the books of the Bible in their sequential order, but you may want to skip around to parts that are of particular interest to you. Here are a few other suggestions that should add to your use of this book.

1. Read the real thing. Since this is a book about the Bible, we'll direct you to important verses and passages from the Bible. Some of them we'll print, and we'll tell you where to find others in the Bible so you can read them for yourself. Nothing can substitute for reading God's Word directly. In chapters 4 through 11, when we cover the books of the Bible, we'll give you a "Cram Plan," which lists the important passages covered by that chapter. We're the first to admit that some Bible passages are a little more exciting or inspiring than others. If you are a first-time Bible reader, the "Cram Plan" will give you a good overview.

2. Get in group discussions. We hope this book stimulates you to discuss the subject of the Bible with other people. Share with someone else what you have learned. Get your questions answered. At the end of each chapter, we have included a list of study questions to help you apply what you know to your life. Of course, you can read and think about these questions if you are studying this book alone, but the questions are designed for groups that are using this book as a study guide to the Bible.

3. Use the index and our appendix. If you have a Bible subject (person, place, principle) that is of particular interest to you, look it up in the index. And don't forget to look at our appendix. We included some charts and lists that we think you will find particularly helpful in using the Bible in your everyday life.

4. Visit with us online. We have put together an interactive online resource exclusively for readers of *Knowing the Bible 101*. All you have to do is click on www.christianity101online.com. There you will find a number of features designed to help you learn even more about God, His Word, and His world. See the details at the back of this book.

If you have a question or a comment, you can contact us through this online resource. Or you can email us directly at info@twelvetwomedia.com.

Or if you are a traditionalist and prefer to stick with the postal service for sentimental reasons, you can send mail to us at

Twelve Two Media
P.O. Box 25997
Fresno, CA 93729

A Final Comment Before You Get Started

If you are sincerely interested in finding out what the Bible has to offer, get ready for an adventure. The Bible is a book like no other.

> *For the word of God is full of living power. It is sharper than the sharpest knife, cutting deep into our innermost thoughts and desires. It exposes us for what we really are* (Hebrews 4:12).

Part I
God's Message for You

*C*hapter 1

Millions of people today are searching for a reliable voice of authority. The Word of God is the only real authority we have. His Word sheds light on human nature, world problems, and human suffering. But beyond that, it clearly reveals the way to God.

The message of the Bible is the message of Jesus Christ who said, "I am the way, the truth, and the life" (John 14:6). It is the story of salvation; the story of your redemption and mine through Christ; the story of life, of peace, of eternity.

Our faith is not dependent upon human knowledge and scientific advance, but upon the unmistakable message of the Word of God.

Billy Graham

Someone may tell you the Bible is the most amazing book ever written, but discovering that for yourself is quite another thing. In this section, we are going to give you reasons why the Bible is both amazing and important—and we're going to show you why you can trust the Bible completely. This is crucial because as you read the Bible for yourself, you're going to eventually ask a very big question: Is this stuff really true? And whether your answer is yes, no, or maybe, another even bigger question will follow right behind: What does it mean for me?

The Bible:
Anatomy of the World's Bestseller

*W*hat's *A*head

- [ ] What Makes the Bible So Popular?
- [ ] How Do We Know the Bible Is the Word of God?
- [ ] Why God Chose Words Over Angels
- [ ] Here's How God Did It
- [ ] It's Greek to Me (But for a Reason)
- [ ] From Stone Tablets to the Internet
- [ ] Can Translations Be Trusted?
- [ ] Bible Warriors

*Y*ou've seen it around for as long as you can remember. That black book with the word "holy" on the cover, the one people swear on when they are asked to tell the truth, the book TV preachers hold up and wave around.

It's the Bible, of course. You probably have a Bible somewhere close by. Maybe you've read parts of it, but you can't remember the last time you opened it. Was it at confirmation class? Was it in that hotel room? And didn't it have all of those "thees" and "thous" in it? And really, how can such an old book be relevant to you now?

How do you feel about the Bible? Are you curious? Intimidated? Since you're reading this book, we'll take a shot and say you're at least *interested* and want to know more. You may even be eager to learn just exactly what the Bible has in store for you.

Where you are coming from doesn't really matter. What counts is where you're going. The fact that you have chosen to read a book about the greatest book ever indicates that you care about your life: how you got here, where you're going, and how you live your life every day in between.

We think that when you finish this book, and (more importantly) when you begin to read the Bible for yourself, you're going to be a different person. And you're going to discover that the Bible will put you in touch with God Himself.

Why I'm Interested in the Bible

Now would be a great time to list your reasons for reading the Bible (might as well be stunningly honest).

_____

_____

_____

_____

You're not alone in your search to find out more about the Bible. The fact of the matter is that the Bible is the bestselling book in the world! No one knows how many people throughout history have actually read the Bible or a portion of the Bible, but we do know that since the invention of the printing press in 1455, more than *6 billion* copies of the Bible have been printed in more than 2000 languages. That means that billions of people in every corner of the world have read at least a portion of the Bible. The Bible has no rival when it comes to popularity.

What Makes the Bible So Popular?

Reading the Bible is unlike any other reading experience. In fact, the Bible is many kinds of books in one:

The Bible is a great story. It's the story of God and man from Creation to the end of the world. The Bible contains hundreds of unforgettable dramas involving nations, families, and individuals. And think of all those Sunday school stories about giants and whales and lovers and dead men rising from the grave....

The Bible is a great literary achievement. The Bible is considered the greatest piece of literature ever written. The Bible contains virtually every type of literary style: drama, historical narrative, instruction, even poetry. The plots, characters, and settings are timeless. The quality of writing is unparalleled.

The Bible is a great history book. The Bible has been proven to be totally accurate in its portrayal of historical events. No other book of antiquity has survived to the present with such integrity.

The Bible is a great book of prophecy. No other book even comes close to predicting the future in such detail and with such amazing accuracy.

The Bible is a great holy book. More than any other holy book in the world, the Bible is read by people looking for spiritual answers to their deepest questions.

Yes, the Bible contains all of these kinds of reading experiences—and more. But this is not why the Bible is read by millions of people every day. For a bigger, more important reason, the Bible is unlike any other book ever written.

The Bible Is God's Message

Here's why the Bible is so unique: *The Bible is God's revelation of Himself to people.* Theologians use a term called "divine revelation." This refers to the fact that God, who is *divine,* has *revealed* Himself to us in various ways, most directly through the Bible, which historically has been accepted by the church as the "final authority." The reason you and millions of other people want to read the Bible is because you believe it is—or might be—God's message for you.

The Bible is often called the "Good Book," and indeed it is. But the Bible is much more than a book, and it is much more than good. Here's the deal: The Bible contains the very words of God. You don't have to *wonder* about God. You can *know* about God because He has left you a message. In fact, when you read the Bible, God is talking to you.

> *You accepted what we said as the very word of God— which, of course, it was. And this word continues to work in you who believe* (1 Thessalonians 2:13).

More than just a collection of books with hard-to-pronounce names, the Bible is God's personal message to you, someone He loves very much.

How Do We Know the Bible Is the Word of God?

Good question! Because the Bible is the written Word of God, we need to know that the Bible—which we are calling God's message—has been accurately written down and copied from the ancient days to today. We don't want to guess and hope that it was correctly duplicated through the ages.

Josh McDowell, noted Bible teacher, says that only God could have created a book that

- has been transmitted accurately from the time it was originally written

- is correct when it deals with historical people and events

- contains no "scientific absurdities"

- remains true and relevant to all people for all time.

Hang on during the next few pages. Some of this stuff could get a little detailed, but you need to know why the Bible you use really is the Word of God. You will have confidence as you read the Bible, and you will also have an answer for those who doubt the authority and authenticity of the Bible.

*T*he Bible is alive, it speaks to me; it has feet, it runs after me; it has hands, it lays hold of me.

Martin Luther, sixteenth-century reformer

Why God Chose Words Over Angels

Think about this: God can communicate to the world in any way He wants. He could send an angel to everybody with a long announcement. Or interrupt your favorite TV show with an important message. Or program His message about life's meaning into your genes. Or arrange things so that if you sit cross-legged while eating Thai noodles, you would suddenly understand everything.

But despite all His options, He has chosen *written* communication as the primary means to deliver His message about the meaning of life.

God chose the written word for a simple reason: For reliability, you can't beat it. You know the drill: If you verbally tell something to someone, and that person tells someone else, you can be sure that the message will change. And the more your original message is passed from one person to another, the more it will change dramatically.

But when you write your message down and give it to someone else, you leave no question as to what you said. The *meaning* of your words may be open to interpretation (more on that

*W*hat's in a Word?

According to the dictionary, the word *word* can have several different meanings:

- *Word*—a sound that has meaning
- *Word*—a promise (as in "I give you my word")
- *Word*—the Bible, the message of the gospel
- *Word*— Jesus Christ, the *logos*, the Son of God

in chapter 2), but the *words* remain intact. That's why we still use the written word for legal contracts even though we could use much more advanced technology to record our words.

Here's How God Did It

We're going to tell you how your Bible went from God to you. This is an amazing question to ponder. Just how does God, who is a Spirit (that is, not of flesh and blood), put His words into a format that we flesh-and-blood humans can read and understand?

One of the foremost authorities on the Bible is Dr. Norman Geisler. In his textbook *A General Introduction to the Bible*, Dr. Geisler says when it comes to the Bible, there are three links in the chain from God to us: *inspiration, canonization,* and *transmission.* Studying each of these will give you greater confidence as you read your Bible.

Link #1—Inspiration: God-Breathed Words

The first link in the chain "from God to us" is *inspiration.* In chapter 3 we'll talk more about the role the Holy Spirit plays in

---

So What Do We Call It Anyway?

The word *Bible* never appears in the Bible. The word comes from the Latin word *biblia,* which means "book." Jesus often referred to the *Scriptures.* Here are some other words used to describe the Bible from Psalm 119:

The *law* of the Lord	(verse 1)
His *decrees*	(verse 2)
His *commandments*	(verse 4)
His *principles*	(verses 5 and 23)
His *commands*	(verse 47)
His *word*	(verse 105)
His *promises*	(verse 140)

helping us to *understand* God's Word. This is a present and ongoing benefit provided by the third Person in the Godhead.

In the past, however, the Holy Spirit did something critically important that made the Bible possible. God used the Holy Spirit to *inspire* 40 different writers over a period of 1500 years to write down His words.

When we get inspired, we get motivated. But in the literal sense of the word, *inspire* means "to breathe or blow into." Webster's dictionary defines *inspiration* as "a divine influence." This is also the meaning of the Greek word that is translated *inspire*. Inspiration describes the process by which God gave His message to human authors who received it and wrote it down.

> *All Scripture is inspired by God and is useful to teach us what is true and to make us realize what is wrong in our lives. It straightens us out and teaches us to do what is right* (2 Timothy 3:16).

Because of this process, you can trust the Bible completely. God, who is perfect, used a foolproof means to get His message into print. He "breathed in" what He wanted. Nothing more, nothing less.

God's breath gives life. When God breathed into the human authors, He gave *life* to His Word. God also gave life to man when He created him. The Bible says that when God formed Adam's body from the dust of the ground, He "breathed into it the breath of life." Dr. R.C. Sproul, one of our favorite Bible scholars, writes in his book *Essential Truths of the Christian Faith* that

> the Holy Spirit guided the human authors so that their words would be nothing less than the word of God. How God superintended the original writings of the Bible is not known. But inspiration does not mean that God dictated his messages to those who wrote the Bible. Rather, the Holy Spirit communicated through the human writers the very words of God.

The result was that the personalities of the authors came through without changing God's message one bit.

Link #2—Canonicity: the Words Measured Up

The second link in the chain "from God to us" is *canonicity*, which is the process by which church leaders recognized individual books of the Bible as being inspired by God. The *canon* describes which books make up the Bible we use today. The word comes from the root word *reed*, which was used as a measuring stick in ancient times.

$\mathcal{O}$ld and Scrolled

Keep in mind that Bible translators work from the most reliable (which usually means the oldest) manuscripts of the original Bible languages available. The oldest and most trusted Bible manuscripts, called the Dead Sea Scrolls, were not uncovered until 1947. Most Bible translations since then have been based on these remarkable Bible manuscripts.

When applied to Scripture, *canon* indicates the measure or the standard used to evaluate which books were *inspired* and which ones weren't. In the first centuries after Christ, several church councils met to determine which books should be included in the canon. Their main task was to evaluate books written during and after the time of Christ (the Old Testament canon had already been determined). The councils followed strict guidelines to determine which books qualified as Scripture. Dr. Geisler lists five checkpoints they used:

1. Does it speak with God's authority?

2. Is it written by a man of God speaking to us as a prophet of God?

3. Does it have the authentic stamp of God?

4. Does it impact us with the power of God?

5. Was it accepted by the people of God?

*I*nfallibility and Inerrancy

When we say that the Bible is *infallible* or *inerrant*, we mean that it is completely true. This is because God, who is the Author, is incapable of error. Dr. Sproul says that "this does not mean that the Bible translations we have today are without error, but that the original manuscripts were absolutely correct."

A key point to remember is that the canon councils did not *declare* a book to be from God. They simply *recognized* the divine authority that was already there.

Link #3—Transmission: Writer's Cramp and Beyond

Transmission is the third link in the chain "from God to us." This describes the total process of transmitting the Bible from the early writers to us today using the most practical and reliable materials available at the time.

The total *canon* of Scripture—that is, all 66 books of the Bible—was recognized as the authoritative Word of God by the fourth century A.D. After that time, the Bible had to be preserved for the future.

What About the Apocrypha?

Some Bibles—most notably the *New Jerusalem Bible*—include a section of books between the Old and New Testaments called the Apocrypha. The name itself means "hidden" or "noncanonical." Although these books have historical value, the early church fathers decided that they were not inspired. More than a thousand years later (in 1546 at the Council of Trent), the Roman Catholic Church declared the following apocryphal books to be canonical: Tobit, Judith, the Wisdom of Solomon, Ecclesiasticus, Baruch, and I and II Maccabees.

*D*etails, Details...

From earliest times, Jewish scribes had to follow detailed procedures for copying Scripture. These rules helped to ensure total concentration and accuracy. Their meticulous approach set the standard for monks and other scholars who have transcribed the Bible through the ages. Of scores of rules for scribes listed by Jewish scholar Samuel Davidson, here are three:

1. No word or letter or any other mark may be written from memory. The scribe must look directly at the original scroll for every stroke.

2. Between every letter, the space of a hair or thread must intervene.

3. Should a king address him while writing the name of God, the scribe must take no notice of him until finished.

According to Geisler, "The Scriptures had to be copied, translated, recopied, and retranslated. This process not only provided the Scriptures for other nations, but for other generations as well."

The accuracy of these copies is critical to the Bibles we currently use. Today, when someone asks you to copy a document, you simply stick it into a photocopier. No big deal. Before copiers, however, documents had to be printed on presses, and before the printing press, documents had to be copied by hand. In His providence, God chose to preserve His Word objectively through *language*.

It's Greek to Me (But for a Reason)

The two major original languages of the Bible are Hebrew (Old Testament) and Greek (New Testament). God did not choose these languages at random, but rather for specific purposes that helped transmit the Bible accurately from ancient times to today.

We take language for granted, but without it we would be hard-pressed to explain something to another person or group of people. Just try explaining the game of football to someone using only hand gestures. Language enables us to explain concepts and ideas—both real and imagined—to others. In His wisdom, God first

A Scholar Speaks Out

Some scholars are reluctant to recognize the accuracy and reliability of the Bible manuscripts because doing so means that you have to recognize the authority of God as well. Not Dr. Clark Pinnock. Here's what he wrote about the Bible:

> There exists no document from the ancient world witnessed by so excellent a set of textual and historical testimonies and offering so superb an array of historical data on which an intelligent decision may be made. An honest [person] cannot dismiss a source of this kind. Skepticism regarding the historical credentials of Christianity is based upon irrational bias.

enabled people to use language, and then He picked the best languages possible for communicating His message to us.

Hebrew

Language experts agree that Hebrew, the principal language of the Old Testament and of the Jewish (or Hebrew) people, is a *precise, pictorial,* and *personal* language. Bible scholar F. F. Bruce wrote that Hebrew is "the right sort of language for the record of the self-revelation of a God who does not make Himself known by philosophical propositions but by controlling and intervening in the course of human history."

In other words, Hebrew perfectly describes a God who is very much involved in the lives of people, especially the Hebrew people. As Geisler says, it was the ideal *biographical* language.

Greek

Greek is the primary language of the New Testament, and again, God chose Greek for a reason. For one thing, it was the language spoken by most of the world at the time of Christ. This meant that the Scriptures that were distributed to the known world after Jesus left the earth could be read by most people. Greek was the ideal language for the transmission of the gospel.

Furthermore, as Geisler says, Greek was an *intellectual* language that was perfect for the expression of the "propositional truth" of the New Testament.

You don't have to read the New Testament very long to realize that the Christian faith is a rational and reasonable faith. Greek is a language of reason. Maybe we should not be surprised that the three greatest philosophers of history—Plato, Aristotle, and Socrates—were all Greek.

---

*M*ore than 6500 languages are spoken in the world. The Bible has been translated into approximately 2400 of them.

From Stone Tablets to the Internet

Just as the two major languages of the Bible were important to its accuracy and reliability, the *materials* on which the words were recorded had to be reliable as well. Here is a list of different materials used to record the Word of God throughout history.

Clay. Used as early as 3500 B.C., clay was practical because the material could be inscribed with a *stylus* while it was still soft.

Stone. The biblical writers *chiseled* the words onto stone tablets. This stuff is pretty permanent, which is probably why God asked Moses to use it to record His law (Exodus 24:12). That was also the first portion of Scripture to go into a second printing (Exodus 32:19; 34:1).

Papyrus. This material was big in Egypt as early as 3100 B.C. Papyrus is a plant with fibers that can be pressed together to create a writing surface.

Vellum, parchment, leather. Various animal skins were popular forms of writing materials (although not as popular with the animals).

Paper. The Chinese invented paper in the second century A.D.

Computer Technology. In the twentieth century new materials have been developed which record and transmit God's Word in practical new ways, including computer discs, satellites, and the Internet.

𝒲ax-Its

During the time of Esther (479 B.C.), scribes and court officials used writing boards covered with a thin coat of wax as quick, reusable "scratch paper."

Can Translations Be Trusted?

God has carefully planned the preservation of His Word through the ages so that the Bible you have today can be trusted completely. But the Bible was originally written in Hebrew and Greek. What about all of the Bible translations in other languages? What about the English translations we read? Are they reliable? Are they accurate? Can you trust them to be the Word of God?

How Did It Happen?

The first book known to be translated into another language was the Old Testament. In the third or second century B.C., the Hebrew Old Testament was translated into Greek. This version was known as the *Septuagint,* and it stayed popular with Jews and Christians alike well into the second century A.D.

In the middle of the third century, however, Latin replaced Greek as the common language. This occurred primarily because the church, the highest authority in the world, was headquartered in Rome. In 405, Jerome finished a translation of the entire Bible into Latin called the Vulgate (which means "Common"). A thousand years or so later, some great men of God took on the daunting task of translating the Bible into English.

The problem was that the Vulgate had become so popular and so identified with the church in Rome that the idea of the Bible being in any other language than Latin was considered blasphemy. With all of the English translations available to us today, we can hardly imagine that owning an English Bible—let alone translating one—was once considered an offense punishable by death. But it's true. Hundreds of men and women gave their lives so that today we can read the Bible in English.

*B*ackup Copies

Copies of ancient Bible documents, called *manuscripts*, are so abundant and so accurate that scholars universally agree the Bible is beyond question a historically accurate document. More than 5000 Greek manuscript portions of the New Testament exist.

Bible Warriors

Here are just a few of the Bible warriors who sacrificed to give us an English Bible we can read and understand:

John Wycliffe. A scholar who taught at Oxford in England, Wycliffe provided the first complete English Bible from the Latin Vulgate in 1384. Wycliffe died of natural causes, but many of his followers, called Lollards, were persecuted and killed for possessing and believing in Wycliffe's Bible.

Martin Luther. The father of the Reformation, Martin Luther translated the Bible into German while in prison in 1522.

William Tyndale. A brilliant man educated at Oxford and Cambridge, Tyndale devoted his life to translating the Bible from the original languages into the language of the common man. His Bible, finished in 1530, had copies burned by the thousands by the king of England, and Tyndale himself was burned at the stake in 1536.

John Knox and Miles Coverdale. In 1560, Knox, a Scotsman, and Coverdale, an Englishman, produced the Geneva Bible. Also known as the "Puritan Bible," this is the Bible the Pilgrims brought to America on the Mayflower in 1620. (This Bible popu-

*I*f God spare my life, I will cause a boy that driveth the plough to know more of the Scripture than thou dost.

William Tyndale, speaking to an official of the church

larly was called the "Breeches Bible" because of the way Genesis 3:7 was translated: "They sewed figleaves together, and made themselves breeches.")

King James. By the time James I became the king of England, the English Bible had become so accepted that the king himself appointed a committee of 47 English Bible scholars to produce an "Authorized Version" of the Bible. First published in 1611, this version became commonly known as the "King James Version."

Ken Taylor. Many modern-language translations have been produced in this century, but none have matched the popularity of *The*

The Gutenberg Millennium

As recently as the fifteenth century, reproducing one copy of the Bible by hand took ten months. A single copy cost more than the average person made in a *lifetime*. All that changed when Johannes Gutenberg designed and built the first Western printing press that worked in Mainz, Germany, in 1455. The first book he printed was a copy of the Bible. Within 50 years, hundreds of Gutenberg presses produced hundreds of thousands of Bibles all over Europe. So powerful was the effect of the printing press on the world that *Life* magazine called this single achievement the most significant event of the last thousand years. On October 22, 1987, a copy of the Old Testament containing Genesis through Psalms, printed in 1455, was sold at Christie's Auction House in New York City for 5.39 million dollars.

Living Bible. Ken Taylor's greatest desire was for his children to understand the Bible, so he single-handedly took on the task of paraphrasing the Bible in a version he called *The Living Bible.* Since it was completed in 1971, more than 40 million copies have been sold.

What These Warriors Fought For

Over the centuries, many people have made great sacrifices to make the Bible available to you. But in the end, what matters more than *having* a Bible is *reading* the Bible. Remember, God has placed an incredibly high value on His Word, both written and living. The Bible tells us that God has exalted Jesus—the living Word—for all eternity (Philippians 2:9-11). The written Word of God has also been preserved for all eternity.

> *The grass withers, and the flowers fade, but the word of our God stands forever* (Isaiah 40:8).

Ever since God inspired human agents to write down His words, He has acted meticulously and miraculously to make sure that we can

- read it
- understand it
- live it

The Bible is God's message for you. And you can trust it completely.

$\mathcal{B}$illions Served

In what was perhaps the greatest broadcast of a Scripture text in history, British Prime Minister Tony Blair read 1 Corinthians 13, one of the most famous passages in the Bible, at the funeral of Princess Diana of Wales. The estimated viewing audience was 2 billion people.

What's That Again?

1. God has chosen written communication as the primary means of delivering His message to us.

2. Inspiration, canonization, and transmission are the three links in the chain from God to us.

3. God has been meticulous in preserving His Word through human language and materials.

4. Thousands of people have sacrificed their lives so that we can have a readable, trustworthy English Bible.

Dig Deeper

Here are some other resources that you might want to read if you are interested in the composition of the Bible:

A General Introduction to the Bible by Norman Geisler and William Nix. In our view, the best and most complete book on the origin and transmission of the Bible.

What the Bible Is All About by Henrietta Mears. Here is the bestselling book about the Bible (more than 4 million sold) ever written. The reason is that it's personal and readable.

A Ready Defense by Josh McDowell. The first section of this book offers a well-documented presentation on the Bible and its reliability.

The Complete Guide to Bible Versions by Philip W. Comfort. A handy (and inexpensive) guide to the major translations and versions of the Bible.

Truth and Power by J. I. Packer. Dr. Packer looks at the authority of the Bible. If you want to learn how to use, rather than abuse, your Bible, read this book.

■ □ □

$\mathcal{Q}$uestions for $\mathcal{R}$eflection and $\mathcal{D}$iscussion

1. If you have avoided reading the Bible until now, explain why. What led to your current interest in the Bible?

2. What might Josh McDowell have meant when he said the Bible contains no "scientific absurdities"?

3. Role play for a moment. Imagine the Bible is on trial, and you have been called to testify. Answer this question: How do you know the Bible is God's Word?

4. What is your favorite Bible story? If you are reading this book in a group study, be prepared to tell the story aloud to the others in your group. If you're going through this book on your own, tell your story to a friend or someone in your family.

5. Review the five strict guidelines that the church councils used to determine which books qualified as Scripture. Describe how each of these impacts you personally as you read the Bible.

6. Did you know that people were actually killed for translating the Bible so others could better understand it? How does that fact affect you as you read your own favorite Bible translation?

7. Read 2 Timothy 3:16 and Hebrews 4:12. What are your top three reasons for reading the Bible regularly?

■ □ □

Moving On...

Congratulations! You've made it through the most technical (and probably most detailed) chapter in our book. Why was all this stuff important? As you read your Bible, we want you to *know* (rather than *feel)* that you can trust your Bible completely. You can have confidence that the Bible isn't something people created out of their imaginations. It is the authoritative Word of God.

Now we're going to talk about the benefits of reading and studying the Bible. We're also going to show you how easily you can *twist* Scripture into something it's not, and how you can unknowingly follow someone who's done that. Ultimately, *your* responsibility is to know the truth of the Bible. But you're not alone. You have the *resources* you need, you can find other *people* to help you, and you have the *Holy Spirit* to guide you. So move on! This story gets better and better.

Chapter 2

Maintain at all costs a daily time
of Scripture reading and prayer. As I
look back, I see that the most formative
influence in my life and thought
has been my daily contact
with Scripture over 60 years.

Frank Gaebelein
Founding headmaster,
Stony Brook School

So far we've tried to establish why you can trust the Bible. By now you're probably wondering *how* to read the Bible. When we say *how*, we aren't talking about the mechanics of reading (as in left to right, front to back), but the proper *approach* to reading the Bible.

The Bible is a big book that could easily seem intimidating. It contains 66 books, 1189 chapters, and 33,173 verses. From Genesis to Revelation, the Bible is a true historical epic, covering a span of time from the beginning to the end of the world—and beyond. There are thousands of characters and story lines. How in the world do you get a hold on such a book?

It's easier than you think, and we'll show you how to get started.

The Bible:
The Deeper You Go...

*T*he Bible requires an activity that must take place before we can enjoy its benefits. It's called *reading*. Because God chose written language as the primary method of communicating His message to us, the Bible is, first of all, meant to be read.

We know that for some people this may be a new idea. After all, throughout history, the Bible has had a number of uses:

- The Bible looks great on a coffee table, especially when the pastor comes for a visit.

- On several documented occasions, a Bible stuffed into the breast pocket of a military jacket prevented a bullet from inflicting mortal harm to a soldier.

- Without the Bible, people in a courtroom would have to swear on a copy of Webster's dictionary.

Read to Live

The Bible is nothing more than a symbol or a prop for many people. It will become meaningful to you under one condition and one condition only: You have to *read* it. And we're not talking about reading it only on special occasions or religious holidays. If you want to experience God and enjoy spiritual results, you need to develop the reading habit.

Here's yet another way to think of it: There's never a day when you don't read your mail. You don't leave it unopened and say, "Someday, when I have time, I'm going to read my mail." You at least open your mail before the end of the day.

If your earthly mail, which is filled with so much meaningless trivia and bad news, has such a hold on your life, how much more should you be eager to read your heavenly mail each day?

Although we're going to spend quite a bit of time in this chapter talking about how to study the Bible, studying should never be a substitute for reading. Here's why. Reading is subjective. Reading is a personal thing between you and the author. Reading is intimate.

Remember, the Bible is God's message to *you*. In effect, it's a collection of letters God has written to you—and He wants you to read them.

$\mathcal{F}$ifteen Minutes a Day

If you started reading the Bible aloud, you could probably read every verse in 80 hours or less. Think about this: You could read the Bible through in two weeks if you spent eight hours a day. You could read the Bible through in a year in just 15 minutes a day.

*Y*our Letter from Home

Read the Bible not as a newspaper, but as a home letter. If a cluster of heavenly fruit hangs within reach, gather it. If a promise lies upon the page as a blank check, cash it. If a prayer is recorded, make it yours and launch it as a feathered arrow from the bow of your desire. If an example of holiness gleams before you, ask God to do as much for you. If the truth is revealed to you, ask God to make it shine through your whole life.

F.B. Meyer

Why Study the Bible?

Let's face it, studying is not the most popular activity in the world. Somehow we've come to view studying as something difficult and unpleasant. True, work is involved. But at its core, studying the Bible will produce such joy in your life that you will be eager to do it on a regular basis.

In fact, that's what the word *study* actually means: "to be eager, or diligent." Once you've gotten into the habit of reading, you need to take the next step and develop a habit of systematic study. You want to be *eager* to learn more about God's Word.

Look at the benefits:

1. You will please God. There is a direct correlation between your eagerness to study and God's approval.

> *Work hard so God can approve you. Be a good worker, one who does not need to be ashamed and who correctly explains the word of truth* (2 Timothy 2:15).

2. You will learn how to live and grow as a Christian. Just as a baby needs and craves his mother's milk, Christians (especially new Christians) must drink in the spiritual nourishment provided by God's Word.

> *You must crave pure spiritual milk so that you can grow into the fullness of your salvation. Cry out for this nourishment as a baby cries for milk* (1 Peter 2:2).

*S*cripture is like a pair of spectacles which dispels the darkness and gives us a clear view of God.

John Calvin

3. You will develop spiritual discernment. The only way to know if others are speaking the truth is to know the truth yourself. When the apostle Paul stopped at a church in Berea, he found believers there studying diligently.

And the people of Berea were more open-minded than those in Thessalonica, and they listened eagerly to Paul's message. They searched the Scriptures day after day to check up on Paul and Silas, to see if they were really teaching the truth (Acts 17:11).

Sweet to the Taste

King David was so in love with God's Word that he could literally taste it: "How sweet are your words to my taste; they are sweeter than honey" (Psalm 119:103). The prophet Jeremiah wrote that the Word of God sustained his life (Jeremiah 15:16).

Sound crazy? Not in the least. In addition to merely reading the Bible regularly (like we would the newspaper), we can really take it in—and let it change our lives. Try these three ways:

- *Study*—Make an effort to learn God's Word (2 Timothy 2:15).

- *Meditate*—Think deeply about God's Word (Psalm 1:2).

- *Memorize*—Be ready to recall God's Word (Psalm 119:11).

4. You will be able to answer the questions of others. Studying the Bible will help you give clear answers to those who ask you about your faith.

> *And if you are asked about your Christian hope, always be ready to explain it* (1 Peter 3:15).

How Do You Interpret the Bible?

The most valuable thing you can do as you read and study the Bible is to *bring out the meaning*. This is also known as *interpretation*. When you interpret something, you make it plain and understandable. Remember what we said in the last chapter about the value of writing something down? There's no mistaking your words. Your *meaning*, however, is a different matter. Any written document—a letter, a novel, a contract—needs to be interpreted if it is to be understood.

The goal of interpreting the Bible should be to apply the meaning of what you learn to your life. As James says, it doesn't do much good to hear (or read, or study) God's message if you don't do anything about it.

> *And remember, it is a message to obey, not just to listen to. If you don't obey, you are only fooling yourself* (James 1:22).

A Few Basic Principles of Interpretation

R. C. Sproul lists three important principles for making the Bible plain and understandable.

1. Interpret the Bible by the Bible. "What is obscure in one part of Scripture may be made clear in another," writes Sproul. "To interpret Scripture by Scripture means that we must not set one passage of Scripture against another passage." This also means that you always read Bible verses and passages *in context*.

Context is a lot like *character*. Just like it's tempting to jump on a rumor about someone even if it's totally out of character, it's tempting to take something in the Bible out of context. In both cases, all that does is make you feel better, even if you're wrong. Here's a guideline:

> When it comes to *people,* consider the *character.*
> When it comes to *Scripture,* consider the *context.*

2. Interpret the Bible literally. What this means is that you should interpret the Bible *as it is written.* Don't read into it something that isn't there, and don't skip over something that is. Because the Bible speaks honestly about the human condition, we sometimes get offended by what we read in the Bible. We would rather *deny* what the Bible says than *deal* with what the Bible says.

*G*ood Form

Interpreting the Bible literally doesn't mean that you read each Bible passage the same way. It's important to know what kind of *literary form* you are reading. The Bible contains historical narratives (or stories), poetry, parables, prophecies, and teaching.

3. Interpret the Bible objectively. It's easy to interpret the Bible subjectively, according to our own viewpoints and desires. This is where people can get into serious disagreements, both with the Bible and with each other. As you read and study the Bible, focus on what it says rather than on what you already believe. As one Bible scholar wrote: "One must first ask what a given Scripture was intended to mean to the people for whom it was originally written. Only then is the interpreter free to ask what meaning it has for Christians today."

Avoid the temptation to stamp your own impressions or feelings on Scripture before you discover the objective truth it contains. Let's say Bruce made a statement regarding an area of law in which he was an authority. But Stan disagreed—not because he knew the law, but because he didn't "feel" it applied to him. Stan's viewpoint would be subjective (and probably wrong), which would prompt Bruce to say, "It's your right as an American to feel that way, but you are wrong."

This doesn't mean that you shouldn't come to your own conclusions about what the Bible means. You aren't obligated to follow someone else's viewpoint. However, your own "private interpretation" will only be meaningful with the guidance of the Holy Spirit combined with your own diligent study. Remember that the Bible bears the authority of God. Trust God's Word to mean what it says.

By following these principles, you will become a person who "correctly explains the word of truth" (2 Timothy 2:15).

Watch Out for Twisted Scripture

The reason it's so important to handle Scripture correctly is that it's the only way God has chosen to speak *directly* to us. That's not to say that God doesn't speak to you *indirectly*. He can and does—through your circumstances, through wise people, and through your own inner sensitivity to the Holy Spirit.

But when you interpret Scripture to fit your own desires and preconceived ideas, you just might change it from truth to error. When you change the Bible's objective truth to fit your life rather than changing your life to fit the Bible, you run the risk of "twisting Scripture."

How to Spot Twisted Scripture

"Scripture twisting" refers to what happens when people interpret the Bible to suit their own false beliefs. The apostle Paul

Cults at Your Door

The difference between a cult and a religion is that the major teachings of a cult come out of someone's false interpretation of the Bible whereas a religion is defined more broadly as any system of faith and worship. The major cults in the world today (these are the ones you will probably encounter) are Jehovah's Witnesses, Mormonism, Christian Science, and the Unification Church.

confronted members of the Galatian church, who were following a "different way."

> *I am shocked that you are turning away so soon from God, who in his love and mercy called you to share the eternal life he gives through Christ. You are already following a different way that pretends to be the Good News but is not the Good News at all. You are being fooled by those who twist and change the truth concerning Christ* (Galatians 1:6-7).

Sometimes entire belief systems will come from people who "change the truth." If such people organize and begin teaching others their beliefs, we can correctly call them a "cult." Josh McDowell defines a cult as "a perversion, a distortion of biblical Christianity." At its core, a cult "rejects the historic teachings of the Christian Church."

I f you believe what you like in the Gospel and reject what you do not like, it is not the Gospel you believe, but yourself.

Augustine

How to Spot a Counterfeit

Think about counterfeit money. A good counterfeit bill is one that looks exactly like the real thing. Do you know how the experts learn to tell the phony bills from the genuine article? They don't study the counterfeit bills (there are too many variations to keep track). They study the real thing (there is only one). Bank tellers are great at spotting counterfeit money because they *handle* the real bills all day long.

Do you think Satan and his demons know the Bible? Absolutely. Better than you do. We sometimes refer to Satan as the "prince of darkness," and that he is. But he's also known as the "angel of light." Satan and his servants work by sneaking up on you with something that looks like the truth. But it's a lie.

> *These people are false apostles. They have fooled you by disguising themselves as apostles of Christ. But I am not*

surprised! Even Satan can disguise himself as an angel of light. So it is no wonder his servants can also do it by pretending to be godly ministers. In the end they will get every bit of punishment their wicked deeds deserve (2 Corinthians 11:13-15).

If you want to get good at spotting false teachings—if you want to develop your spiritual discernment—then spend time with the real deal. Learn to correctly handle the Word of Truth (2 Timothy 2:15). Then, like the Bereans who checked out Paul, you will be able to see if the people you hear or the books you read are "really teaching the truth" (Acts 17:11).

---

*T*he devil can cite Scripture for his purpose.

William Shakespeare

Get Alone—and Get a Group

Studying the Bible on your own is an important and practical way to approach Bible study. You can set your own schedule and read and study in your own room.

What counts to God is your *heart*. This prayer of King David should be our prayer every time we approach God's Word:

Create in me a clean heart, O God. Renew a right spirit within me (Psalm 51:10).

As you study alone, you could do one of the following:

- Follow a self-study guide through a particular Bible book.
- Explore a topic using various Bible-study resources.
- Study groups of Bible books, such as the Gospels.

What If You Just Don't Get It?

Just because you pray for guidance and study hard doesn't mean you are going to understand everything in the Bible. Since the Bible is God's Word, and because there are things about God that are a mystery, it is inevitable that there will be things in Scripture that you don't understand. This doesn't make them wrong, and it doesn't mean that God has made a mistake.

Think of it this way. God is an infinite being. We are mere finite mortals. Likewise, God's Word is eternal (Isaiah 40:8), and our minds, even when we fix our minds on heavenly and eternal things, are still limited.

Rather than concentrate on what we don't know, we need to value and obey those things God has revealed to us, especially the truths in His Word.

> *There are secret things that belong to the LORD our God, but the revealed things belong to us and our descendants forever, so that we may obey these words of the law* (Deuteronomy 29:29).

The Advantages of a Group

In addition to studying on your own, we advise that you also participate in a *group* Bible study on a regular basis. It could be

What About Bible Difficulties and Weird Stuff?

There are things about God and the Bible that will take time to understand (we'll talk about some Bible "difficulties" as we get into the Bible books). Be confident in knowing that as you carefully study God's Word, He will be faithful to reveal answers to you through the Holy Spirit (1 Corinthians 2:12-16). But don't expect to grow in your understanding of Scripture if you don't spend any time with it.

On the other hand, don't expect to know everything about God and the Bible. You can't. God is simply too vast for you to know everything. Trust God that He will show you what you need to know when you need to know it.

once a month or once a week. Again, the goal should be consistency.

When you're a part of a group Bible study, you have the advantage of learning and gaining insights from other people. Getting together with others who are eager to study God's Word can create a kind of *synergism* (the whole is greater than the sum of the individual parts). Plus, you can be an encouragement to others, and there may be times when you need encouragement yourself.

Do's and Don'ts of Group Bible Studies

Do study on your own before you meet with your group.

Don't show up without first doing your homework, depending on the Lord to "speak to you" with profound truth. God gets the credit for too many dumb ideas.

Do feel free to disagree with someone else's interpretation of a particular verse or Bible passage.

Don't intimidate or make other people feel inferior. Disagree in love and with diplomacy. And don't dominate the conversation when you're in a group. Remember, your own voice sounds better to you than to other people.

Do be honest as you share your questions or confusion.

Don't go for "shock value." Be sensitive to your group as you open up.

Ways to Get Involved in a Group Bible Study

- Meet with an existing organization, such as Bible Study Fellowship or a Sunday school class.

- Help organize a home Bible study where you meet with friends in various home locations.

- Volunteer to *disciple* someone else one-to-one (a disciple is a *learner*). There are some excellent materials available for this, most notably the "Operation Timothy" study guides.
- You may want to be discipled yourself. Seek out someone who knows more about the Bible than you do and whose life demonstrates the kind of Christlike qualities you want in your own life.

Seekers Wanted

Does everyone in a group Bible study need to be a Christian? That's up to you, but our suggestion is that you include seekers who really want to learn what the Bible has to say. In this way a Bible study can be a means of telling others about the good news of the Bible.

Begin to Build a Bible Study Library

The more you study the Bible, the more you will want to use some Bible study resources. At the end of each chapter of this book, we give you a short bibliography of recommended books and other resources.

Right now we want to give you some *categories* of Bible study resources that you will want to begin adding to your personal library. These are listed in a kind of priority order. The best place to purchase these types of materials is at your local Christian retail store. You can also find these materials in your church library.

Bible concordance. A concordance lists the words found in the Bible and tells you which verses in the Bible contain each word. An *exhaustive* concordance will list every word (except *and, a, an,* and *the*) and then give you the original Hebrew (if the word is found in the Old Testament) or Greek (if the word is found in the New Testament) meaning of the word. The original meanings of words can provide amazing insight into your Bible study. The concordance found at the end of some Bibles will simply tell you where to find certain key words.

Bible dictionary. Like a Webster's dictionary, a Bible dictionary will give meanings and, in some cases, the history of significant Bible words, people, and places.

Bible handbook. Books of this type provide a basic overview of the Bible and a book-by-book synopsis of all 66 books.

Bible commentary. You can get commentaries for each book of the Bible, but we suggest you start by adding a single-volume Bible commentary to your library. It can help you with the background of the Bible, as well as provide insights when you study a particular word, verse, passage, chapter, or book in the Bible.

Which Bible Is Right for You?

Choosing a Bible to read and study can be confusing. You'll find dozens of different Bible translations (or versions) available in English. Which one is the best?

Actually, there is no "best" Bible, although there may be a Bible that's best for you. Don't be concerned that you are going to end up with a "bad" Bible translation. "Translating" simply means changing from one language to another. Where different Bible versions may differ is in the *method* used to translate them.

Here are some examples of popular Bibles that were translated according to three different methods:

Word for word. This approach, technically called literal, or *complete equivalence,* translates each word of the Hebrew and Greek as closely as possible in order to keep the meaning and structure of the original language. These translations are generally more difficult to read because they often use long sentences and complicated grammar.

King James Version (KJV)
New King James Version (NKJV)
New American Standard Bible (NASB)
New Revised Standard Version (NRSV)

Thought for thought. This approach, technically called *dynamic equivalence,* focuses more on ideas than word-for-word translation. The emphasis in these Bibles is on translating the Hebrew and Greek into contemporary English "idioms," or concepts, while keeping the original meaning.

Today's English Version (TEV)
New International Version (NIV)
Contemporary English Version (CEV)
New Living Translation (NLT)

Paraphrase. This approach simplifies or expands the author's words to make the Bible easier to understand. A paraphrase is not a translation in the literal sense.

The Living Bible
The Message

Take a Test Drive

With a car, there's no substitute for getting behind the wheel. When it comes to a Bible, a test drive involves reading it for yourself. Have some favorite verses picked out in advance so that you can read them in different translations when you get to the Christian bookstore. For example, here's Psalm 1:1 in three different translations:

> *Blessed is the man that walketh not in the counsel of the ungodly, nor standeth in the way of sinners, nor sitteth in the seat of the scornful—* Kings James Version.

> *Blessed is the man who does not walk in the counsel of the wicked or stand in the way of sinners or sit in the seat of mockers—*New International Version.

> *Oh, the joys of those who do not follow the advice of the wicked, or stand around with sinners, or join in with scoffers—*New Living Translation.

*G*od used the scriptural Gospel to bring me to saving faith in Jesus Christ. He has also convinced me that the Scriptures are utterly true, inerrant, if you will; they are the "swaddling clothes in which Christ is laid." Some will call this conviction hopelessly naïve or a refusal to look at the findings of twentieth-century science. So be it. If the scientist is our authority, ask him if dead men rise.

Karl Barth, twentieth-century theologian

Once you've decided which Bible translation you want, you will need to select your *options*. Here's a handy checklist:

❐ Text Only   ❐ Cross-References
❐ Concordance   ❐ Study Notes
❐ Hardback   ❐ Leather Cover
❐ Small Print   ❐ Medium Print   ❐ Large Print

Keep in mind that your options will affect the size of your Bible.

Fortunately, the Bible publishers have come up with some wonderful Bible packages which provide practical features helpful in your Bible study. Our personal favorite is the *Life Application Bible* (a type of study Bible which includes thousands of helpful notes, references, and personal applications) in the *New Living Translation* (the translation we are using in this book). Most study Bibles are available in a variety of translations.

You Have All the Help You Need

There's no question that the Bible has a lot of words (773,692 in the King James Version). But it doesn't have to be intimidating. God wants to talk to you through His Word, regardless of where you are in your spiritual journey:

• searching but skeptical
• exploring with an open mind
• interested but ignorant
• eager for more

And all you have to do is begin reading with a sincere desire to learn.

When you begin to search for God through His Word, He will meet you where you are. He has promised...

> *"If you look for me in earnest, you will find me when you seek me. I will be found by you,"* says the LORD (Jeremiah 29:13-14).

What's That Again?

1. Because reading is a personal thing between you and the author, reading the Bible should be your first priority.

2. Studying the Bible offers many benefits, not the least of which is that it pleases God.

3. When you interpret the Bible, you bring out the meaning.

4. When people interpret the Bible to suit their own false beliefs, they are engaging in Scripture twisting.

5. Satan and his followers are very good at creating counterfeit beliefs.

6. Group Bible studies give you the advantage of learning and gaining insights from other people.

7. There is no "best" Bible, but there is probably a Bible which is best for you.

Dig Deeper

Here are some great books that explain how to read and study the Bible:

Living by the Book by Howard Hendricks and William Hendricks. With wit and wisdom, legendary Bible teacher Howard Hendricks and his son, William, tell you how to study the Bible so it will affect your life.

How to Read the Bible for All Its Worth by Gordon Fee and Douglas Stuart. This very popular book is a step-by-step guide to understanding the Bible.

How to Study Your Bible by Kay Arthur. The founder and president of Precept Ministries shows you how to study the Bible *inductively*, which means directly interacting with God's Word.

735 Baffling Bible Questions Answered by Larry Richards. If you've got questions about the Bible, Dr. Richards has the answers. A great resource.

Unmasking the Cults by Alan W. Gomes. An inexpensive booklet which gives you the characteristics of a cult.

■ ■ ■

*Q*uestions for *R*eflection and *D*iscussion

1. You've read the benefits of reading the Bible. What influences keep you from reading and studying the Bible on a regular basis? What can you do to overcome them?

2. How can R.C. Sproul's three principles of interpretation help you get more out of your Bible reading? Give one benefit for each principle.

3. Have you ever "twisted" Scripture to suit your own false beliefs? Have you ever twisted Scripture to justify your own wrong behavior? What happened, and how did you straighten out?

4. List three things you can do—starting immediately—to correctly handle the Word of truth (hint: quick fixes and magic formulas won't work).

5. Does anything in the Bible really bother you? What is it? (Don't be afraid to be honest. God isn't going to hit you with a bolt of lightning.) What are three practical things you can do deal with your dilemma?

6. Can people who disagree with each other's interpretation of a particular Bible verse or passage still get along? Is "agreeing to disagree" always enough when interpretations differ?

7. Review the two different methods of Bible translation (word for word, thought for thought) and Bible paraphrasing. Is your Bible a paraphrase, a word-for-word translation, or a thought-for-thought translation? How did you happen to choose your Bible? Is reading and studying from more than one Bible translation a good idea? Why or why not?

■ ■ ■

Moving On...

We hope that you're getting the idea that the Bible is a very personal thing between you and God. The more you read and study the Bible, the more you're going to know about God. And the more you know about God, the more you're going to love Him.

In the next chapter, we're going to show you how the Bible is arranged, and then we're going to do something a little daring. We're going to give you the story of the Bible in 22 minutes. Frederick Buechner wrote that the Bible is "a book with a plot and a plot that can be readily stated." Well, we're going to state the plot for you. The idea is to give you a view of the forest before we tackle the trees in Parts II and III.

*C*hapter 3

Preparing for a long trip, a traveler said to his friend: "I am just about packed. I only have to put in a guidebook, a lamp, a mirror, a microscope, a telescope, a volume of fine poetry, a few biographies, a package of old letters, a book of songs, a sword, a hammer and a set of books I have been studying."

"But," the friend replied, "you can't get all that into your bag."

"Oh, yes," replied the traveler, "it doesn't take much room." He placed his Bible in the corner of the suitcase and closed the lid.

The Employment Counselor

When we took our families to see *Phantom of the Opera* and *Les Miserables,* we read the synopsis in the program before the play started. Knowing the plot in advance didn't spoil the play. Just the opposite. With the intricate story line fresh in our minds, our enjoyment of the entire play increased. It actually helped us to know what was going to happen next.

We think that same principle applies to reading the Bible. What follows is our synopsis of the entire Bible.

We admit that it is incomplete. But in about 22 minutes, you can get the entire incredible story under your belt. Your understanding of what God is up to in this world will never be the same.

Proceed with...anticipation!

The Bible:
Never a Dull Moment
(The Greatest Story Ever Told in 22 Minutes)

*W*hat's *A*head

- One Book, One Story, One Plot
- Prologue: Once upon an Eternity
- Act I: The Human Race Was Lost As Soon As It Began
- Act II: How Odd of God to Choose the Jews
- Act III: The Rise and Fall of Israel
- Act IV: Jesus—A Very Personal Plan to Save the World
- Act V: Christianity Spreads Around the World
- Epilogue: The End of the World (As We Know It)

*T*he Bible follows a chronological order—sort of. Sometimes the story line jumps out of order, and many parts give lessons about God and life which aren't part of a plot.

One Book, One Story, One Plot

One reason we want to summarize the story of the Bible is to help you see that it really is one story— even though it consists of 66 books, written by about 40 different authors over hundreds of years. But these books all have one predominant theme (with a lot of subplots).

"Christ is not only the *theme* of both Testaments of the Bible," writes Norman Geisler in *A General Introduction to the Bible,* "but He may also be seen as the *subject* in the sequence of each of the eight sections of the Scriptures."

Henrietta Mears put it this way: "The Bible is one book, one history, one story—His story. Behind 10,000 events stands God, the builder of history, the maker of the ages. You can go down into the minutest detail everywhere and see that there is one great purpose moving through the ages: the eternal design of the Almighty God to redeem a wrecked and ruined world."

Too Grand to Grasp?

Does that description still sound too grand to grasp? "Give it to me quick," you say. Try this three-sentence mini-summary of God's book:

1. God is the author.

2. We are the characters.

3. Jesus is the theme.

Now let's flesh out the mini-summary:

1. God is the author. The Creator of the universe wrote the Bible, which is the record of how God has chosen to work through history.

> *All Scripture is inspired by God and is useful to teach us what is true and to make us realize what is wrong in our lives. It straightens us out and teaches us to do what is right. It is God's way of preparing us in every way, fully equipped for every good thing God wants us to do* (2 Timothy 3:16-17).

2. We are the characters. One of the unique things about the Bible is how much it focuses on us—God's human creation. Every book of the Bible describes how God has interacted with people. He is not some distant deity who has no interest in His creation. The Bible tells us in great detail how God has reached down to bring us back to Himself.

> *From one man he created all the nations throughout the whole earth. He decided beforehand which should rise and fall, and he determined their boundaries. His purpose in all of this was that the nations should seek after God and perhaps feel their way toward him and find him—though he is not far from any one of us* (Acts 17:26-27).

3. Jesus is the theme. Evangelist Ken Poure once said that when an author writes a book, the characters don't know him. It would be impossible, for example, for Hamlet to know Shakespeare, the one who created Hamlet in the first place. And yet that's exactly what God did when He sent Jesus. In the great drama of human history, God has written Himself into the plot. He did it 2000 years ago when He came to earth in the Person of His Son, Jesus Christ.

> *But God showed his great love for us by sending Christ to die for us while we were still sinners* (Romans 5:8).

The A+ Once-Over

Any A+ student will tell you that before you read a book front to back, you need to scope it out first. Read the covers and the flaps. Peruse the table of contents. Check out the pictures, if any. Fan the pages.

Same goes for the Bible. We'll be able to skim faster and with more understanding if we give it the once-over first.

Old + New = A Binding Agreement. Open your Bible to the table of contents. You'll notice that there are two parts: the Old Testament and the New Testament. The word *testament* means "covenant," which is a compact or agreement between two parties.

The 39 books of the *Old Testament* tell about the agreement between God and His chosen people, the Israelites (or Hebrews, or Jews). It also records how well each party lived up to the agreement (hint: One side did a lot better than the other).

The 27 books of the *New Testament* tell about the covenant, or agreement, between God and the rest of humankind through the life of Jesus and His followers.

The Old Testament. The *Old Testament* is basically a historical record of one group of people, the Hebrews, up to 432 B.C. As you might expect, all of the books in the Old Testament were written by Jewish authors (28 in all) in their native language, which was (you guessed it) Hebrew.

Traditionally, the books of the Old Testament have been divided into four sections:

OLD TESTAMENT BOOKS

The Books of Moses

Genesis	Leviticus	Deuteronomy
Exodus	Numbers	

The Books of Generals, Judges, and Kings

Joshua	1 & 2 Samuel	Ezra
Judges	1 & 2 Kings	Nehemiah
Ruth	1 & 2 Chronicles	Esther

The Books of Poetry and Wisdom

Job	Proverbs	Song of Songs
Psalms	Ecclesiastes	

The Books of Prophets

Major Prophets

Isaiah	Lamentations	Daniel
Jeremiah	Ezekiel	

Minor Prophets

Hosea	Jonah	Zephaniah
Joel	Micah	Haggai
Amos	Nahum	Zechariah
Obadiah	Habakkuk	Malachi

In Part II of this book, we're going to devote one chapter to each of these sections.

The New Testament. The *New Testament* is the historical record of the birth and life of Jesus and the ministry of His followers, who continued working after His death and resurrection. Nine different authors wrote the books in the New Testament, and all but one were Jewish. The New Testament was originally written in Greek (the common language of the day) and covers a time span of less than 100 years.

Like the Old Testament, the books of the New Testament have been divided into four sections:

NEW TESTAMENT BOOKS

The Gospels

Matthew	Luke	
Mark	John	

The Book of Acts

Acts

The Epistles

Romans	Colossians	Hebrews
1 & 2 Corinthians	1 & 2 Thessalonians	James
Galatians	1 & 2 Timothy	1 & 2 Peter
Ephesians	Titus	1, 2, & 3 John
Philippians	Philemon	Jude

The Book of Revelation

Revelation

In Part III of this book, we're going to devote one chapter to each of these sections.

The End Is Only Minutes from Right Now...

Now it's time to strap on your seat belt and get ready to fly through the Bible at warp speed. (You might not think that 22 minutes is warp speed, but consider that we are taking you from eternity past—before the creation of the earth—to eternity future, all in 1320 seconds. That's moving!) Start your stopwatch because the story begins...now!

Prologue: Once Upon an Eternity

Before time began, God existed. He has always existed. We can't explain it. That's just the nature of God.

Mutiny in the Heavens

In the ages preceding the creation of our universe, God created an army of angels who served and worshiped Him. But something went wrong. In the most ill-fated tactical maneuver of all time, one

So Where Did God Come From?

The first verse of the Bible starts off with: "In the beginning." The Bible explains the beginning of everything—except for God. That's because God never had a beginning. He always existed. Even though God created all things (Genesis 1:1), He didn't create Himself. God is self-existent, and He's the only such being who has ever lived.

For every house has a builder, but God is the one who made everything (Hebrews 3:4).

of the angels attempted a mutiny. Lucifer (also known as Satan), believing that he was better than God, recruited some other over-confident angels. The heavenly revolt was easily squashed. (Perhaps Satan forgot that you can't catch God by surprise because He is "all-knowing," and it is impossible to conquer Him because He is "all-powerful.")

Satan and his other angel stooges were kicked out of heaven. God planned eventual punishment for them in a lake of fire (hell), but God's timetable spans eternity, so that penalty is yet to come.

And Then Creation

That's just a flashback. In the first verse of the Bible, things get down to earth. Literally. God decides to make His move. Out of darkness and nothingness, God began to make a world.

Act I: The Human Race Was Lost As Soon As It Began

At the first stage in His plan for mankind, God spoke our universe into existence by the mere command of His voice. God created in the solar systems a planet which was specifically and uniquely designed as a habitat for humanity. Every detail, from the atmosphere, to the seasons, to the animals and vegetation, was part of God's grand design. Consider the created world as the setting for

God's sweeping epic about to unfold. (For more information, see chapter 4 of this book.)

We don't know what God called it—except "very good." But we call it planet Earth.

A Man and a Woman Made for Each Other

Now with everything in place, God was ready to make His characters: humans. But this creation was special. God designed man in God's own image, meaning that humans would have a spiritual dimension to their lives. God formed a man's body from the dust of the ground, and God breathed life into it.

Meet Adam, the first man. God placed him in a beautiful oasis (called the "Garden of Eden"). Next, God created Eve, the first woman. He commissioned Adam and Eve to raise a family (Bible words: "Be fruitful and multiply").

God placed Adam and Eve in charge of all of His other creations. They had only one restriction: God told them not to eat the fruit from a tree at the center of the garden (the "tree of knowledge of good and evil") because its fruit would cause death.

Then Sin Slithered In

Meanwhile, Satan still roamed the universe, exiled from heaven. He and his "hell's angels" decided to establish their "kingdom" on planet Earth. They knew God had given them a death sentence without the possibility of parole, but until their punishment was imposed, they intended to thwart God's plan.

Disguised as a snake, Satan told Eve that she wouldn't die if she ate the fruit from the forbidden tree. (Remember, Eve may have been only a few days old, so maybe she thought a talking snake was normal.) Not content with just one lie, Satan also said that the fruit would make her as smart as God.

Another rebellion seemed to be brewing.

Free Will Runs Amok

Complication: God had equipped Adam and Eve with a "free will." Unlike robots, they were free to make their own decisions. Confronted with Satan's lie, they were free to choose between the sly words of the serpent or the instructions of the Creator of the universe. The choice seemed obvious, but they made their decision based on selfish desires. They chose wrong. They picked the fruit and ate it. Immediately, they knew they had rebelled against God.

Suddenly, the happy days were over. Life in God's new world got tragically messed up. Why? Because a violation of God's law (Bible word: sin) brings consequences. God can't tolerate sin because He is holy. So God had to deal with Adam and Eve's sin.

- **Consequence #1—Exiled**

    Adam and Eve were banished from the Garden of Eden. Their life would now be filled with hardship instead of the bliss they had previously experienced. They would experience physical death.

- **Consequence #2—Guilty**

    The sin of Adam and Eve tainted the entire human race that would follow them. Every member of humanity is now born into a sinful world and will be guilty of his or her own sins. Our sins must be punished by eternal spiritual death.

- **Consequence #3—Waiting for Rescue**

    Satan will continue to plague mankind, but eventually God's plan will bring a descendant of Eve who can be a Savior for mankind and who will conquer Satan forever. This Savior can pay the penalty for our sins so that we can have eternal life with God.

From Bad to Worse

Kicked out of the Garden of Eden, Adam and Eve got serious about God's "be fruitful and multiply" command. They did a good job of populating the earth, and within ten generations the population had grown rapidly.

But Adam and Eve and their descendants weren't the only ones who were busy. Satan promoted evil at every turn, and because humans were now all infected with the sin virus, evil was rampant. The first crime was committed by Cain, the oldest son of Adam and Eve, who murdered his brother Abel.

*T*emptations are certain to ring your doorbell, but it's your own fault if you ask them in to stay for dinner.

As the centuries passed, the people of the world ignored God. They weren't atheists—they believed in gods—just not in the real God. Instead, they worshiped idols.

By the time of Noah, only one decent family remained on earth. In anger and disappointment, God let loose with an awful flood to clean the slate. But the flood solution didn't seem to wash either. The slate of the human heart just wouldn't come clean.

At this point God's story of beginnings leaves the grand scale of "eternity," "universe," "Earth," and "civilizations." Instead, in what we're calling Act II, the story focuses on the origins of one particular family.

Act II: How Odd of God to Choose the Jews

God still intended to implement His plan to provide a permanent sacrifice for the penalty of sin. Not just for Adam and Eve's sin, but for all of the sins of all mankind. As part of that plan, God would select a certain group of people to be His "chosen nation." God would reveal Himself to the entire world through this one extended family. His chosen people would be evidence of the blessings that come from obedience to God and the consequences that accompany disobedience.

So God's story narrows drastically. For the next 2000 years, the Bible saga reads like a generational epic, or maybe just a family scrapbook. And it starts with one man and one woman who had a very special character quality: faith.

The Fathers of a New Nation

The scene is an ancient city, Ur. Meet Abraham, a man devoted to God.

God selected Abraham to be the patriarch of this new nation. God directed Abraham to journey to a new home with his wife, Sarah. They were to leave Ur (near present-day Iraq) and move about 500 miles to the land of Canaan (present-day Israel). Abraham obeyed without any objections. God made a multi-pronged promise to Abraham (Bible words: Abrahamic Covenant):

- His descendants would become a great nation (what we now call "the Jews").
- The land of Canaan would be their homeland.
- All of mankind would be blessed by one of his descendants.

I will make you into a great nation and I will bless you; I will make your name great, and you will be a blessing. I will bless those who bless you, and whoever curses you I will curse; and all peoples on earth will be blessed through you (Genesis 12:2,3 NIV).

But wait. This happy-ever-after promise came wrapped in suspense. You see, Abraham and his wife, Sarah, didn't have any children (which makes it difficult to have descendants). To add another wrinkle, Abraham was about 100 years old by now, and Sarah was 90. Their biological clocks were unwound and shut down. Despite these obstacles, Abraham had faith in God's promise.

*F*aith sees the invisible, believes the incredible, and receives the impossible.

It's a good thing that God is not restricted by the laws of nature (since He controls them). Eventually, Isaac was born to Abraham and Sarah, just as God had promised. This was the start of the Hebrew nation (also known as Jews, children of Abraham, Israelites, or nation of Israel).

The "new nation" was getting off to a slow start because Isaac only had two sons, Jacob and Esau. But then Jacob did his best to expand the population with his 12 sons (whose respective descendants would become the 12 tribes of Israel). Fleeing a years-long drought,

Jacob moved his clan to Egypt where one of his sons, Joseph, landed a job as chief administrative assistant to the Pharaoh.

Enslaved in Egypt

The sounds change. Instead of the cozy sounds of babies gurgling and grandpas chuckling, we hear whips cracking and work gangs groaning in the hot sun. The date is about 1800 B.C. (For more information, see chapter 4 of this book.)

What happened? Over 400 years, Jacob's clan had gotten a little too prolific for the Pharaohs. The population of the Jews had exploded. Now worried Pharaohs had two problems: how to keep these prolific foreigners under control, and how to get a lot of work done. They hit upon a two-for-the-price-of-one solution: Make slaves of the Israelites.

> *Then a new king, who did not know about Joseph, came to power in Egypt. "Look," he said to his people, "the Israelites have become much too numerous for us. Come, we must deal shrewdly with them or they will become even more numerous and, if war breaks out, will join our enemies, fight against us and leave the country." So they put slave masters over them to oppress them with forced labor* (Exodus 1:8-11 NIV).

The Great Escape

Moses, the leader of the Jews, persuaded Pharaoh to "Let my people go!" Actually, the Egyptian ruler agreed only in principle. It took God sending plagues on the Egyptians to get Pharaoh to shriek, "Please, get out now!" (There's nothing like millions of frogs in the palace to make a Pharaoh jump.)

The Jews left their prison blues behind, picked up their belongings, and made their getaway. God miraculously parted the water of the Red Sea to help the Jewish caravan of approximately 2 million people escape the Egyptian soldiers. Moses continually relied on God to rescue the Jews from desperate situations:

> *Do not be afraid. Stand firm and you will see the deliverance the Lord will bring you today* (Exodus 14:13 NIV).

God's Top-Ten List

Scene: The Jews are camped at the base of Mount Sinai, resting from the dash for freedom. Everywhere you look are tents flapping, sheep bleating, kids playing. Above the scene loom rocky desert peaks.

The Jews spent time here preparing to journey to the homeland which God had promised to their ancestor Abraham.

At God's request, Moses trekked up Mount Sinai, where he met with God. God wrote out ten commandments on stone tablets and gave them to Moses. God's commandments told the Jews exactly how God wanted them to worship Him and treat each other.

Soon after this point in our story, the action unexpectedly stalls. Just when this dramatic journey from slavery to nationhood seemed to be leading them home, the Jews got lost on the trail....

A 40-Year Detour

God wanted the Israelites to invade Canaan, the "Promised Land," which had been given to their forefather Abraham. To do so, they would have to battle the pagan nations that inhabited the land. But when Jewish warriors saw how strong the enemy was, they lost faith in what God could do for them.

For the next 40 years, God's people wandered in the desert until a whole generation had passed off the scene. During this long, sad sojourn, God miraculously provided His children with food and water every day (but that didn't keep them from whining).

Act III: The Rise and Fall of Israel

Moses died, and Joshua took over as general and leader of the Jews. About 1400 B.C., Joshua led the Jews across the Jordan River into their first battle to recapture the Promised Land. (For more information, see chapter 5 of this book.)

God had given the Jews specific instructions to annihilate the pagan Canaanites. But they didn't follow God's instructions exactly. Their period of conquest should have ended quickly, but the Jews frequently lost faith in God's provision and protection, and they didn't completely drive out the pagans. This fatal mistake would present continual problems for them.

As Israel recaptured the Promised Land, Joshua assigned certain regions of Canaan for each of the tribes to live in. After Joshua's death, God appointed "judges" to lead the nation and give spiritual guidance.

Several hundred years passed. Canaanites and Jews lived side by side. They seemed to either be marrying each other or at war with each other. It was an era of violence, lawlessness, and immorality—a time when "the people did whatever seemed right in their own eyes" (Judges 17:6). Freedom fighters like Gideon, Deborah, and Samson brought only temporary relief.

When a King Is Second-Best

Remember the whiners in the wilderness? Well, 400 years later their descendants were still at it. The calendar says it's about 1000 B.C. Now the Jewish tribes wanted a king like all of the surrounding nations. They didn't need a king because they had God. Of course the other nations needed a king because their gods were carved out of stone and sat on a shelf.

But God gave the Jews what they wanted, even though He knew it wasn't what they needed. In fact, over the next 120 years, Israel ascended to the height of its military and cultural powers.

Meet a genuine hero—handsome, romantic, and a warrior too. His name is David, who became Israel's most famous and admired king. He loved God dearly and wrote many poems (Bible word: psalms) to and about God, which are included in the Bible. (For more information, see chapter 6 of this book.)

As the deer pants for streams of water, so my soul pants for you, O God (Psalm 42:1 NIV).

David was a great military leader and established the capital of the nation in the city of Jerusalem.

After David's death, his son Solomon became king. During his reign, Israel's borders reached to their furthest extent, and the nation prospered. The Bible says he was the wisest man who ever lived. The Bible includes many of his wise sayings and practi~ for life (Bible word: proverbs).

He who is slow to anger has great understanding, but he
who is quick-tempered exalts folly (Proverbs 14:29 NASB).

But this climax of national unity and power was short-lived.
God's people went to war again. This time it was with each
other....

---

*T*he children of Israel didn't recognize their greatest enemy—
themselves.

A Divided Kingdom Is Taken Captive

Only days after Solomon's death, civil war broke out. The ten
northern tribes formed their own confederacy, calling themselves
"Israel." The two southern tribes (with Jerusalem as their capital)
took the name of "Judah."

These two Jewish nations didn't always get along with each
other, and they were always battling invaders. The kings of Israel
were pretty much all losers and certainly uninterested in leading
their people back to God. Several kings of Judah proved to be
devoted to God, but usually the effect of any spiritual revival was
quickly lost with the next corrupt king.

Years passed. Pages turn. Meanwhile, powerful nations to the
east like Assyria and Babylonia rose up to threaten little Israel. To
the south, Egypt waited for an opportunity.

Like a parent warning His delinquent children, God warned His
people that they were in for trouble unless they turned their
hearts back to Him. This alert was sounded by several messengers
whom God designated (Bible word: prophets). God would reveal
His message to prophets like Amos and Isaiah, and they, in turn,
would speak to the king or directly to the people. The message of
the prophets was clear: Turn back to God or you will be taken captive by invaders. (For more information, see chapter 7 of this
book.)

Seek the Lord while you can find him. Call on him now
he is near. Let the people turn from their wicked
·m banish from their minds the very thought

of doing wrong! Let them turn to the LORD that he may have mercy on them. Yes, turn to our God, for he will abundantly pardon (Isaiah 55:6-7).

Israel in Exile

The tension reached a breaking point. When God speaks, you ought to listen. But the Jews failed to listen, and the imminent doom the prophets predicted came true.

- The northern nation of Israel was invaded from the north by the Assyrians in 722 B.C.; the cities were destroyed, and the Jews were taken into exile, never to see their homeland again. In fact, these tribes dispersed into the local populations and were never heard from again.

- The southern nation of Judah was captured by the Babylonians in 586 B.C. The city of Jerusalem was destroyed, and the beautiful temple was looted and leveled. All but the poorest people were taken as prisoners to Babylon.

Now the scenery in God's storybook fades to dark—like the darkness before the dawn, but no one could even hope for a dawn. The exile period is definitely the low point in the biblical account of the Jews.

Think about it: Their homeland had been destroyed. They were scattered across the foreign cities of the Middle East and living in slavery. They had no future. Jeremiah spoke for his people after the fall of Jerusalem:

I cry out, "My splendor is gone! Everything I had hoped for from the LORD is lost!" (Lamentations 3:18).

Had God finally given up on Abraham's children? Only a fool would talk about the bright side of things now.

But God had a few fools in mind.

Messengers of Hope

He had not forgotten His promise to Abraham to bring a Savior to the world through Abraham's descendants. During these years when hope had died, God continued to speak through prophets, some living in exile and others who remained in the ruins of Jerusalem.

And His message was full of hope. In fact, God made the most encouraging promises imaginable:

- God would send a Savior (Bible word: Messiah) who would lead Israel out of slavery. But He would also be a suffering servant who would carry the sorrows of His people.

- The place and circumstances of His birth, and His lineage as a descendant of King David, were predicted.

Returning and Rebuilding

Within a couple of generations, the Babylonians were conquered by the Persians. Then miraculously, Cyrus, king of Persia, allowed the Jews to begin returning to their homeland. Best of all, he gave them permission to rebuild Jerusalem and the temple. Leaders like Nehemiah and Ezra took charge.

But it soon became clear that life in rebuilt Jerusalem wasn't all that different than life in exile. Israel remained a servant state to foreign powers. The Jews were back home, but their spiritual relationship with God was on-again, off-again.

Their only hope was the promised Messiah. They hoped He would come soon to deliver them from their trials.

But something soon became clear. God's first agreement with the Jews was drawing to a close. How could they tell? For the next 400 years...

- God didn't send another leader (like Moses), general (like Joshua), judge (like Gideon), or king (like David) to deliver them and make them great again.

- And most troubling of all, God stopped talking to them. He sent no more prophets.

The first agreement (testament) was over. A worrisome silence brooded over the land.

Who's in Charge Now?

During the 400-year gap in the action between the Old Testament and the New Testament, the Jews continued to be under the authority of other empires. Alexander the Great asserted Greek control of the Jews in Israel in about 300 B.C. By about 50 B.C., Israel was part of the Roman empire. The Jews were miserable under Roman control.

Act IV: Jesus—A Very Personal Plan to Save the World

How would God break through the silence? With the rumble of chariots coming to the rescue?

How about with a baby cooing in a barn? That would certainly make quite a scene!

God never forgot His promise to Abraham that his descendant would be a Savior for the entire world. As our story suddenly begins again, the New Testament traces the bloodline of Abraham all the way through the generations to a baby named Jesus. (For more information, see chapter 8.)

God Gets Down to Earth

A young couple named Joseph and Mary were engaged to be married. An angel appeared to both of them and said that Mary had been selected by God to be the mother of the Messiah. They were told that God's Spirit was inside her and she would give birth to a son, to be named Jesus, who would be the Savior of the world.

On a late evening in the small village of Bethlehem, Mary gave birth to Jesus. This birth was announced to nearby shepherds by a group of angels, and a star appeared and shone so brightly that it was noticed by astronomers in a far eastern land (Bible term: the wise men).

This was no ordinary baby. The wise men were familiar with the writings of the Hebrew prophets. They knew that the star was a sign of the promised Messiah. They traveled to Jerusalem and inquired about the birth of the "King of the Jews." All of this was news to

Herod, ruler of Judea. The wise men found Jesus and presented Him with valuable gifts. Meanwhile, Herod felt threatened by this toddler and issued a decree that all male baby boys must be killed. An angel warned Joseph in advance, and he escaped with his wife and child to Egypt. They returned only after Herod had died.

Not much is reported about the childhood of Jesus. He lived in relative obscurity with His parents in the town of Nazareth. We next see Him at the age of 12, when Jesus traveled with His parents to Jerusalem. There He astounded the teachers in the temple with His understanding of Jewish law and of spiritual matters.

In the Public Spotlight

Let's set the scene: the rolling hills of Judea and Galilee. Or sometimes a local synagogue. Either way, the focal point is a young teacher and healer named Jesus. As Roman chariots clatter by and priests look on suspiciously, Jesus talks about another kind of country, "the kingdom of God." He sounds as if He knows the place—as if we can too....

Most of the stories about Jesus contained in the Bible start when He was about 30 years old. It was at this point in His life that people began to take notice of who He was, especially when He said that He was the Son of God who came to earth to be the sole means of salvation for mankind:

> I am the way and the truth and the life. No one comes to the Father except through me (John 14:6 NIV).

Jesus was immediately recognized as the Messiah by some.

- **By John the Baptist.** John the Baptist was an itinerant preacher who challenged people to return to God. If people confessed their sins, he would immerse them in the Jordan River (Bible term: baptize) to symbolize how God can cleanse a person from sin. Some thought he might be the Messiah, but when he saw Jesus he proclaimed:

    > Look! There is the Lamb of God who takes away the sin of the world! (John 1:29).

- *By God.* When Jesus was baptized by John, the Spirit of God descended on Jesus and a voice from the sky said:

  This is my beloved Son, and I am fully pleased with him (Matthew 3:17).

- *By Satan.* Satan confronted Jesus in the wilderness. He offered Jesus all the fame and fortune of the world if Jesus would bow down to him.

For everyone else, the fact that Jesus was God should have been obvious because of the supernatural things He did (Bible word: miracles).

- He gave sight to the blind. He made the lame to walk. He cured leprosy. He brought dead people back to life.

- He turned water into wine. He calmed a storm by telling it to be quiet. He fed 5000 people by multiplying the food in a sack lunch.

Jesus and His Band of Hairy Men

Jesus attracted large crowds wherever He went, but He tried to spend quality time with 12 close followers (Bible term: disciples). The disciples were a ragtag group of relatively uneducated working men who were especially close to Jesus.

Jesus knew that His disciples would be responsible for carrying His message to the world after He was gone. He spent most of His three-year ministry teaching them what they needed to learn about God's plan for mankind. The disciples proved to be well-intentioned, but they were often a little dense.

What a Way to Teach

Tension mounted. The religious and political establishment was threatened most by the teachings of Jesus. What He said was radical. The religious leaders (Bible terms: Pharisees, Sadducees, and scribes) interpreted the laws literally, so they considered themselves righteous if they obeyed every one of them. Jesus taught that no man could ever be righteous in God's sight because God's laws also apply to feelings and attitudes.

Jesus explained many concepts through the use of stories with a point (Bible term: parables). Sometimes His disciples understood what He was getting at; the meaning of other parables was not plain to them until later. These lessons were about God's kingdom, service to others, God's love, and the circumstances when Jesus will return to earth.

Jesus Was Dying for a Chance to Save You

After three years of His public ministry, Jesus returned to Jerusalem for what would be the last week of His life. The city was bustling with visitors for the Jewish holy celebration of Passover. By this time, the common people were so enthralled with His miraculous abilities, they were declaring Him to be the Messiah. The disciples thought that His coronation was imminent; the religious leaders worried about the same thing, and they plotted His murder.

Only Jesus understood that His divinely appointed purpose was to die.

Several days later, Jesus had a special dinner with His disciples (Bible term: the Last Supper). He tried to explain to them that He was going to be crucified. Later that night, Jesus was arrested on false charges trumped up by the Pharisees.

He went through a series of phony trials in the middle of the night, and He was sentenced to death. The next day He was hanged on a cross on a hill (Bible name: Calvary) with several common criminals. Within hours, Jesus was dead.

Someone arranged for Him to be buried in a tomb (which in those days was an underground vault sealed by a large rock). Fearing that He would come back to life as He had previously predicted, the Pharisees prevailed upon the Roman authorities to post armed guards around the tomb.

At this point, our story gets lost in darkness again—this time the darkness of one small tomb on a Judean hillside.

Had the hopes of all Israel died too? Had Jesus' band of fishermen been seriously duped?

*N*o revolution that has ever taken place in society can be compared to that which has been produced by the words of Jesus Chirst.

Mark Hopkins

You Can't Keep a God-Man Down

Morning sun. It's the third day following those terrible executions....

Some of the women followers of Jesus went to visit His tomb. Suddenly, an earthquake struck and an angel rolled the rock away. When the women leaned down to look into Jesus' tomb...it was empty! The angel spoke directly to the women:

> *Do not be afraid, for I know that you are looking for Jesus, who was crucified. He is not here; he has risen, just as he said. Come and see the place where he lay. Then go quickly and tell his disciples* (Matthew 28:5-7 NIV).

The guards were so frightened that they went into shock. Later, when they told their superiors what had happened, the Pharisees bribed them to say that the disciples had stolen the body of Jesus.

He'll Be Back

What an amazing few weeks followed! Jesus appeared to more than 500 people at different times after He came back to life (Bible term: the resurrection). They could see His body, they watched Him eating and drinking, they saw the nail prints in His hands. Yet something about Him was different. He was able to pass through walls and vanish out of sight.

Jesus made a final appearance and explained to the disciples and the other followers that He was going back to heaven. He told this group that they should spread the message of His salvation for all people around the world. He said that He would return again sometime in the future to establish His kingdom on earth. In the meantime, He promised to send God's Spirit (Bible name: the

Holy Spirit) to live inside those people who believed in Him. Wait in Jerusalem, He said, until My Spirit comes.

Now imagine this scene: While they stood listening on the hillside, the disciples saw Jesus begin to float up from the ground. He rose up higher and higher into the sky. Soon clouds seemed to wrap God's Son in an embrace of welcome, and the God-Man disappeared from sight.

Jesus returned to the Father in heaven (Bible term: the ascension).

ACT V: Christianity Spreads Around the World

The news of the resurrection of Jesus spread quickly throughout Jerusalem and the neighboring regions. It was witnessed by so many people that the facts weren't really a cause of controversy. *The only question that people faced was whether to believe the claims that Jesus Christ made to be the Son of God.* (For more information, see chapter 9 of this book.)

If you think about it, the whole rest of God's story for the human race from those exciting weeks around Jerusalem until now swirls around the same question: *Do you believe that Jesus is the Christ, the Son of God?*

The Holy Spirit Arrives on the Scene

The scene shifts from a hillside to an upstairs room in Jerusalem. The place is packed with Jesus' followers. Everyone is doing exactly what Jesus had told them to do—wait.

One night, what seemed like a mighty wind entered that house, and all of them were filled with the Holy Spirit. This was the supernatural power that Jesus had promised to send them. A crowd gathered outside the house. The Holy Spirit enabled the disciples to speak to them in foreign languages that were recognized by all of the foreigners in the crowd.

The Holy Spirit empowered the disciple Peter, the gruff fisherman, to give an eloquent speech about God's plan for the salvation of mankind. He traced the predictions of the ancient prophets and explained how they pointed to Jesus as the Messiah. He reminded them of the wonders and signs, which proved that Jesus was God. He showed them how the crucifixion was necessary for the forgiveness of their sins. The evidence was overwhelming, and about 3000 people made decisions to believe in Jesus.

A New Kind of Family—the Church

The ragtag group turned into a major news story and then into a movement. "Go into all the world with My message," Jesus had told them. With the Holy Spirit's power, it began to seem almost possible.

The followers of Jesus became known as "Christians." Each local group became known as a "church."

Almost immediately, Christians had to sort through a serious question: Was the salvation of Jesus Christ restricted only to Jews? After all, Jesus was a Jew. Abraham had been a Jew. Non-Jews (Bible name: Gentiles) had been allowed in the church in Jerusalem only if they followed some of the Jewish traditions.

But God revealed in a dream to Peter that the Gentiles, and even the Jews, were no longer bound by the ceremonial Jewish traditions. As the apostle Paul would later teach:

> *Jew and Gentile are the same in this respect. They all have the same Lord, who generously gives his riches to all who ask for them* (Romans 10:12).

An incredible realization was now dawning on the church. What had started as a story of God's dealings with one "family"— the Jews, all descendants of Abraham—had now widened again to include all the families of the world. God's plan of salvation was for every color, every race.

The Pharisee Who Became a Missionary to the World

But opposition to these new religious fanatics mounted. The Jewish establishment still refused to acknowledge Jesus as the Messiah, and it conspired with the Roman government to persecute the Christians. A Pharisee named Saul dedicated himself to stoning Christians or throwing them in jail. On one of his excursions, however, he was blinded by a light from heaven and the voice of Jesus spoke from heaven:

Saul, Saul! Why are you persecuting me?... I am Jesus, the
one you are persecuting (Acts 9:4-5).

This experience was enough to make a believer out of Saul. He later changed his name to Paul and became a missionary to bring the message about Jesus to distant cities throughout the Roman empire. On three different missionary journeys, Paul either established new churches or encouraged the Christians in existing churches.

The original Jesus Movement was quickly spreading to the horizons of the known world.

---

*T*he Christian church is the only society in the world in which membership is based upon the qualification that the candidate shall be unworthy of membership.

Charles C. Morrison

Take a Letter to You

Much of the New Testament is comprised of letters written by Paul and by the disciples Peter, James, and John to churches or individuals. (For more information, see chapter 10 of this book.) The disciples (later called apostles) and Paul (also called an apostle) were recognized as experts in understanding the spiritual concepts about Christianity. Since they couldn't be at all of the churches all of the time, they wrote letters to

- Explain how to know Jesus personally and know Him better.

- Give reassurance of God's care during times of hardship and persecution.

- Describe Jesus' principles for relationships with family, friends, and enemies.

- Provide instructions for organizing the church.

With these intimate and inspiring letters, the story of the New Testament races toward its conclusion. But it's an open-ended story because we are part of it.

Why? Because the movement Jesus started is still fanning out across the globe. We're still studying His teachings, learning from the letters of His disciples, telling others the good news of the gospel: *Jesus is alive! And we too can have new life if we believe in His name!*

You see, the second agreement God made with the human race is still good. How good? *It's guaranteed with God's own blood.*

That's why the story of God's dealings with men and women is being written these days by another set of interesting characters— ones like you and me.

Epilogue: The End of the World (As We Know It)

The story of the Bible begins in eternity past, so it should be no surprise that it ends in eternity future.

In the last book of the Bible, the disciple John, old and in exile, wrote about visions he received from God concerning the end of the world. These are symbolic visions of hope and warning. (For more information, see chapter 11.)

What should God's people keep in mind about the future?

- At a time unknown to any man, and when people least expect it, Jesus is going to return to earth from the heavens. This "second coming" of Christ will be accompanied by heavenly fanfare, which will be heard throughout the universe.

- This will be a time of judgment for sins. Those who accepted Jesus and His death as the sacrifice for their sins will be spared, and they will enter the presence of God in heaven for eternity. Everyone else will be sentenced to eternity in hell as the punishment that their sin deserves.

The end of the world will also be marked by the greatest and last battle between God and Satan. God will prevail, and Satan and his demon forces will be thrown into hell forever. Sin and rebellion and death will be no more.

Then, and only then, will God finally write down in the Book of books, *"The End."*

What's That Again?

1. Man's sin in the Garden of Eden interrupted a perfect and personal relationship with God. God's holy nature cannot tolerate the evil of sin, and all of mankind that would follow were separated from God. All along, God had devised a plan to restore that relationship.

2. God chose the Jews as the people through whom He would teach the world about Himself and through whom He would send a Savior to earth.

3. God sent His own Son, Jesus, as the promised Savior of the world. But many ignored the miracles, which prove who Jesus is.

4. The crucifixion of Jesus was all part of God's plan to provide a perfect sacrifice for the sin of mankind. Jesus displayed His divine nature by defeating death and rising from the grave.

5. A personal relationship with God is possible for those of every race who accept Christ's death as the sacrifice for their sin.

6. Jesus is going to return to the earth again to establish a permanent kingdom. Those who have rejected Jesus will be doomed to hell. Those who have accepted Jesus as their Savior will live forever with God.

Dig Deeper

Here are a few books that will give you an excellent overview of the Bible from the beginning to the end.

Talk Through the Bible by Bruce Wilkinson and Kenneth Boa. Lots of charts, tables, and outlines.

Adventuring Through the Bible by Ray C. Stedman. The narrations and explanations in this book are very descriptive.

Nave's Topical Bible by Orville J. Nave. This is one of the most popular texts on Bible topics.

■ □ ■

Questions for Reflection and Discussion

1. Why must God be self-existent? What if God had been created?

2. What if God had not given Adam and Eve a free will, and they had no choice but to obey God? Would that change the way we relate to God? If so, how?

3. Even though God chose the Jews to be His people, they rarely acted like it. Why did they have such a hard time obeying God? Why would anyone—including people living today—rebel against a loving, caring, all-knowing, all-powerful God?

4. In what way are you a character in God's story? Is the story still being written? How?

5. After reading through the entire Bible summary, what do you consider to be the major theme of the Bible? How does this affect your Bible reading?

6. Discuss the characteristics and personality of God as revealed in the Bible. Give specific examples.

7. How does the Bible impact your thinking about sin? Life? Death? Jesus?

■ □ ■

Moving On...

Now that you've read the synopsis, you're ready to study the Bible in more detail.

In the next chapter, you'll be starting back at the beginning of the Bible. It's not only the beginning of the Bible, but it also starts at the beginning of the world. There are lots of other "beginnings" and "firsts" in the next chapter, like the beginning of humanity, the beginning of sin, the first murder, and the first weather forecaster.

Part II
The Old Testament

Chapter 4

If I were God,
And man made a mire
Of things: war, hatred,
Murder, lust…
I would sweep him
To one side and start anew.
(I think I would.)
If I did this,
Would I be God?

The Evangelical Beacon

How did the world begin? Where did man come from? What is the purpose and meaning of life? These are baffling questions that have perplexed humanity down through the ages. But you can find the answers to all of these questions in the first five books of the Old Testament.

These books also answer big questions about God: Who is He? What is His plan for the world? What does He think of me? But you'll notice that the stories mostly address these human concerns *by showing what God says and does.* As one scholar put it, "The Bible does not argue for the existence of God. It reveals Him."

You may be surprised to see God presented from many different perspectives: as mighty Creator of the universe, as a loving Father who desires an intimate relationship with His children, as a holy and righteous God who cannot tolerate sin.

As you begin your book-by-book journey through the 66 books of the Bible, get ready to see the real you revealed in new ways too.

The Books of Moses:
How It All Began

What's Ahead

- Seeing God in the Big Picture
- Five-in-One Review
- All in a Week's Work
- Fig Leaves and Forbidden Fruit
- It Looks Like Rain
- A Bunch of Babbling Fools
- Abraham—a Man of Promise
- Joseph—a Dreamer Saves the Nation
- Moses—Leader (and Chief Baby-Sitter) of a New Nation

*Y*es, the Bible *is* a religious book—it wrestles with the deepest questions humans ask about meaning and purpose in life. But the Bible is more than just religion. It is also a historical record of how the world came into existence and how humankind began.

This information isn't hard to find in the Bible. It starts in the very first verse:

> *In the beginning God created the heavens and the earth* (Genesis 1:1).

In this chapter, we will review the contents of the first five books of the Bible. You will be amazed what you can learn about archaeology, science, astronomy, geography, and sociology. No trustworthy book can be true about who God is but false about what God does.

Seeing God in the Big Picture

Moses is generally credited with writing the first five books of the Bible: Genesis, Exodus, Leviticus, Numbers, and Deuteronomy. These books are collectively called "the Pentateuch."

For the Jewish religion, these first five books are called "the Torah" (which means "the law").

Before we review with you the books and true-life stories written by Moses, it will be helpful to understand what lies behind these historical adventures. Moses was not just interested in creating material for children's bedtime stories or Sunday school lessons. (That's obvious, because some of these stories are way beyond a "G" rating.) We believe that it was the intention of Moses to present God. Let's face it—much of what you can learn about God from the Old Testament comes from reading what God did and how it related to humanity.

Through all of the books of Moses we learn a tremendous amount about His character and His purposes. (God is still pretty mysterious in Genesis.) As you read this chapter's review of the contents of Genesis, Exodus, Leviticus, Numbers, and Deuteronomy, we think you'll discover these things about God:

God is present. He is not just hanging around in outer space. He appeared to Moses in the burning bush and on Mount Sinai. His presence was revealed to the Jews in the cloud and the pillar of fire. He had a permanent dwelling place in the "Holy of Holies" portion of the Tabernacle.

God is supernatural. He is the Creator of the universe. His miracles reveal that the laws of nature are subject to His orders.

God is a Savior. The rescue of the Jews from captivity in Egypt is just an illustration of how God desires to rescue us from sin.

God is faithful to His promises. True to His word, God moved in the events of the world to keep His promise to raise a nation from Abraham's descendants. His promises will never be broken.

God is holy. God's holiness is revealed by His expectation that His chosen people will be holy in every aspect of their lives.

God is personal. This may be the most important part about God. He is not a distant alien being who has no comprehension of you. He created humanity in His own image. He continued to pursue a relationship with humanity, despite mankind's rebellion. He is a personal God who knows you by name and is interested in reestablishing a personal relationship with you.

Now, with that as a background, let's see how Moses lays it all out.

Five-in-One Review

Genesis: the Book That Started It All

This is the book of beginnings: of Creation, of humankind, of evil on earth. And, most importantly, the beginning of God's plan to rescue humankind from its sin.

Some of the most famous events of the Bible are recorded in Genesis: Creation, the fall of man, the flood, and the Tower of Babel. It also contains the first mention of these names: God, Satan, Adam and Eve, Noah, Abraham, and Joseph.

The name *Genesis* means "origin."

Exodus: This Way Out

Genesis ends with Joseph dying in Egypt. Exodus begins three centuries later with the Hebrews trapped under Egyptian persecution. In the first chapter, we are introduced to Moses. We see Moses confronting Pharaoh, king of Egypt, and leading the children

The Books of Moses

What's in the Bible?		What's in the World?
Creation	? ▼	
The Flood	? ▼	
	3500 B.C. ▼	Animals used in agriculture
	2600 ▼	First of the great pyramids built in Egypt
	2500 ▼	Farmers cultivate rice crops in China
Abraham born	2160 ▼	
Abraham enters Canaan	2095 ▼	
Isaac born	2065 ▼	
Jacob born	2006 ▼	
	1750 ▼	Babylonian culture develops
Moses born	1526 ▼	
Exodus	1446	

Promised Land

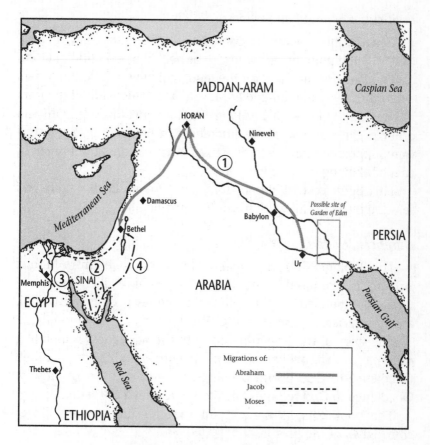

Travels of the Patriarchs

1. Abraham takes a hike to the "Promised Land."
2. Jacob moves his family to Egypt.
3. Moses leads the children of Israel out of Egyptian slavery.
4. Forty years of wandering in the wilderness.

of Israel to freedom. In the desert, God gives His people the Ten Commandments.

A key message of the book is how God saves His people from the slavery of sin and provides them with a new way of life.

Leviticus: a Manual on Holiness

Genesis and Exodus are packed with action, but Leviticus is, well, to put it politely, a slow read. The book is a collection of God's civil and ceremonial laws for the Jews, which were given to Moses when the Jews were camped at Mount Sinai. God wanted the Jews to live holy lives, with lifestyles separate and distinct from the other pagan nations. Their differences in behavior and worship were supposed to be an example to all other nations about the benefits of obeying the one true God.

This book gets its name from the tribe of Levi, which was selected by Moses to work in the Tabernacle.

Numbers: Wilderness Wanderings

The Book of Numbers tells how the Jews moved from Mount Sinai to the Promised Land. The trip should have taken about two weeks, but it ended up taking 40 years. The key people in this book are Moses, Aaron, Joshua, and Caleb.

The story of the Jews wandering in the wilderness is a perfect example of the covenant God made with the children of Israel: Obedience to God brings blessings; disobedience brings misery. Obedience to God requires faith to move ahead as He directs.

The book gets its name from the two times when Moses counted all of the people.

Deuteronomy: a Final Pep Talk (Actually, Three of Them)

Like a football coach who wants to motivate his team before the big game, Moses—now an old man—wants to psych up the Israelites before they invade the Promised Land and tackle the Canaanites. So he is giving them a series of stirring speeches. The content boils down to themes coaches use all the time: "This is who we are. This is who we're up against. This is why and how we can win."

But Moses is dying, so these words also stand as his farewell address. The name *Deuteronomy* means "the second law" because Moses repeated the Ten Commandments for a second time in his remarks.

Now we're ready to look at the books of the Pentateuch in more depth.

One-Hour Cram Plan for the Books of Moses

There are 1189 chapters in the entire Bible. You may think that is too much to read all at once. So, as we go through the Bible, we'll be giving to you a list of the chapters that might be of most interest to you.

In the books of Moses, there are some really great stories about God and people. If you want to get finished in an hour, select six from the list below (or skim them all).

- Genesis 1–2—the Creation
- Genesis 3—the fall
- Genesis 6–8—the flood
- Genesis 12:1-9—the call of Abraham (Will he leave home?)
- Genesis 22—the test of Abraham (Will he sacrifice his son?)
- Genesis 29–30—Jacob, Leah, and Rachel make babies
- Exodus 2–3—the call of Moses (Will he stand up to Pharaoh?)
- Exodus 12—Passover and the escape from Egypt
- Deuteronomy 1; 5–6—Moses tells stories from the wilderness: spies, rebellion; the Ten Commandments

All in a Week's Work (Genesis 1)

The Bible reports that God created everything that exists—the earth, our solar system, the entire universe—and that He did it all in six days. Here's how the account in Genesis breaks the process down:

Day #1: God created light.

Day #2: God created Earth's atmosphere and water.

Day #3: God created land to separate the water into the "seas," and vegetation was created.

Day #4: God created the sun and moon.

When?

The three questions most people ask about Creation are "Who?" "How?" and "When?" The answer to *who* made the universe is the most important. Only God was capable of bringing about our world. *How* God did it is next in importance. The Bible tells us that "God said," and it happened:

God said, "Let there be light," and there was light (Genesis 1:3).

The entire universe was formed at God's command (Hebrews 11:3).

From God's perspective, the least important issue is *when*. Why? Because the answer is not clear from Scripture. The six days of Creation could be six literal days, or they could be six ages, because in the Hebrew language, the word *day* can mean 12 hours, 24 hours, or a long period of time. And because God can do anything, He could have created everything in six milliseconds if He had wanted to.

When did all of this happen? We don't know. The date of Creation (and the events through Noah's flood) are pretty much open for debate. What is not debatable is that the events actually happened and how they occurred.

Day #5: God created the creatures which inhabit the sea and the air.

Day #6: God created the animals and mankind.

Fig Leaves and Forbidden Fruit (Genesis 2–3)

God's last act of Creation was different from the others. The first man, Adam, and the first woman, Eve, were created by God "in the image" of God:

> *So God created people in his own image; God patterned them after himself; male and female he created them* (Genesis 1:27).

God breathed into man the "breath of life" (Genesis 2:7). The special imprint that God gave to humanity was a soul—an eternal, spiritual element in each human being. It is our soul that separates us from the animals and the vegetables. It is our soul that allows us to connect with God.

God created a special paradise for Adam and Eve, which He called the Garden of Eden. Everything was perfect and complete. Adam and Eve lived in harmony with each other and with all the animals. More importantly, they enjoyed personal friendship with God Himself. God considered His total creation to be excellent. When the work of Creation was done, God exclaimed, "It is very good."

---

*A*dam and Eve—Seeing a Family Resemblance

What do you suppose Adam and Eve looked like? They were the first ones into the gene pool, so Adam never wondered if baldness was an inherited trait from his father's or mother's side of the family.

The Bible says that Adam and Eve were created in God's own image. Think about that for a moment, because there are implications for you. Every person who has ever lived—including you—is a descendant of Adam and Eve. You are made in God's image. You have dignity and value because of your divine imprint.

Adam and Eve Choose Door Number Two

But the perfection didn't last long. Satan tempted Eve to eat fruit from a tree that God had specifically prohibited. Rather than obey God, she chose to gratify her own selfish desires. Adam wasn't any better because he ate the fruit too. Their actions were in direct and blatant defiance of God's instructions.

Rebellion against God is "sin." God is so holy and perfect that sin cannot exist in His presence. In fact, the penalty for sin must be spiritual death:

For the wages of sin is death (Romans 6:23).

Because of their sin, Adam and Eve were kicked out of the Garden of Eden and cut off from their intimate friendship with Him. God said that they would suffer physical death, but He had a plan to eventually restore the relationship between Himself and humankind that could save humanity from suffering spiritual death.

Sin, the Secondhand Virus

Adam and Eve's sin is bad news for *you*. They were representatives for the entire human race. Their rebellion against God tainted all of humanity with the stain of sin and death:

When Adam sinned, sin entered the entire human race. Adam's sin brought death, so death spread to everyone, for everyone sinned (Romans 5:12).

But the penalty isn't being imposed on the innocent. Each of us has sinned too. If we're honest, we know we are guilty of acts and thoughts that would displease God.

For all have sinned; all fall short of God's glorious standard (Romans 3:23).

Don't despair! As we'll see in chapter 8, God makes a plan to save humanity from the sin virus and its terrible aftereffects:

But God showed his great love for us by sending Christ to die for us while we were still sinners (Romans 5:8).

It Looks Like Rain (Genesis 6–9)

Sin had a predictable dastardly effect on the human race. Cain, the oldest son of Adam and Eve, murdered his brother Abel. Following generations were equally wicked. There came a point when the entire population of the earth was so perverted and corrupt that God was compelled to destroy them all—except for a man named Noah and his family. Noah was the only remaining man who obeyed and worshiped God.

God revealed to Noah that He was going to obliterate all of humanity for its wickedness. Only Noah and his family would be spared. The plan went something like this: Noah would build a boat (Bible term: ark) large enough for his family and two of every kind of animal. With all of the passengers inside, God would send enough rain to flood the world and destroy its wicked inhabitants.

Noah was a righteous man, the only blameless man living on earth at the time. He consistently followed God's will and enjoyed a close relationship with him (Genesis 6:9).

Sensing rain in the forecast, Noah did as he was told. With his family and menagerie in the boat, God sent the rain—for 40 days straight. The whole earth was flooded, and everything but the ark and its cargo was destroyed.

---

*N*oah: The Ark Architect

The comedian Bill Cosby says that Noah responded to God's command to build an ark with this question: "What's an ark?" That joke probably isn't too far from what actually happened.

Noah was a man of incredible faith. He believed that God would flood the earth, even though he had never seen a flood. And he followed God's plans to build an ark, even though he had never seen such a craft. In fact, Noah is in the Faith Hall of Fame, found in Hebrews 11, because "he obeyed God...and was made right in God's sight" (Hebrews 11:7).

The Bible describes Noah as a "righteous" and blameless man. This doesn't mean he was perfect. He messed up at the end of his life and embarrassed himself in front of his sons. But he stood out in a world filled with evil.

When the floodwaters receded, the family and animals disembarked. God was pleased with Noah's loyalty, and He promised never to permit another flood that would destroy all life. As a sign of this eternal promise, God invented the rainbow. Noah and his wife, and his sons and their wives, then set about to repopulate the earth.

A Bunch of Babbling Fools (Genesis 11)

In the generations that followed Noah, the people all spoke the same language and basically lived in the same region. Together they made great advancements. Unfortunately, they were so proud of their own accomplishments that they completely ignored God.

When they decided to build a huge tower as a monument to themselves, God decided to mix things up a little bit. He miraculously gave them different languages. Everybody wandered around jabbering until they found a group that shared the same language. This event scattered the people across the earth based on their common languages.

Abraham—a Man of Promise (Genesis 11–25)

The time is about 2100 B.C. The world was inhabited by immoral and corrupt people. Except for a man named Abraham. Despite man's wickedness, God wanted to keep the promise He had made in the Garden of Eden to provide a way to save humankind from the penalty of sin. God chose Abraham to be the beginning of the plan to save the world.

Abraham is known for his great faith and obedience to God. He lived in the city of Ur, near the present-day Persian Gulf. At God's direction, Abraham packed up his wife, Sarah, and his nephew, Lot, and left his home, his friends, and his pagan culture. It was God's plan to set Abraham and his descendants apart from the rest of the pagan world. God wanted a "chosen people" to

- be the recipients of God's laws and holy Scriptures
- be an example to the pagan nations of the world
- be the lineage for the birth of the promised Savior

*W*hat's in a Name?

Actually, their names were originally Abram and Sarai. After God made a covenant with them, He changed their names to Abraham and Sarah. Abraham means "father of many." Every time someone called Abraham by his new name, he was reminded of God's promise.

A Promise You Just Gotta Believe

God made a promise (Bible word: covenant) with Abraham. Because of Abraham's faithfulness, God promised...

- Abraham would be the *father of a great nation.* This promise is all the more amazing if you know that Abraham and Sarah were already well past their seventies and didn't have any children.

  Look up into the heavens and count the stars if you can. Your descendants will be like that—too many to count! (Genesis 15:5).

  I will guarantee to make you into a mighty nation (Genesis 17:2).

- Abraham and his descendants would be given *a homeland* in Canaan (now the region of Israel and Palestine).

  Yes, I will give all this land of Canaan to you and to your offspring forever (Genesis 17:8).

- Through one of Abraham's descendants, *salvation would be available to all of the people of the world.*

  All the families of the earth will be blessed through you (Genesis 12:3).

These promises are referred to as the Abrahamic Covenant.

God—the Original Promise Keeper

God kept His promise to Abraham. He moved Abraham to the land of Canaan, and Sarah gave birth to a son, Isaac, when Abraham was 100 years old and Sarah was 90. The start of the great nation had begun.

Isaac. He was the only child of Abraham and Sarah. The covenant promises were reiterated by God to Isaac. He had twin sons, Jacob and Esau.

Jacob. Jacob was a scoundrel in his younger years, but he later got things straight with God. He had 12 sons. God repeated to Jacob the covenant promises which were originally made to his grandfather, Abraham.

Abraham, Isaac, and Jacob are often referred to as the "patriarchs." This means that they were the honorable ancestors.

*G*ive Me Back My Miracle...

In one of the most dramatic and instructional stories in the entire Bible, God tested faithful Abraham by asking him to take the life of his only son, Isaac, as an offering to the Lord (Genesis 22:1-19). Why would God do such a thing? He had already told Abraham that a great nation would come through Isaac.

Sometimes God's ways are inexplainable in human terms. Maybe God wanted to see if Abraham loved Him more than His miracle gift of a son in Abraham's old age. Abraham passed the test, and God provided a substitute—a ram—which Abraham sacrificed in place of his son.

Joseph—a Dreamer Saves the Nation (Genesis 37–50)

Jacob's eleventh son, Joseph, is more connected to God than are the other brothers. In fact, they threw him into a pit to kill him but then decided to sell him into slavery. His new owners took him to Egypt. God gifted him with the ability to interpret dreams, and he came to the Pharaoh's attention. The king was having nightmares. When Joseph was able to decode his dreams, Pharaoh rewarded him with a high position in the government.

Later, during a severe famine, Jacob sent his sons to Egypt to buy some food. Through Joseph, the family was reunited and saved from starvation. At the Pharaoh's invitation, Jacob's clan settled in Egypt.

$\mathcal{G}$od Was in Control All Along

Genesis 50:19-20 shows that Joseph recognized that God can work through the events in a person's life. Nothing catches God by surprise. He can use what looks bad, and He can make it turn out good in the end. This principle was repeated by the apostle Paul in the New Testament:

And we know that God causes everything to work together for the good of those who love God and are called according to his purpose for them (Romans 8:28).

If there was a television show about bad things happening to good people, Joseph could be the celebrity spokesperson. The life of Joseph shows that God can bring good results out of difficult circumstances. In a touching face-off with his brothers, Joseph tells them:

> *Don't be afraid of me....As far as I am concerned, God turned into good what you meant for evil. He brought me to the high position I have today so I could save the lives of many people* (Genesis 50:19,20).

$\mathcal{Y}$ou Otta Be on Broadway, Baby!

If you think that the life story of Joseph would make a good script, you're right. His life is the subject of Andrew Lloyd Webber's blockbuster musical *Joseph and the Amazing Technicolor Dreamcoat.*

Moses—Leader (and Chief Baby-Sitter) of a New Nation

After Joseph died, the memory of his importance quickly faded. Meanwhile, the descendants of Jacob's 12 sons multiplied. Over the next 400 years, the descendants of Jacob had grown to well over 2 million. Out of fear of being overwhelmed by the Hebrews, the Egyptians forced them into slavery.

But the more the Jews were oppressed, the more they multiplied. It got so bad that Pharaoh ordered that all newborn Jewish males must be killed by the Egyptian midwives. In the midst of all of this hardship and anguish, the descendants of Abraham, now called the Hebrews, cried out to God to be rescued.

The Riverboat Baby (Exodus 2:1-10)

Although they had forgotten Him, God never forgot His "chosen nation." His plan for the rescue of the Jews began with a Jewish baby named Moses.

To avoid the death decree, the mother of Moses kept his birth a secret. When she couldn't hide him any longer, she made a papyrus basket and set him afloat in the Nile (sending his older sister to watch what would happen). In God's designed plan, Pharaoh's daughter was bathing in the Nile and found the basket. She fell in love with the baby but needed someone who could nurse the infant. The sister leapt out of the bushes, and guess who she recommended? So, Moses was allowed to be raised through his early childhood by his mother (being taught about God and his Jewish heritage) until he was older. Then he was "adopted" by Pharaoh's daughter and received a royal upbringing.

How Many Names Do They Need?

The descendants of Abraham are called by several different names in the Bible:

- The Jews
- The Hebrews
- Israel (except sometimes Jacob was called "Israel")
- The children of Israel (because Jacob's 12 sons were the start of 12 separate tribes of the Jews)
- The nation of Israel
- The Israelites

Don't get confused. They all refer to the same group.

An Unlikely and Reluctant Leader (Exodus 2:11–4:17)

As a young man, Moses had all the trappings of an Egyptian, but he remembered his Hebrew roots. When he saw a slave master beating a Jewish slave, Moses came to the rescue and killed the Egyptian. He thought the Jews would rally around him, but they weren't ready to recognize him as their leader. Feeling estranged from the Jews, and fearing Pharaoh's reprisal for the murder he had committed, Moses fled to the desert, where he lived for years as a reclusive goatherd.

One day, while Moses was wandering around in the desert, God appeared to him in the form of a burning bush. How could he be sure that this was God? Well, the bush was not consumed by the fire, and it talked. Those are pretty good clues. God told Moses that he was God's chosen leader to bring the Jews out of their slavery in Egypt.

Whose God Is Greater?

The plagues proved that Moses' God was greater than all of the false gods of the Egyptians. Bible scholar William Hendriksen says it this way:

- The Nile (whose waters were turned into blood) was considered a god.
- The frogs (which came swarming into kitchens and bedrooms) received divine honors.
- The cattle (afflicted by later plagues) were objects of worship.
- The sun (darkened during the ninth plague) was identified by the Egyptians with deity.
- And the crown prince (slain during the last plague) was believed to be in very close touch with the heavens.

With the plagues, Moses proved that there is only one true God.

Exit This Way (Exodus 5:1–11:10)

Following God's instructions, Moses confronted Pharaoh with the famous "God says, 'Let My people go!'" speeches. It took a series of plagues to convince Pharaoh that God was serious. These plagues were subtle hints, like Egypt being invaded by grasshoppers (Bible terminology: locusts) and the Nile water turning to blood. These plagues proved to Pharaoh and to the millions of Jews that Moses was God's appointed representative and that God was serious about getting His chosen nation out of slavery.

It took a plague that killed his son to convince Pharaoh to release the Jews (and the Egyptians were so glad to get rid of them and the plagues that they gave them animals, gold, silver, and jewels as lovely parting gifts).

Divine Direction in the Desert (Exodus 12:37–18:27)

With a cloud during the day and a pillar of fire in the sky at night, God led the group of more than 2 million Jews across the desert.

Pharaoh changed his mind and sent his army to recapture the Jews. When the Jews were stuck between the mountains and the Red Sea, with no way of escape, 2 million people started complaining that Moses didn't have a boat. Moses confidently announced that God would deliver them from this calamity (but he had no idea how).

> But Moses told the people, "Don't be afraid. Just stand where you are and watch the LORD rescue you....The LORD himself will fight for you. You won't have to lift a finger in your defense!" (Exodus 14:13-14).

Then God miraculously caused the water of the Red Sea to separate and reveal a path to the other shore. With walls of water on each side and with the ground completely dry, the Jews crossed through the Red Sea. The Egyptian army, apparently slow to understand God's special protection of the Jews, came charging through the same pathway. But when they got halfway through, God caused the walls of seawater to let go. Pharaoh's army drowned.

With supplies running low, God miraculously provided meat, bread (called "manna"), and water for His chosen people while they were in the wilderness. Even with all of these freebies, the Israelites kept constantly complaining about the living conditions.

Laws Written in Stone (Exodus 19:14–24:18)

After a three-month trip, God led the Jews to the base of Mount Sinai (pronounced "sigh-nigh"). They were supposed to

God's Top-Ten List (Old Testament Version)

Here is the list of the Ten Commandments, which God gave to Moses. The first four deal with our relationship to God; the next six deal with our relationship to each other (Exodus 20:1-17).

1. Do not worship any other gods.
2. Do not make any idols to worship.
3. Do not misuse God's name.
4. Keep the Sabbath day holy.
5. Honor your father and mother.
6. Do not murder.
7. Do not commit adultery.
8. Do not steal.
9. Do not be a false witness.
10. Do not covet.

God's Top-Two List (New Testament Version)

Jesus said that these ten commandments (and all of the other laws given by God) could be summed up in two principles:

1. Love the Lord your God with all your heart and with all your soul and with all your mind and with all your strength (Mark 12:30).

2. Love your neighbor as yourself (Mark 12:31).

Metaphors You Can Use

The books of Moses are filled with symbolism and foreshadowing that can help you understand the meaning of the New Testament. For example:

- God provided a ram for Abraham to sacrifice in place of Isaac. The ram represents Jesus (the sacrifice God sent to die in place of you).

- God brought Joseph through some utterly humiliating circumstances so that he could be in a place to rescue his family (thereby saving the entire nation of Israel) when everyone else was starving during the famine. This is a picture of how Jesus left His privileged place in heaven to suffer death on earth, in order to rescue humanity dying in sin.

- Moses brought the children of Israel out of slavery. Moses' role as "deliverer" illustrated in advance the role of Jesus, who came to deliver all of mankind from the slavery of sin.

rest up and get ready to invade and recapture Canaan, the land given by God to their ancestor Abraham.

God called Moses to come to the top of Mt. Sinai alone. It was there that God gave Moses the stone tablets, which contained the Ten Commandments.

God gave other instructions to Moses—instructions for how the people should deal with each other and how to perform the ceremonies for worship. This included God's famous promise to the Jews (the Mosaic Covenant) that He would bless them if they obeyed Him and punish them if they disobeyed Him.

Now if you will obey me and keep my covenant, you will be my own special treasure from among all the nations of the

earth; for all the earth belongs to me. And you will be to me
a kingdom of priests, my holy nation (Exodus 19:5-6).

Sacred Ceremonies at Sinai (Exodus 19:1–40:38; Leviticus)

During these days at camp at the base of Mount Sinai, God
taught His people through Moses. He defined their purpose, which
was to be His holy nation. He also gave instructions about how to
build the Tabernacle (which would be the temporary tent of worship until a permanent temple could be constructed in Jerusalem).

The people responded by making solemn promises to obey God.

Through Moses, God gave the Jews detailed rules and regulations
for daily life and worship:

- civil and criminal conduct (rules for living together as a
  nation)
- health and safety tips (proper diet and avoiding germs
  and disease)
- ceremonies and rituals for worship (sacrifices, offerings, and
  festivals)

From the 12 tribes (descendants from each of Jacob's 12 sons),
God chose the tribe of Levi to work in the Tabernacle. From the
same tribe, God chose Aaron (Moses' brother) to be the high
priest. Once a year, the high priest would enter the "Holy of
Holies" in the Tabernacle, into God's presence, to offer sacrifices for
the sins of all the people. The high priest served as a type of mid-
dleman between God and the people. Jesus would later be called
"the great high priest" for all those who believe in Him (Hebrews
2:17; 4:14-15).

---

*G*od's Nobody

Moses spent 40 years thinking he was somebody; 40 years learning he
was nobody; and 40 years discovering what God can do with a nobody.

Dwight L. Moody

Whining in the Wilderness (Numbers 13:1–14:24)

During the 400 years when the Jews were in Egypt, many pagan nations had occupied the Promised Land. Now the Jews were going to have to invade and recapture their own homeland.

In preparation for the invasion, Moses sent 12 spies to check out Canaan. The spies returned with good news and bad news.

- *The good news:* Canaan is "a land flowing with milk and honey" (which is a Bible way of saying it was a great place to live).

- *The bad news:* The cities were fortified and inhabited by giants (which is a Bible way of saying that the residents of Canaan were very large and very mean).

Ten of the spies recommended aborting the mission. The other two, Joshua and Caleb, trusted in God's power to bring victory. They were fired up to go ahead with the planned invasion.

Unfortunately, the people sided with the cowards. In what would become a pattern for the Jews over the next 1000 years, they forgot all about how God had rescued them from slavery and the miracle of the Red Sea. They forgot about the provision of manna and quail for food. Instead, they whined and complained. They even said they would have preferred to die as slaves in Egypt.

---

*W*hat Has God Done for Me Lately?

Two of the spies had faith that God could give them victory in the Promised Land. Ten of the spies were faithless. How quickly they had forgotten God's miracles in Egypt and at the Red Sea. Their *faithlessness* was the result of their *forgetfulness*.

As a result of their ingratitude and unbelief, God sent the Jews wandering around in the desert for 40 years until everyone over the age of 21 (except Joshua and Caleb) died. Listen to His anger in these verses:

> *Not one of the men who saw my glory and the miraculous signs I performed in Egypt and in the desert but who dis-*

obeyed me...will ever see the land I promised on oath to
their forefathers. No one who has treated me with contempt
will ever see it (Numbers 14:22-23 NIV).

During this time, God continued to miraculously provide for the Jews. He gave them water and food, and their shoes and clothes did not wear out. Regardless of God's provision, they continued to complain. It's a little ironic that the Jews are called the "children of Israel." So much of the time that's exactly how they acted—just like children.

By the end of the 40 years, Moses gathered the Jews together for a series of sermons to remind them of God's promises. Moses was close to death, and he wanted to help the people think ahead to the future God wanted to give them. His moving sermons, collected as the Book of Deuteronomy, could have been titled "Lessons from the Desert."

He challenged God's people to be obedient and faithful to God. Then just before he died, Moses passed the role of leadership to his general, Joshua.

What's That Again?

1. The books of Moses, or the Pentateuch, explain beginnings—of the world, of the human race, of the Jewish nation.

2. Genesis reveals that God created everything. He created mankind with a spiritual nature, a soul, so that we could have a relationship with Him.

3. The sin flaw, which has marked human nature since Adam and Eve disobeyed God in the Garden of Eden, sent the human race on a downward spiral. Yet after the flood, God promised not to destroy the earth again out of anger.

4. From Genesis 12 on (to the New Testament), we see God working through one family—Abraham and Sarah and their descendants—to bring His salvation plan to humans. God promised Abraham that his descendants would grow into a great nation.

5. Exodus shows that God is in the business of rescuing mankind from bondage—as He had done for Joseph, so He freed the Jews from slavery.

6. At Mount Sinai, God gave His people the Ten Commandments and other rules for life and worship. But Numbers through Deuteronomy show the Israelites mostly rebelling against God. They wandered in the desert, living with the miserable consequences of disobedience.

Dig Deeper

Here are some other books you can use for a further exploration of the people, the places, the events, and the God of the books of Moses:

Thru the Bible by J. Vernon McGee. This is a five-volume set taken from the "Thru the Bible" radio broadcasts. The first volume covers the books of Moses. J. Vernon McGee was a country preacher who taught in a down-home style. You'll find this commentary set to be easy reading.

Paradise to Prison—Studies in Genesis by John J. Davis. This is a scholarly work, but it includes an interesting analysis of the archaeological and scientific accuracy of the Bible.

Joseph by Charles R. Swindoll. The famed writer and radio preacher is writing a series of books called

"Great Lives from God's Word." This book contains great lessons for today from the life of Joseph.

Book of Genesis: Inspiration Bible Study Guide by Max Lucado. You'll find this book to be a helpful study guide to reading the Book of Genesis.

Genesis: Discovering God's Answers to Life's Ultimate Questions is from our series of Christianity 101 Bible Studies. You'll learn how God's record of ancient times applies to your life.

■ ■ ■

Questions for Reflection and Discussion

1. Review the six characteristics of God listed at the beginning of the chapter. List at least one way each characteristic affects your life.

2. Why is the "when" of creation less important than the "who" or the "how"? What is your position on the six Creation "days"? Explain why you take this position.

3. What is the significance of God's specific creation of humans? What would be the difference if humans had simply evolved from some gooey blob that crawled out of a swamp?

4. Abraham is called a "man of faith." Why does he deserve this distinction? Give three examples from his life.

5. In what ways does the life of Moses foreshadow the life of Christ?

6. Review God's Top Ten list. Is keeping all ten of these commandments humanly possible? Why or why not?

7. Explain how God's Top Two list (Mark 12:30-31) summarizes God's Top Ten list. Do we still need to pay attention to the longer version, or only to the shorter version? Why?

_____

■ ■ ■

Moving On...

When you think about the first five books of the Bible, think water....In Genesis, God's Spirit hovered over it and divided it from the land. In Exodus, God divided the Red Sea and let the Israelites pass through to safety.

In Deuteronomy, God is about to divide water again. At the close of the book, only the raging Jordan River separates the Jews from the Promised Land (but the river is at flood stage). When Joshua takes the reins of leadership, guess what God's first miracle is on his behalf? (See Joshua 3.)

To get his people ready, Joshua tells them, "Purify yourselves, for tomorrow the LORD will do great wonders among you" (Joshua 3:5).

In the next chapter, you'll see plenty of "great wonders." For example, the Israelites win battles without even lifting a weapon. You'll also see humiliating defeats when they trust in their own power. But the most amazing thing in the stories ahead is God's loving patience with His foolish "kids." Think of it as His water of life to sustain them in a new land.

Chapter 5

If men could learn from history, what lessons it might teach us! But passion and party blind our eyes, and the light which experience gives us is a lantern on the stern, which shines only on the waves behind us!

Samuel Taylor Coleridge

The first five books of the Bible are about the *birth* and *early years* of the human race. They tell the story of God establishing His relationship with people on His terms. These next 12 books are about the *adolescence* of the human race. They are like the teenage years, when the desire to rebel and go it alone is strong. God cares deeply about His people. He cares deeply about you. That's why He won't let us live in rebellion for long without suffering the consequences. We may not understand everything God does in history—or in our lives, for that matter. But we can trust Him to always act with our best interest in mind.

The Books of Generals, Judges, and Kings:
War and Peace

*S*tan's wife, Karin, loves history. She reads books about history, watches the history channel, and has traced and tracked the history of her own Swedish ancestors. Perhaps she is motivated by that great insight of George Santayana: "Those who cannot remember the past are condemned to repeat it." Karin says she just enjoys finding out where she came from, both in the context of her family and her culture.

Karin also loves studying the Old Testament and the history of Israel. "By discovering how God has dealt with His people," she says, "I can learn a lot about how He is dealing with me."

Bible history can do that. So rather than skipping over the Old Testament books of history, which we are calling "the Books of Generals, Judges, and Kings," you can learn a lot about God and how He deals with people by studying these books. True, there are a lot of stories about wars and battles and conquest in these books. It may take some doing to understand how and why God chose to work in this way during this time in history, but hang in there. Try to put yourself in the middle of this history. Focus on the lessons and personal applications of the major characters and stories.

Bible History 201

The first period of Bible history is recorded in the five books of Moses (see chapter 4). We could call it Bible History 101. Approximately 700 years go by from the time of Abraham (Genesis 12) to the death of Moses (Deuteronomy 24), bringing us to another watershed in the history of Israel. We're ready for Bible History 201.

It is now around 1400 B.C. God has used Moses to both deliver His people and also to give them His law. God did *not* use Moses to lead His people into the Promised Land. That responsibility would fall to Moses' protégé and successor, Joshua. The Jewish nation is about to cross the Jordan River into Canaan, the Promised Land, under the leadership of General Joshua, son of Nun.

In this chapter, we are going to cover the next thousand years in the history of God's chosen people, beginning with the conquest of the Promised Land (around 1400 B.C.) and concluding with the end of Old Testament history (around 425 B.C.). The story told by these 12 books is one of war and peace. It's a history of the spiritual triumphs and tragedies of God's people.

When reading the Old Testament, we must be careful to remember that it is the record of God's dealing with the Jews. We must keep everything we read in this context. The whole Bible is the story of God's plan of salvation for fallen man. But God has dealt with people in different ways throughout history. In other words, although God does not change, His methods do.

Conquer and Divide (Joshua)

The Book of Joshua, named for the great military hero who succeeded Moses, is proof that the key to success in life is to obey God by obeying His Word. It also shows the benefits of obedience and the consequences of disobedience to God. One of the themes in Joshua is that the people of God have to make a conscious decision

One-Hour Cram Plan
for the Books of War and Peace

If we figure about ten minutes per passage, you can read six passages in an hour. We would be hard-pressed to select just six passages from these great books, so we'll let you choose your own.

- Joshua 1–4—Joshua leads Israel into the Promised Land...

- Judges 1—...but they don't know what to do with it.

- Judges 6—Gideon gets brave.

- Judges 16—Samson goes blind for Delilah.

- Ruth 1—Naomi comes home.

- 1 Samuel 1—Samuel leaves home.

- 1 Samuel 17—Goliath gets stoned.

- 2 Samuel 5—David gets crowned.

- 1 Kings 3—Solomon gets smart.

- 1 Kings 21—Ahab loses a steal.

- 2 Chronicles 20—Jehoshaphat steals a win.

- 2 Chronicles 36—Jerusalem falls.

- Ezra 9–10—Ezra leads a revival.

- Nehemiah 4—Nehemiah builds a wall.

- Esther 2—Esther wins a beauty contest.

The Books of Generals, Judges, and Kings

What's in the Bible?		What's in the World?
Israel enters Canaan	1406 B.C.	
Judges begin to rule Israel	1375	
	1250	Early musical instruments developed in Europe
	1100	Greek culture begins to develop
David becomes king of Israel	1010	
Solomon becomes king	970	
Temple completed	959	
Kingdom divides	931	
	900	Celts invade Britain
	776	First Olympic Games in Greece
	753	Rome founded
Israel taken into captivity	722	
	604	Nebuchadnezzar becomes king of Babylon
Judah taken into captivity	586	
	544	First public library founded in Greece
First exiles return to Jerusalem	538	
New temple completed	516	
Esther saves Jews in Persia	473	
Israel returns to Canaan	448	Parthenon built in Greece
Nehemiah rebuilds the wall	445	

Conquest, Capture, and Return

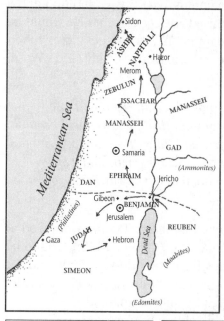

SETTLEMENT AREAS, MILITARY CONQUESTS, AND ENEMY KINGDOMS

→ Arrows indicate Joshua's military conquests, circa 1300 B.C.

TRIBE — Names in capital letters show settlement areas for 12 tribes of Israel

(Enemy Kingdom) — Names in parentheses show enemy kingdoms

---- Kingdom divided in 930 B.C.

⊙ Capitals of Israel (Northern Kingdom) and Judah (Southern Kingdom)

CAPTIVITY AND RETURN

→ Northern Kingdom, Israel, taken captive by Assyria

⟶ Southern Kingdom, Judah, taken captive by Babylon

→ → Return of exiles

to follow Him. God doesn't tolerate halfhearted devotion. "Honor the Lord and serve him wholeheartedly," Joshua tells the people.

Joshua was in a giant pressure cooker. Moses, the great deliverer of Israel, had died, and it was up to Joshua to successfully lead God's anxious and fickle people into enemy territory. God didn't allow Joshua to go in alone. He promised His general that He would be with him, and He told Joshua that he would be successful in everything he did as long as he did one thing—study God's Word. Here's what God told Joshua:

> Be strong and very courageous. Obey all the laws Moses gave you. Do not turn away from them, and you will be successful in everything you do. Study this Book of the Law continually. Meditate on it day and night so you may be sure to obey all that is written in it. Only then will you succeed (Joshua 1:7-8).

Here it is. God's blueprint for true success. Do you want God to lead you? Do you want God to use you? Do you want God to be with you? Then obey the things He has written in His Word. For Joshua, it was the "Book of the Law." For us, it's God's entire Word, the Bible, the world's greatest success manual.

Here are more highlights from this action-packed book:

God tells Joshua how to succeed. In the first chapter, God tells Joshua, "You're My man." He then tells the willing warrior that his success will be in understanding and obeying God's laws.

Joshua tells the people how to succeed. Joshua's no dummy. Throughout his life, Joshua repeats God's instructions like a broken record (or whatever they had in those days). He never lets the people forget where their strength and success come from.

Disobedience affects everyone. A little weasel named Achan (Joshua 7) disobeyed God, and Joshua's entire army paid the price of defeat.

Joshua conquers the land. Another key theme in Joshua is "conquest." God required His people to completely conquer the Canaanites and their sinful ways.

Joshua

Joshua was born a slave in Egypt, but he was destined for greatness in the Promised Land. Joshua never wavered from his commitment to serve God by obeying His commands, and he expected no less of the people he led.

Joshua didn't put up with people who were ambivalent about God. "You don't want to serve the Lord?" Joshua would say. "Then find who you're going to serve and get on with it. But you better think long and hard about the consequences." If he were around today, Joshua definitely wouldn't tolerate wimpy Christians.

At the end of his life, after he had successfully conquered the Promised Land for God's people, Joshua divided the land among the 12 tribes of Israel. He instructed each tribe to keep control of the land by staying devoted to God. "If you are unwilling to serve the LORD, then choose today whom you will serve," Joshua declared. You can almost see the proud warrior, standing strong at the end of his life, as he shouts to the throng, "As for me and my family, we will serve the LORD" (Joshua 24:15).

The Human Sin Cycle (Judges)

Have you ever made a promise to God and then failed to live up to your promise? At the end of Joshua's life, the people of Israel promised to serve God and obey Him alone (Joshua 24:24). The problem was that their commitment didn't last very long.

The Book of Judges tells the story of a people who repeatedly failed to keep their promises to God. In fact, within one generation after Joshua died, the people "did not acknowledge the LORD or remember the mighty things he had done for Israel" (Judges 2:10).

Israel Then Versus Israel Today— Not Much Has Changed

From Bible times to today's headlines, Israel has been hounded and harassed by other nations. Right now it may be Iraq or Syria. Thirty years ago it was Egypt. Three thousand years ago, during the time of Judges and Kings, it was the Philistines.

The Philistines were a powerful, organized, religious (in a pagan sense) people who hated the Hebrew people (sound familiar?). They occasionally dominated Israel (during the time of the judges) and generally gave them fits until David gave their biggest warrior, Goliath, a giant-sized headache.

Here Come the Judges

God sent a series of "judges" or "deliverers" to lead the people out of their sin and back to God. The most famous judge was Samson (Judges 13–16), who illustrates the cycle of sin and repentance that characterized Israel (and us, too). First, Samson was strong (no kidding). Then he fell into sin and paid a dear price when he lost his strength and position. Finally, he recommitted his life, regained his strength, and delivered his people once again.

So How Do You Get Out of the Sin Cycle?

The sin cycle is one of the most frustrating experiences of the Christian life. It goes something like this. You make a decision to live for God, and you really want to do the right thing. Then something happens, you give in to temptation, and you lose all of your spiritual momentum. The problem is that we want to do what we want or what we think is right rather than what God wants. This was true in the days of the judges:

In those days Israel had no king, so the people did whatever seemed right in their own eyes (Judges 21:25).

And it's true today (sound familiar?). The apostle Paul said it this way: "When I want to do good, I don't. And when I try not to do wrong, I do it anyway" (Romans 7:19).

So how do you overcome this frustrating and destructive sin cycle? Only Jesus in you has the power to resist temptation and do the right thing. Paul answered his own question when he said, "Who will free me from this life that is dominated by sin? Thank God! The answer is in Jesus Christ our Lord" (Romans 7:24-25).

Do what's right in God's eyes, not your own.

Love in a Dark Time (Ruth)

The Book of Ruth is one of the shortest and sweetest books in the Bible. Take ten minutes right now and read this tender love story (even if you're a guy). Then come back and read on.

Notice how loyal Ruth was to her mother-in-law. And how about that Boaz? What an honorable man. Can you imagine how different our world would be if men treated women with this kind of respect? The Book of Ruth demonstrates that it is possible to live by godly principles in a society that does just the opposite. All around you people lie, cheat, steal, gossip, and take advantage of each other. But you don't have to live that way. God has called you to live at a higher standard. His standard.

God honored Ruth for her loyalty, and He honored Boaz for his faithfulness. After Ruth and Boaz got married, they had a son named Obed, who was the grandfather of David, Israel's greatest king and an ancestor of Jesus.

A Heart for God (1 and 2 Samuel)

First and Second Samuel are named for Samuel, the last judge and the first prophet of Israel. God called Samuel as a boy to speak to His people (1 Samuel 3:19-21). Essentially, Samuel served as a bridge between the judges and the kings. The primary focus of 1 and 2 Samuel is David, one of the greatest characters in all Scripture.

God Looks on the Inside

Israel badly wanted a king. The fierce and intimidating Philistines, Israel's worst enemy, continually hounded, harassed, and hammered God's people. Like the big bullies they were (and Goliath was their biggest), the Philistines even stole the ark of the covenant, Israel's holiest artifact (it contained the Ten Commandments). Israel couldn't take it anymore. They cried out for a king.

Of course, the people of Israel already had God, the greatest King of all. But they refused to serve Him (1 Samuel 8:7-9). They wanted a tall, dark, spear-throwing king like every other nation. So God gave them the king they asked for (Saul), who wasn't God's choice.

When Saul turned against God and his own people, God stepped in and asked Samuel to find and anoint David, who was God's choice. The people looked on the outside and chose Saul; God looked at the heart and chose a young shepherd named David.

People judge by outward appearance, but the LORD looks at a person's thoughts and intentions (1 Samuel 16:7).

David is called the man after God's own heart (1 Samuel 13:14). You can see his devotion to God in the many psalms he wrote. His lifelong passion for seeking God never wavered, even though he committed some serious sins. His most famous failure was committing adultery with a married woman named Bathsheba and then arranging for her husband to die in battle. David reigned over Israel for 40 years.

Despite his human failings, God used David to bring Israel to a place of glory and honor:

- He united all the tribes under one monarchy.

- He established the capital at Jerusalem.

- He defeated Israel's enemies (some, like the Midianites, Amalekites, and Philistines never troubled the nation again).

- He expanded the nation's region of influence from Egypt in the south to Syria in the north.

- He founded a royal family line (the house of David) into which Jesus was born (Romans 1:3).

David and Solomon

David and Solomon illustrate two sides of what it means to have a "heart after God." As a father and son, they also show the powerful impact—both good and bad—a family can have on the world around it.

David's life can be divided into four parts:

- the brave and gifted *shepherd boy* who protected his sheep from wild animals and defeated Goliath;

- the *fugitive* who fled for his life from King Saul, whose place he would eventually take;

- the *triumphant king,* who established his throne in Jerusalem and built the nation into a world power;

- the *suffering father,* whose sons Absalom and Amnon brought shame to his household after David's acts of adultery and murder.

Solomon's life can be divided into two parts. As David's son by Bathsheba, the woman David stole away from her loyal husband, Solomon inherited the throne. In the first part of his life he honored God and prospered in both wisdom and wealth as no man before or since.

In the second part of his life, Solomon turned away from God and gave himself over to pleasure and idolatry, leading to the division and demise of Israel.

From Glory to Captivity (1 and 2 Kings)

The history of Israel continues in 1 and 2 Kings with David's son Solomon taking over the kingdom, and ends with a divided nation being taken captive by oppressive kings. In between is an amazing story of triumph and tragedy.

Solomon is known as the richest and wisest man who ever lived. His palace, the temple he built for God, and the lavishness of his lifestyle must have been incredible to behold. Yet despite his wisdom and the blessing of God (1 Kings 3:10-14), Solomon "refused to follow the LORD completely, as his father, David, had done" (1 Kings 11:6).

He married many foreign wives and allowed pagan worship in Jerusalem.

> *Thus, Solomon did what was evil in the LORD's sight; he refused to follow the LORD completely, as his father, David, had done* (1 Kings 11:6).

Despite his sin, David's heart never turned from the God he loved. Throughout his life he served the Lord, always coming back to Him after he sinned (Psalm 51). And although his personal life suffered, God preserved David's kingdom. But Solomon, who had every advantage, turned away from God, and his kingdom broke apart as a result.

---

*T*he Wisdom and Splendor of Solomon

Solomon used his wisdom to build tremendous wealth for himself and his country. Israel prospered through foreign trade, mining, and massive building projects, including Solomon's temple. More of a chapel than a cathedral, Solomon's ornate and beautiful temple was really God's temple because it was the dwelling place of God (1 Kings 6:13). Yet when Solomon dedicated the temple, he made it clear that no building could ever really contain the God of heaven.

God Doesn't Like Second Place

As the leader goes, so go the people. The people of Israel turned away from God, and God punished them for it.

Just as He promised He would do if Solomon and his descendants abandoned Him, God uprooted the nation (1 Kings 9:6-7). The once-mighty kingdom was divided in two: Israel in the north with 10 of the 12 tribes of Israel, and Judah in the south with the other two tribes. Each was ruled by a succession of kings—some good, but most as wicked or more wicked than the people.

The big problem with these people was their tendency to turn from the one true God to a bunch of worthless idols. God doesn't tolerate second place. (Now would be a good time to consider if God is in first place in your life.)

> *Turn from all your evil ways. Obey my commands and laws, which are contained in the whole law that I commanded your ancestors and which I gave you through my servants the prophets* (2 Kings 17:13).

Eventually Israel was taken into captivity by the Assyrians in 722 B.C., and Judah by the Babylonians and King Nebuchadnezzar in 586 B.C. Even though His people continued to be disobedient, God continued to show mercy. He sent a succession of prophets to warn the people and to call them back to right living—prophets like Elijah, Elisha, Isaiah, and Jeremiah (see chapter 7 of this book). Sometimes the people and their king responded to the prophet's plea and asked God to forgive them. And every time they did, God forgave them and gave them another chance.

---

*J*erusalem: God's 3000-Year-Old City

Jerusalem celebrated its three-thousandth birthday in 1997. Today it is a troubled city of 600,000 (70 percent of its inhabitants are Jews, and 30 percent are Arabs). Founded during the time of Joshua, Jerusalem has experienced great glory—as in the time of King Solomon—as well as disaster. On many occasions Jerusalem has lain in complete ruins. One destruction occurred when the Babylonians carried Judah, the southern kingdom, into captivity in 586 B.C. Another occurred in A.D. 70 when Jerusalem was leveled and its citizens massacred by the Romans. The temple and the temple worship the Jews valued so highly were destroyed both times.

More than Genealogies (1 and 2 Chronicles)

A lot of people skip 1 and 2 Chronicles because these two books cover the same historical period as 1 and 2 Kings. Besides, there are a lot of genealogies—more than any other book in the Bible—and these lists are just no fun to read. You may have to do some digging to uncover the gems in these two books, but they are there, including one of the most memorable promises God ever made to His people:

> Then if my people who are called by my name will humble themselves and pray and seek my face and turn from their wicked ways, I will hear from heaven and will forgive their sins and heal their land (2 Chronicles 7:14).

The Chronicles were compiled during and after the exile, the darkest period in the Jews' history. The prophet Isaiah described their sorrow this way in a desperate plea to God:

> Zion is a desert, Jerusalem a desolation. Our holy and glorious temple, where our fathers praised you, has been burned with fire, and all that we treasured lies in ruins. After all this, O LORD, will you hold yourself back? Will you keep silent and punish us beyond measure? (Isaiah 64:10-12 NIV).

The main purpose of these history books, then, was to try to face up to some very painful national questions: *What happened? Where did we go wrong? Will God ever bless us again?* These questions are also eloquently addressed in the psalms that were written during the exile (see especially Psalm 74, 89, and 137). No wonder, then, that we find some recurring themes in the Chronicles:

- Wholehearted allegiance to God, not hedging bets with idols or making alliances with evil political powers, is the true source of security for a person or a nation.
- God takes away His blessings when His people turn away from Him.

• God rewards those who wholeheartedly devote themselves to Him.

The eyes of the LORD search the whole earth in order to strengthen those whose hearts are fully committed to him (2 Chronicles 16:9).

Israel Returns (Ezra, Nehemiah, and Esther)

The books of Ezra, Nehemiah, and Esther focus on getting the Jews out of exile from their Babylonian captivity. They tell the story of Israel's rebuilding process, both physically and spiritually. When the Jews were in captivity in Babylon, they were unable to

Post-captivity Time Line

722 B.C.   The ten northern tribes of Israel were captured by the Assyrians (2 Kings 17).

586 B.C.   The two southern tribes of Judah were conquered by the Babylonians and taken into captivity for 70 years (2 Kings 25). When the Persians conquered Babylon, the Jews were allowed to return to their homeland (Ezra 1).

537 B.C.   Zerubbabel led the first expedition of 50,000 Jews back to Jerusalem (Ezra 2).

516 B.C.   The temple in Jerusalem was restored (Ezra 6).

479 B.C.   Esther married King Xerxes and became queen of Persia, preserving the Jews who remained there (Esther 1–10).

458 B.C.   Ezra led the second group of 2000 Jews back to Jerusalem (Ezra 7).

445 B.C.   Nehemiah rebuilt the wall around Jerusalem (Nehemiah 6).

worship God according to their traditions and ceremonies. Also, living in exile brought with it the risk of intermarriage with people who did not love and honor God.

Not Everybody at Once

The Book of Ezra picks up where 2 Chronicles left off. Judah had been in captivity in Babylon for about 70 years when Persia invaded and conquered Babylon. The king of Persia, Cyrus, allowed the Jews to return to Jerusalem.

Interestingly, not many Jews wished to return to their own country, which was 900 miles away. Most of them were caught up in the pagan culture, which was pretty comfortable for them. Those Israelites who decided to return (called the "remnant") faced the difficult task of restoring the destroyed city of Jerusalem as well as restoring their relationship with God. Here is the sequence of events which followed:

Structural rebuilding (Ezra 1–6). Of the 2 to 3 million Jews in captivity, only about 50,000 decided to return to Jerusalem with a guy named Zerubbabel. Despite considerable opposition from outsiders, this remnant rebuilt and dedicated the new temple.

Spiritual rebuilding (Ezra 7–10). Fifty-eight years after the completion of the temple, a priest named Ezra led about 2000 more people (mostly priests) from Persia back to Jerusalem. He noticed that the new temple didn't solve the people's spiritual problems. They still weren't following God's instructions. They were mixing their spiritual culture with the pagan cultures of their neighbors. Ezra challenged the people to confess their guilt and disobedience to God. In response, they committed themselves to living according to His guidelines.

Physical protection (Nehemiah 1–7). As the chief administrative assistant to King Cyrus, Nehemiah had considerable political power. He was a mover and a shaker. When he heard that the rebuilding of Jerusalem had bogged down, he put his reputation (not to mention his cushy lifestyle) on the line and asked the king if he could go to Jerusalem to help his people.

*S*kill comes so slow, and life so fast doth fly. We learn so little and forget so much.

Sir John Davies

The king not only sent Nehemiah to Jerusalem but also gave him his blessing (see how honesty and integrity pay off, especially when you are serving a pagan boss).

When he got to Jerusalem, Nehemiah determined that the wall around the city needed to be rebuilt in order to protect the Jews from the influences and attacks of their pagan neighbors. Nehemiah rallied all of the citizens of Jerusalem to participate in the rebuilding of the wall. Remarkably, they completed the job in a mere 52 days.

Spiritual protection (Nehemiah 8-13). With the newly rebuilt wall surrounding the city, the Jews were able to once again worship God the way they were supposed to. In a citywide revival, Ezra read from the Scriptures to all of the people, who made a covenant with God to obey Him and resist evil.

> *Ezra had determined to study and obey the law of the* LORD *and to teach those laws and regulations to the people of Israel* (Ezra 7:10).

Restoration of our relationship to God involves repenting (turning our backs to sin) and rebuilding our moral and spiritual lives.

*T*his Was No Picket Fence!

This was no little fence Nehemiah and the people built. The city of Jerusalem was about one mile square, shaped like a squashed New Jersey. The wall, when finally constructed, was very high and about 27 feet wide. It served as protection from invaders, and security patrols would ride their horses on the top.

Esther

Ezra and Nehemiah tell the story of the Jews who returned to Jerusalem. But what about those who stayed in Persia? The Book of Esther answers that question. It's a true-life story of romance and intrigue. And although the name of God is never mentioned in the book, it clearly shows how God can and does direct the events and circumstances of life to protect His children.

The story centers around Esther, a young and beautiful Jewish girl, and her older cousin, Mordecai. It just "so happened" that Esther became queen of Persia, and it just "so happened" that Mordecai thwarted an attempt to assassinate the king. Because Esther and Mordecai were faithful to God, He used the "coincidences" in their lives to protect and preserve the Jews when they were threatened with genocide.

If you keep quiet at a time like this, deliverance for the Jews will arise from some other place, but you and your relatives will die. What's more, who can say but that you have been elevated to the palace for just such a time as this? (Esther 4:14).

God Stops Talking

Chronologically, Nehemiah is the last book of the Old Testament. Its story ends in approximately 425 B.C. and, in effect, the recorded history of the Old Testament stops, too.

"Wait a minute, there are still, let's see, five books of poetry and wisdom, and 17 books of prophecy left. What gives?"

Yes, and we're going to cover those in chapters 6 and 7. But right now, at the end of Old Testament history, something very profound occurs—God stops talking. Not a word to anyone for 400 years.

Timing Is Everything

What was God doing in that "400 years of silence"? Well, for one thing, keep in mind that God exists outside of time. So it wasn't like He was yawning the time away.

No, God was preparing the world for the greatest event in the history of the world. He was getting the world ready so He could send His Son.

> *But when the right time came, God sent his Son* (Galatians 4:4).

God may have been silent, but He was actively arranging world events so everything would point to Jesus. Here are a few highlights from the 400 silent years:

333 B.C. Alexander the Great defeats Persia and ushers in the golden era of Greek culture and language. By the time Jesus was born, the Greek language was spoken by most of the world, which helped spread the Good News in the first century.

285 B.C. The Old Testament is translated into Greek (remember the Septuagint from chapter 1?). This made the Scriptures, which pointed to the coming Messiah, more available to people.

63 B.C. Rome takes over Palestine, where the Messiah would be born. You've heard the expression, "All roads lead to Rome." It was true. The Romans built a highly advanced transportation system, which meant that the Good News could literally be carried by land and sea to the ends of the known world with great efficiency. And even though the Roman government was tyrannical in many respects, its power ensured peace throughout the land.

Yes, the world was being prepared. It was only a matter of time. God had a better idea. It wasn't another military campaign. It wasn't a powerful young general or prince. He had let the secret slip hundreds of years earlier through the prophet Isaiah:

Then Isaiah said, "Listen well, you royal family of David! You aren't satisfied to exhaust my patience. You exhaust the patience of God as well! All right then, the Lord himself will choose the sign. Look! The virgin will conceive a child! She will give birth to a son and will call him Immanuel— 'God is with us' " (Isaiah 7:13-14).

What's That Again?

1. God has used human history—particularly the history of His chosen people—to prepare the world for His plan of redemption.

2. Joshua, who based his success on God and His Word, led the nation of Israel into the Promised Land.

3. God sent a series of judges to lead His people out of their sin.

4. God chose David to be His greatest king because of his heart.

5. After generations of poor leadership and religious compromise, God allowed Israel to be taken captive.

6. Men faithful to God led the remnant back to Jerusalem, where the temple and the wall were rebuilt. God used a faithful queen to protect and preserve the Jews who remained.

7. During the so-called 400 silent years, God prepared the world for the coming of His Son, the long-awaited Messiah.

Dig Deeper

You should have no trouble finding additional reading material about these Old Testament books. Here are a few that have earned the "Bruce and Stan Seal of Approval."

David: a Man of Passion and Destiny by Charles Swindoll. One of the "Great Lives from God's Word" series, this book on David combines the ancient true-to-life story with contemporary insight and application.

Esther: a Woman of Strength and Dignity by Charles Swindoll. If you really want to capture the world of Queen Esther and apply it to your life today, this is a great book.

Wilmington's Bible Handbook by Harold C. Wilmington. No pictures, no charts, just the facts. This handbook gives a passage-by-passage synopsis of the Bible, and there are also some great character studies. This book would be especially helpful as you study the Bible history books.

■ ■ ■

*Q*uestions for *R*eflection and *D*iscussion

1. Do you think God's methods have changed throughout human history? Why or why not? Give an example if you think they have.

2. Read Joshua 1:7-8 again. How consistent are you in following the advice of these verses? How can knowing Scripture make you strong and courageous?

3. Can we succeed without obeying God's Word? Define success from the world's standards. Now define success from God's standards.

4. Why are so many Christians reluctant to serve God wholeheartedly (see Joshua 24:14-15)? What has held you back? What could motivate you to join with Joshua and say, "As for me and my family, we will serve the Lord"?

5. Why do you think the Bible talks so much about sin? What can you learn from the lives of Bible characters who sin greatly?

6. What is a person "after God's own heart"? How can you know the heart of God? How do you follow after it?

7. Why must God always be in first place? What are the benefits, if any, for Him? What are the benefits for you?

8. God's chosen people have had a rough time over the years (including today). Is being chosen by God a blessing or a curse? Why?

9. God prepared the world for the first coming of Jesus. How is God preparing the world for the second coming of Jesus?

■ ■ ■

Moving On...

So far in the Bible, God has been like a father who carefully instructs and sometimes lovingly disciplines his children. Now, in this next part, it's as if God steps back and says, "Okay, what do you have to say?"

More than any other section of the Bible, the books of poetry and wisdom are a record of man's response to God. You see, God really cares about what we think and how we feel. He doesn't want our relationship with Him to be a one-way street.

So read on and drink in the emotion and creative expression of the next five books in the Bible. And remember, even though God has a lot to say to you, He's listening, too.

Chapter 6

Books of Wisdom:

Job—how to suffer;
Psalms—how to pray;
Proverbs—how to act;
Ecclesiastes—how to enjoy;
Song of Songs—how to love.

Oswald Chambers

Sometimes God blesses you so much that you feel like echoing the words of King David: "Who am I, O Sovereign Lord, and what is my family, that you have brought me this far?" Other times, when you are going through a dark time, you want to cry out like Job: "I wish I'd never been born!"

The Bible tells us that it's okay to relate to God from your heart whether you're on top of the world or under its weight. It's okay to tell God how you feel.

The books of poetry and wisdom show that God is interested in your heart. He doesn't want your phony lip service. He wants you to express your deepest emotions. If you are open to God, you will find that He always listens and that He is always worthy of your praise.

The Books of
Poetry and Wisdom:
You Sure Have a Way with Words

*P*oetry has been called the purest form of literary expression. Through the ages, poets have expressed majestic—as well as intimate—thoughts about life and love and heaven and earth in a way that captures the imagination like nothing else.

No less a poet than Shakespeare wrote:

> *The poet's eye, in a fine frenzy rolling,*
> *Doth glance from heaven to earth, from earth to heaven.*

Is it any wonder that the Bible, the greatest piece of literature ever written, should contain some of the most magnificent poetry ever written? Not at all. God, who inspired the biblical writers, is the Source of creativity and imagination. We shouldn't be surprised that so much poetry speaks of God because, as poet Thomas Gray wrote, "Genuine poetry is conceived and composed in the soul."

In this chapter we're going to look at the five books of poetry and wisdom: Job, Psalms, Proverbs, Ecclesiastes, and Song of Songs. Contained in these five books are some of the world's most memorable and often-quoted verses. And it's not just because they're beautifully written. They have been composed from the heart and therefore express so much of what we think and feel about our lives and about God.

Heart and Soul

Let's take a minute to place these more literary works in the context of the Old Testament:

- The *first 17 books* of the Old Testament are *historical* in nature. And as we learned in chapter 5, the history of the Old Testament ends in Nehemiah with the building of the wall around Jerusalem by the Jewish remnant.

- The *last 17 books* of the Old Testament are *prophetic* in nature. We'll talk about those in chapter 7.

Between these two groupings are the five poetic and wisdom books. They form the heart of the Old Testament in more ways than one:

- They are in the middle.

- They deal with the issues of God's people as they lived in the presence of God and His prophets.

$\mathcal{T}$hey Were Poets and Didn't Know It

The books of poetry and wisdom were written over a period of more than a thousand years by a group of distinguished writers. Job was written by an unknown author (possibly Job himself) in about 2000 B.C., which would make it the oldest book in the Bible. Various writers, including Moses, David, Asaph, and Solomon, penned the Psalms. Solomon wrote or collected most of the Proverbs, and he is named as the author of the Song of Songs and Ecclesiastes.

- They will speak to your heart as you relate to God.

For these books, the Jewish reader changes questions, and so should we. For the first five books of the Bible, the reader asks, "Where did we come from?" and "Who are we?" In the history books, the reader asks, "What made us the nation we are today, and what are we supposed to learn from it?" Here, the questions are more reflective: "Where is God when it hurts?" "How can I tell God what's really on my heart?" "How can I live well?"

If It's Poetry, Why Doesn't It Rhyme?

There's no literary rule which says a poem has to rhyme. We're just used to it. In the English language, a poem or a song that rhymes is easier to remember. In the Hebrew language, however, the mark of a good poem is the *repetition,* not the rhyme. Rather than making words sound alike, in Hebrew poetry a word or idea is repeated or elaborated upon. This is referred to as parallelism. Here's an example (Psalm 9:9) of parallelism where one line repeats the other:

The Lord is a shelter for the oppressed,
A refuge in times of trouble.

Here's an example (Psalm 103:16-17) where one line is in contrast to the other:

The wind blows, and we are gone—
As though we had never been here.

And here's a verse (Psalm 27:1) where the second line completes the first:

The LORD is my light and my salvation—
So why should I be afraid?

Parallelism is very common in Proverbs as well. Read how one idea is repeated in Proverbs 3:19:

By wisdom the LORD founded the earth;
By understanding he established the heavens.

The Books of Poetry and Wisdom

What's in the Bible?		What's in the World?
Job lives in the land of Uz	2000?	Stonehenge is built in England
	▼	
Moses writes Psalm 90	1406?	
	▼	
	1100	Chinese artists develop sculpture
	▼	
David is a shepherd boy	1025	
	▼	
David becomes king of Israel	1010	
	▼	
	1000	Greek mythology is written
	▼	
Solomon becomes king	970	
	▼	
Temple completed	959	
	▼	
Death of Solomon	931	
	▼	
Kingdom divides	931	

The themes of these books are both contemporary and timeless:

Job—suffering and faith

Psalms—our dependence on God for help, forgiveness, praise, and thanksgiving

Proverbs—the practical consequences of wisdom and foolishness

Ecclesiastes—the meaning of life

Song of Songs—the beauty and power of love

Proverbs, along with Job and Ecclesiastes, can also be categorized as wisdom literature. Job is essentially a narrative drama in three acts, while Proverbs addresses the practical issues of life. Ecclesiastes considers the human tendencies toward pessimism and materialism.

One-Hour Cram Plan for the Books of Wisdom and Poetry

These chapters will give you a nice sampling of the wisdom and poetry books. But we're willing to bet that once you start reading a few chapters, particularly in Psalms and Proverbs, you'll be intrigued to read more.

Job 1–3; 23—Bad things happen to good people.

Psalm 1; 23; 70; 139—Good things come from God.

Proverbs 3; 10—Smart people cooperate.

Ecclesiastes 3—Life can be bitter.

Song of Songs 3—But it can be so sweet.

Job: Faithful Servant

According to God Himself, Job was "the finest man in all the earth—a man of complete integrity" (Job 1:8). It is unlikely that he did anything to deserve hardship and pain. Yet that's exactly what Job got.

The Book of Job begins with a rare glimpse into the heavenlies, where we observe as Satan and God make a deal. God allows Satan to "test" His "faithful servant" Job first by destroying all his possessions, then his children (1:9-22), and then by taking away his health (2:4-10). It's an amazing series of events which leaves Job in a state of suffering "too great for words" (2:13).

God and Satan Have a Little Talk

Job contains one of only three recorded conversations between God and Satan in the Bible (Job 1–2). The first took place in the Garden of Eden, when God cursed Satan for tempting Adam and Eve (Genesis 3:14-15). The other took place when Satan tempted Jesus in the wilderness (Matthew 4:1-11).

As he's sitting on an ash heap and scraping away on the boils that cover his body, Job's wife tells him things are so bad he should just curse God and die. But three "friends" come alongside Job and tell him that he has offended God with his sin and arrogance, and that God is punishing him. With friends like that, who needs...well, you get the picture. Most of the Book of Job is a record of these discussions, with Job pleading his innocence. He may not understand God's ways, but Job sticks up for Him. He tells his friends he can't believe God would go around punishing people for no reason. And he certainly isn't about to curse God.

"Why Me, Lord?"

God answers Job's desperate question personally when He speaks to Job and the others from the middle of a whirlwind (God often has a flair for the dramatic). But God's answer is indirect—mostly, He fires back more questions. God tells these mere mortals

*A*ction is transitory—a step, a blow,
The motion of a muscle, this way or that—
'Tis done, and in the after-vacancy
We wonder at ourselves like men betrayed:
Suffering is permanent, obscure and dark,
And shares the nature of infinity.

William Wordsworth

that He is beyond human understanding. He is worthy of our worship despite our circumstances, good or bad.

Where were you when I laid the foundations of the earth?
Tell me, if you know so much (Job 38:4).

It's important to understand that God is sovereign, which means that nothing happens in heaven or on earth outside His control. This doesn't mean that God causes suffering or evil. Nor does Satan cause all of the wickedness in the world. Ultimately, nothing happens—and no one does anything, not even Satan— unless God allows it. We're called to have faith that God's ways are ultimately best.

So Why Does God Allow Suffering?

The Book of Job wrestles with this question, one of the toughest that humans ask. Philosophers and theologians also refer to it as "the problem of evil." It's as near to our era as the Nazi death camps, and as close to our families as a favorite cousin who gets paralyzed for life in a car accident.

Suffering is not always the result of sin, just as prosperity is not always the result of faithfulness. In fact, at times just the opposite appears to be true. Only God understands why things sometimes work this way. Very often God is beyond our comprehension, and that's not easy to accept. What we can accept, however, is that God wants us to remain faithful to Him, just as Job did.

The Problem of Evil (Why Would a Good, Strong God Allow It?)

So where does suffering come from? There are three primary sources:

1. Satan and his forces do cause significant suffering and pain in the world and to individuals, as he did to Job. However, Satan is not free to do anything he wants. As in the case of Job, God may—and probably does—impose limits. Otherwise, Satan would probably kill us all (John 8:44).

2. We bring much of the hardship we experience on ourselves through bad choices. It is common for unbelieving people to blame God for the consequences of their own bad behavior. Likewise, Christians too often blame Satan for the consequences of their sinful behavior (James 1:14-15).

3. There is a "principle of evil" in the world because of sin. Since Eden, the world has existed in a state of rebellion against God (Romans 1:28-32). It is only by the restraining force of the Holy Spirit, who is in the world to convict us of sin and to lead people to God, that we don't destroy each other because of our utterly sinful natures (Titus 3:3-6).

Saving Faith

The ultimate message of Job is one of hope. Job was faithful—to his God, and to his sometimes unhelpful friends. God restored his health and his fortunes. Yet even if God had not, He still would have been God. Job knew this even before he was restored, as evidenced by his cry in the middle of his deepest pain and sorrow:

> But as for me, I know that my Redeemer lives, and that he will stand upon the earth at last. And after my body has decayed, yet in my body I will see God! (Job 19:25-26).

Somebody Let Me Out of the Zoo

Never believe that God doesn't have a sense of humor, or that He doesn't delight in the unusual and sometimes funny creatures He has made (including us). It isn't until the thirty-eighth chapter of Job that God finally answers His suffering servant, but it isn't in a way you might expect. You would think (humanly speaking, of course) that God would say to Job, "There, there, Job, everything's going to be all right." Instead, God goes off on a kind of animal roll call, asking Job if he knows "Who makes the wild donkey wild?" This wild donkey "hates the noise of the city." God also asks if Job has ever seen an ostrich as she "flaps her wings grandly." God must really like the crocodile, because He talks to Job about this creature for an entire chapter (Job 41). The point—one which Job no doubt understood—was that God's grace and "amazing handiwork" can be seen everywhere. He is Lord of all, and He gives us all we have.

What faith! At another point in the story, Job asks for a mediator to bring him and God together (9:33). Two thousand years before Jesus, Job believed *by faith* that God would send a Redeemer to heal his body and buy him back from the slave market of sin forever.

The story of Job comes to a close with an ironic twist: The one who longed for a mediator with God is himself asked by God to be a mediator for his friends. God tells the three friends to make a sacrifice for their sin of misrepresenting God and to ask Job to pray for them. After Job prays for his friends, the Lord makes him prosperous again and gives him twice as much as he had before, including seven sons and three daughters (Job 42:10-13).

Psalms: Songs in the Key of Life

Pick up your Bible and hold it in front of you. Find the middle and open it up. *Voilà!* You've found the Book of Psalms—the longest and probably most commonly quoted book in the Bible. Every one of the 150 psalms is a gem. Some are very short (Psalm 117 has only two verses), and some are very long (Psalm 119 has 176 verses). Many are cries for help. Almost all express praise to God.

There's a reason why Psalms is in the middle of your Bible. It's the *heart* of the Bible.

If the Bible is God's message to humanity, then the Book of Psalms is humanity's response to God.

The Psalms were actually songs and prayers written in Hebrew-style poetry. The Psalms were set to music, collected in a kind of hymnbook (called a Psalter), and sung by the Jewish people in the temple. The songs were gathered over a period of nearly a thousand years, from the time of Moses to the Babylonian captivity. Moses wrote at least one psalm (Psalm 90), and King David probably wrote half of them. Various musicians and wise men wrote the others.

Traditionally, the 150 psalms have been divided into five parts, or "books." According to the *Life Application Bible,* each "book" corresponds to a different book of the five books of Moses. This poetic connection shows just how important the Psalms are to the history and worship of Israel.

Book I: Psalms 1–41. The emphasis is on God's relationship to human beings and vice versa. These psalms correspond to the Book of *Genesis,* which records the Creation, fall, and planned redemption of humankind.

Book II: Psalms 42–72. The emphasis is on God's relationship to Israel. These psalms are similar in content to the Book of *Exodus,* which focuses on God's rescue of His chosen nation.

Book III: Psalms 73–89. The emphasis is on the sanctuary, or the church. The Book of *Leviticus,* which corresponds to these psalms, deals with the Tabernacle and God's holiness.

Book IV: Psalms 90–106. The emphasis is on the earth and all that is in it. These psalms can be compared to the Book of *Numbers,* which considers Israel's relationship to surrounding nations.

Book V: Psalms 107–150. The emphasis in these psalms is on the Word of God. The central theme of *Deuteronomy,* the fifth book of Moses, is God's Word.

The Psalms Tell Us About God and Us

What the Psalms Tell Us About God:

1. God is the Creator, and His creation does what He wants.

   You make the clouds your chariots; you ride upon the wings of the wind. The winds are your messengers; flames of fire are your servants. You placed the world on its foundation so it would never be moved (Psalm 104:3-5).

2. We cannot ultimately comprehend God, except to the extent that He has revealed Himself to us.

   When I look at the night sky and see the work of your fingers—the moon and the stars you have set in place—what are mortals that you should think of us, mere humans that you should care for us? (Psalm 8:3-4).

3. God has revealed Himself to Israel.

   For he issued his decree to Jacob; he gave his law to Israel (Psalm 78:5).

4. God has revealed Himself to all people.

   The heavens declare his righteousness; every nation sees his glory (Psalm 97:6).

What the Psalms Tell Us About Ourselves:

1. We aren't much.

   O Lord, what are mortals that you should notice us, mere humans that you should care for us? For we are like a breath of air; our days are like a passing shadow (Psalm 144:3-4).

2. We are not an accident; God has given us a purpose on this earth.

   The heavens belong to the LORD, but he has given the earth to all humanity (Psalm 115:16).

3. We are corrupted by sin.

   For I was born a sinner—yes, from the moment my mother conceived me (Psalm 51:5).

4. Our only hope—the only remedy for sin—is God.

   Whom have I in heaven but you? I desire you more than anything on earth (Psalm 73:25).

A Psalm for Every Purpose

Intensely personal and transparent, the Psalms literally sing in praise to the majestic God of the universe (Psalm 96). Sometimes they cry out to the God of mercy (Psalm 51). Other times they express the desire of a nation to turn back to God (Psalm 106). And sometimes they ask God to bring about justice in a world seemingly out of control (Psalm 43).

The Heart of the Matter

Do you have a difficult time opening your heart to God? Start your personal prayer time with a psalm. Get to know these marvelous expressions of faith, hope, and love. Find your favorites and bookmark them. You will be amazed at how your heart will open and how God will fill your every longing with His presence.

The Lord is my shepherd; I have everything I need (Psalm 23:1).

---

*P*raise Completes Us

I think we delight to praise what we enjoy because the praise not merely expresses but completes the enjoyment; it is its appointed consummation.

C.S. Lewis

Proverbs: Wisdom Is the Key

You see them everywhere. Those little instruction books that combine practical advice with homespun homilies. They're supposed to help us do better as we live our lives. And you know what? They're not bad. But if you want to read the all-time greatest book of wisdom, turn to the Book of Proverbs.

Proverbs is one of three wisdom books written by Solomon, the wisest man who ever lived. First Kings 4:32 says that King Solomon composed 3000 proverbs and more than 1000 songs (about 800 of his proverbs are included in the Bible).

How did one man acquire such wisdom? First Kings 3:5-14 says that Solomon asked God for wisdom above all else. This pleased God so much that He gave Solomon "a wise and understanding mind such as no one else has ever had or ever will have."

In the second verse of Proverbs, Solomon tells us that he wrote this book for two reasons:

- to teach people wisdom and discipline
- to help them understand wise sayings

By definition, a proverb is a short poem intended to teach wisdom and common sense. Unlike the common one-line proverbs you may be familiar with (for example, "A stitch in time saves nine"), Solomon's proverbs are two-line, and they take on four basic forms:

1. *Synonymous* proverbs, where the second line repeats the first line in a little different way:

   Pride goes before destruction,
   And haughtiness before a fall (Proverbs 16:18).

2. *Antithetical* proverbs, where the second line is contrary to the first line:

   Hatred stirs up quarrels,
   But love covers all offenses (Proverbs 10:12).

3. *Synthetic* proverbs, in which the second line adds to the idea of the first line:

   Commit your work to the LORD,
   And then your plans will succeed (Proverbs 16:3).

4. *Comparative* proverbs, where a truth is explained by some experience or something in nature:

   As a dog returns to its vomit,
   So a fool repeats his folly (Proverbs 26:11).

More than anything else, the Book of Proverbs is all about *wisdom*: how to acquire it and how to apply it. At its root, *wisdom* means "skill." When you are skilled at doing something, you're good at it. So what is this book suggesting you get good at? It's not a mystery. The answer is found in one of the most-often-quoted verses in the Bible:

> *Trust in the Lord with all your heart; do not depend on your own understanding. Seek his will in all you do, and he will direct your paths* (Proverbs 3:5-6).

Trusting God depends on knowing God. Living right before God depends on knowing what pleases God. When you both know what is right and do it, *that* is wisdom!

Did You Say *Vomit?*

Proverbs is full of witty, funny, and sometimes earthy sayings. Here are a few examples:

As a dog returns to its vomit, so a fool repeats his folly (Proverbs 26:11).

Lazy people are a pain to their employer. They are like smoke in the eyes or vinegar that sets the teeth on edge (Proverbs 10:26).

It is better to live alone in the desert than with a crabby, complaining wife (Proverbs 21:19).

Practical Wisdom from Above

Proverbs is a Bible book for those who think the Bible is all about theology or weird men with unpronounceable names. Proverbs is about how to have friends, how to resolve conflict, what to do with your money, how to find a good wife, and so on. In the process, it teaches the fundamental character qualities of a man or woman who's headed for a happy life. Forget about the self-help books. Stick to Proverbs and find the best advice in the world.

Don't lose sight of good planning and insight (3:21).

Lazy people are soon poor; hard workers get rich (10:4).

A relaxed attitude lengthens life; jealousy rots it away (14:30).

*W*anna Be a Wise Guy?

Do you want to gain wisdom? Here's a practical exercise anyone can do. Proverbs has 31 chapters. Read one each day every day for a month. Then repeat the process next month, and the month after that. In fact, do it *every* month. After you're familiar with Solomon's opus, start meditating on just one saying a day. You'll be amazed at how your spiritual and mental conditioning will improve.

A gentle answer turns away wrath, but harsh words stir up anger (15:1).

We could go on, but you get the idea. Proverbs are good for life!

Ecclesiastes: Is That All There Is?

What if you could sit down with the richest, most powerful, most famous person who ever lived, and ask him any question you wanted? What would you ask? Well, we would ask him one simple question: "What's it like to be the richest, the most powerful, and most famous person who ever lived?"

So, What Is It Like?

Solomon wrote Ecclesiastes, the second wisdom book, toward the end of his life. His glory years had passed. His kingdom was about to split in two. Clearly, Solomon had not lived up to his promise to serve God wholeheartedly. His life became consumed with pleasure, political compromises, and idolatry (1 Kings 11:3-6). Ecclesiastes is his reflection on an incredible life that had drifted from God.

The tone and style of Ecclesiastes is definitely unique among the books of the Bible. It shows that the writer, inspired by God to record the words and ideas in this book, understands the skeptical side present in all people. And it shows that sometimes the strongest faith comes out of great doubt.

Some scholars feel that Ecclesiastes balances the practical wisdom of Proverbs. And while the book doesn't follow any clear outline, it does cover several themes. Here are ten of the most practical:

Themes of Ecclesiastes/Themes of Life

- Wisdom is more valuable than folly (2:13).

- The enjoyment of life and satisfaction in work are gifts of God (2:24), but even these don't satisfy (2:26).

- There is injustice in the world (4:1), and our earthly political systems are oppressive (5:8-9).

- Money doesn't buy happiness, and even those who love money will never have enough (5:10).

- Sometimes the good die young (7:15).

- Even though you determine to let wisdom guide your life, wisdom can be very difficult to find (7:24).

- There's nothing wrong with enjoying life (8:15).

- It's important for a young person to honor God (12:1).

- Often, everything seems meaningless (12:8).

- Despite life's hardships and injustice, fear God and obey His commands (12:13).

Like Proverbs, the Book of Ecclesiastes doesn't hide its purpose. It also gives you Solomon's answer to our question:

> *"Everything is meaningless," says the Teacher, "utterly meaningless!"* (Ecclesiastes 1:2).

The God-Shaped Vacuum

"Everything" refers to everything apart from God. Remember when we talked in chapter 4 about people being made in God's image? In this confession, Solomon writes, "God has...planted eternity in the human heart, but even so, people cannot see the whole scope of God's work from beginning to end" (Ecclesiastes 3:11). In addition to having an eternal soul, bearing God's image means we have a "God-shaped vacuum," or emptiness, in the very heart of our being.

We all experience a longing for the eternal, and only God—not money, power, fame, or pleasure—can fill it. Solomon recognized this firsthand, and he wrote down his conclusions for all to read:

Here is my final conclusion: Fear God and obey his commands, for this is the duty of every person (Ecclesiastes 12:13).

As you read Ecclesiastes, you may find it to be negative and depressing. Keep in mind that this book—or the entire Bible, for that matter—is not about finding happiness in your circumstances. It's about facing the truth and finding ultimate and lasting fulfillment in God. Compared to God, everything else really is meaningless.

Why Be So Negative?

Besides showing the futility of life lived apart from God, Ecclesiastes bares the soul of a man steeped in cynicism. One of the marvelous things about the Bible is that it presents people—even people who followed God faithfully—with all of their flaws intact. We can learn from their lives, including the mistakes. It's as if God wants to make sure we know that life can be difficult, and sometimes it can be *really* difficult. Only by turning to God and depending on Him faithfully can we live our lives with any meaning.

Song of Songs: More Than Meets the Eye

Here's a "Bruce and Stan Bible Quiz." Give us your best answer to this multiple-choice question: The Song of Songs (also known as the Song of Solomon) is...

a. a beautiful story about the love between a husband and a wife

b. an allegory about the love of God for His people and the love of Jesus for His church

c. the one Bible book that makes young men snicker in church

d. all of the above

If you answered "d" to the question, you are correct. This love poem written by Solomon is about a peasant girl and a king who falls for her. Its descriptions of love, courtship, and marriage are among the most beautiful in all of literature.

Written a Good Love Poem Lately?

When the Song of Solomon is interpreted literally as a love poem between a husband and a wife, it provides a pretty decent example of how effective good old-fashioned love poetry can be. The book also shows how much God values the purity and passion of love within marriage. Hey, when the *Young Man* says,

> *You are like a private garden, my treasure, my bride! You are like a spring that no one else can drink from, a fountain of my own* (4:12),

and the *Young Woman* answers,

> *Oh, lover and beloved, eat and drink! Yes, drink deeply of this love!* (5:1),

that should be enough wood for a pretty hot fire!

Once Upon a Time

Merrill Unger, in his classic book *Unger's Guide to the Bible*, retells the Song of Songs in a fairy-tale fashion. Only this isn't a fairy tale. It's the truth. As Unger tells it, King Solomon owned a vineyard, which he rented to a family. The two sons in the family treated one of their sisters, known as the Shulammite (we would call her Cinderella), like a slave. Read what happens to the young lady.

> One day a handsome stranger came to the vineyard. It was Solomon in disguise. He took notice of her, and she became embarrassed about her personal

appearance (1:6). She thought he was a shepherd, and inquired about his flocks (1:7). He replied evasively, but spoke loving words to her (1:8-10), promising rich gifts for the future (1:11). He won her love and departed with the promise that he would return. She dreamed of him at night and felt him near (3:1). Finally, he did come back in all his royal grandeur to take her as his bride (3:6-7).

The Song of Songs also depicts in allegorical fashion God's love for Israel (Hosea 2:16-20) and the love of Jesus, the Bridegroom, for His bride, the church (2 Corinthians 11:2).

How beautiful you are, my beloved, how beautiful! (Song of Songs 1:15).

What's That Again?

1. The books of wisdom show us how to ask God reflective questions.

2. The Book of Job tells us how to deal with suffering without losing faith.

3. The Psalms tell us about God and us.

4. The Book of Proverbs teaches us not only to know what is right but also to do the right thing.

5. Ecclesiastes offers this big idea: Life is not about finding happiness but facing the truth and finding ultimate fulfillment in God.

6. The Song of Songs proves that God loves love, and He wants us to love it too.

Dig Deeper

These books can provide you with interesting details about the Old Testament's wisdom and poetry books, and details about the authors, too.

An Introduction to the Old Testament Poetic Books by C. Hassell Bullock. A scholarly but interesting volume on the five wisdom books of the Bible.

The Treasury of David by Charles Spurgeon. This three-volume set is a classic. The most prolific preacher and Christian writer of the nineteenth century lovingly comments on each verse in the Psalms. Be prepared for nineteeth-century English.

Psalms by Charles Spurgeon. This two-volume set, which is from the Crossway Classic Commentaries, is a condensed, easier-to-read version of *The Treasury of David.*

The New Unger's Bible Handbook by Merrill Unger. Probably our favorite Bible handbook, especially for the books of poetry and wisdom. Each book of the Bible is treated in colorful detail.

■ ■ ■

*Q*uestions for *R*eflection and *D*iscussion

1. Give three reasons why you think the books of poetry and wisdom are in the middle of the Old Testament.

2. Look up the word "sovereign" in the dictionary (if you have a Bible dictionary, that's even better). In what ways are sovereign rulers on earth like the sovereign God? In what ways are they different?

3. How God can permit suffering without causing it?

4. Give an example of a bad choice that leads to suffering. Give an example of suffering that has nothing to do with choices. Why might people tend to blame God for much of the suffering and evil in the world?

5. How could Job know—2000 years before Jesus was born—that his Redeemer lived? What does this imply about the nature of Jesus?

6. Here's your chance to be a poet. Write an eight-line psalm that expresses how you feel about God (remember, it doesn't have to rhyme).

7. Why might King Solomon, the wisest and richest man who ever lived, have been so cynical and ultimately realistic about life?

■ ■ ■

Moving On...

When you look only on the surface, it might seem a bit odd that God stuck the Song of Songs, a rather sweet little book, right before the Book of Isaiah and the rest of the prophets, who have never been described as "sweet." But, as always, Bruce and Stan ask you to look *below* the surface to discover the beauty of God's plan. That's why we've come up with a little analogy we like to call, "Sometimes you need a little sherbet."

Have you ever been to a fancy restaurant where they give you a scoop of sherbet ice cream between two courses of food? The sherbet is a "palate cleanser" that refreshes your mouth and gets you ready for the next course.

The Song of Songs and the other books of poetry and wisdom are like sherbet. They're sweet and they're cleansing. And they set you up for the books of the prophets. The love allegory of the Song of Songs in particular also helps us understand that the prophets weren't a bunch of noisy lunatics, condemning everything and everyone around them. As much as they spoke of God's judgment, they also spoke of His love—the same kind of love Solomon wrote about.

So read on and open your heart. The prophets of God are about to speak.

Chapter 7

Note posted on conference-room door: The regularly scheduled meeting of the Psychic Society has been cancelled due to unforeseen circumstances.

As you get ready to read about the last section of books in the Old Testament, maybe this is a good time for a quick review:

Chapters 4 and 5. The story of the Old Testament starts at the dawn of time in Genesis and winds through 17 books to Esther. But the story stops in about 400 B.C. By this time, some of the Jews have left exile in Babylonia and returned to Jerusalem to rebuild the city of Jerusalem and its temple.

Chapter 6. The next five books of the Bible (Job through Song of Solomon) are poetry books. They don't extend the historical time line. They were written during the events described in chapters 4 and 5.

Now we're at the books of the prophets. Like the poetry books, they don't add to the time line either. The books of prophecy were written just before, during, and after the Jews were taken captive and lived in exile in Assyria, Babylonia, and Persia.

But that doesn't make them outdated manifestos written by a bunch of lunatics. For example, every single one of the prophets' predictions about the birth and death of Jesus came true. With that kind of accuracy, we ought to pay close attention to what they wrote about God and their predictions for the end of the world.

The Books of the Prophets:
Grumpy Old Men

*W*hat's *A*head

- ☐ How to Make a Prophet
- ☐ Who Are These Guys?
- ☐ Now Hear This
- ☐ The Major Prophets: Profiles in Neglect
- ☐ The Minor Prophets: Deep Thoughts in Small Packages

*W*e think you'll find the Old Testament prophets to be fascinating reading. First of all, some of their biographies are pretty colorful:

- Hosea was married to a prostitute.
- Jonah took a famous cruise *inside* a fish.
- Ezekiel lay on his side for 390 days and ate only one meal a day cooked over manure.

But the books of the prophets are much more than the collected memoirs of men who behaved strangely and had questionable hygiene routines. When these guys were walking around on the earth, they were the recognized "spokesmen" for God Himself. If you wanted to know what God was thinking, you would listen to what these men were saying. And beyond that, they gave many clues to identify Israel's long-awaited Messiah. They even gave clues about what is in store for *your* future.

How to Make a Prophet

During the period of the Old Testament, God spoke to the Jews (and the rest of the world) through men and women who were chosen by God for that specific purpose. After all, the Jews didn't have the Bible that is available to us. So, God used certain people to communicate His messages, and these messengers were called "prophets." Their job was to be God's mouthpieces.

Bruce and Stan's Apology

We expect that we will meet all of these prophets someday up in heaven. (We probably won't recognize them at first because we don't know what they look like, although Ezekiel might be easily identified if the stench still lingers from his manure barbecues.) So, to avoid any hard feelings or misunderstandings (and because these guys were tight with God), we want to apologize in advance for calling the prophets "grumpy old men." Let us explain what we mean.

These prophets spent years telling the Jews that they should repent from their rebellious ways and turn back to God. The Jews were going about their everyday lives with indifference and disregard toward God, and the prophets predicted that bad stuff was going to happen as a result of the Jews' attitude. Most of the time the prophets were ignored. Oftentimes they were ridiculed. They were considered to be on the lunatic fringe of society. Basically, the Jews considered the prophets to be eccentric, grumpy old men.

So, if we ever get cornered by these guys in a dark alley in heaven, we hope that this clears things up.

Long ago God spoke many times and in many ways to our ancestors through the prophets (Hebrews 1:1).

While the circumstances of each prophet were different, they all spoke about God's holiness. Whether they were speaking directly to the king or to the people at large, the prophets fearlessly condemned sin and spiritual indifference. As you can expect, they weren't always very popular, and they were often ignored.

Usually the prophet presented his message orally, but not always. Sometimes it was done in writing. Other times it was done with a bit of symbolic theatrics for added emphasis:

- Jeremiah smashed pottery.
- Ahijah ripped his new coat into shreds.
- Isaiah walked naked and barefoot through the city.

One-Hour Cram Plan for the Books of the Prophets

Even the heartiest Bible readers don't always make it through all of the prophet books. However, there are some tremendous passages that you shouldn't miss. At a minimum, be sure to read these:

- Isaiah 6—Isaiah gets his assignment from God.
- Isaiah 53—The Messiah will be a suffering servant.
- Jeremiah 36—An old-fashioned book burning
- Ezekiel 37—Them bones, them bones, them dry bones
- Daniel 1—Daniel resists peer pressure.
- Daniel 3—Three friends in a fiery furnace
- Daniel 5—Daniel reads some holy graffiti.
- Daniel 6—Daniel in the lion's lair
- Jonah 1–4—Jonah has a whale of a time.

The Books of the Prophets

What's in the Bible?		What's in the World?
Kingdom divides	**931** B.C. ▼	
Ahab becomes king of Israel	**874** ▼	
Elijah begins his ministry	**874** ▼	
Jonah (reluctantly) becomes a prophet	**793** ▼	
	753 ▼	Rome founded
Isaiah begins his ministry	**740** ▼	
Israel taken into captivity by Assyria	**722** ▼	
Jeremiah begins his ministry	**627** ▼	
Daniel exiled to Babylon	**605** ▼	
Judah taken into captivity by Babylon	**586** ▼	
Daniel begins his ministry	**580** ▼	
	559 ▼	Cyrus becomes king of Persia
	539 ▼	Persia conquers Babylon
First exiles return to Jerusalem	**538** ▼	
Nehemiah rebuilds the wall	**445** ▼	
Malachi's ministry	**430**	

How Did the Prophets Get the Message?

The prophets didn't make stuff up. They only repeated what God told them to say. But how did God communicate with them? That's a good question. It wasn't always done in the same way. The prophet Samuel heard a voice. The prophet Daniel had dreams. But usually, it was a matter of the prophet being so completely devoted to God that he felt compelled and prompted by the Spirit of God to speak a certain message. When you read about the prophets in the Bible, you will see this phenomenon explained with phrases like:

The word of the Lord came to...

The Lord touched the mouth of...

However it happened, the important thing to realize is that the prophet was speaking what God wanted to say:

Above all, you must understand that no prophecy in Scripture ever came from the prophets themselves or because they wanted to prophesy. It was the Holy Spirit who moved the prophets to speak from God (2 Peter 1:20-21).

Who Are These Guys?

God gave prophets to the Jews as His special representatives throughout their history. During the gaps between the prophets' presence on the national stage, the Jews felt afraid and abandoned. One psalmist wrote, "We see no miraculous signs as evidence that you will save us. All the prophets are gone; no one can tell us when it will end" (Psalm 74:9).

The word *prophet* also described a person who conducted his ministry in a variety of ways. These are a few of the best-known prophets:

- Abraham, the father of the Jewish nation, was referred to as a prophet in Genesis 20:7, but he didn't function in the traditional capacity since there wasn't a nation yet. Angels appeared to him on several occasions.

- Moses was a prophet, bringing the messages of God to the Israelites at Mount Sinai and as they wandered in the

One Mistake and You're Dead

God had a special relationship with His prophets, and He didn't want any fakes or pretenders to claim the position. So He imposed a simple test. If anyone claiming to be a prophet made a wrong prediction, even once, then he was to be sentenced to death by stoning (Deuteronomy 13:10). It was a severe penalty, but God doesn't like people lying about being His messengers. And it made it easy to tell the phony from the real thing.

False prophets were a real problem for Israel. Know why they were so appealing? Right. *They said what people wanted to hear!* Read about Jeremiah's encounter with one phony in Jeremiah 28, or Ezekiel's nasty prediction in chapter 13 for "the foolish prophets who follow their own spirit and have seen nothing!" (verse 3, NIV).

wilderness. He was known as the prophet "whom the LORD knew face to face" (Deuteronomy 34:10).

- Nathan was the prophet during the reign of King David, when the nation of Israel was united. He told the king that God knew about his sin with Bathsheba. Nathan also wrote a national history (2 Chronicles 9:29), but we have no book with his name on it.

- Elijah and Elisha were prophets during the time when Judah (the southern kingdom) and Israel (the northern kingdom) were divided. They are both known for their many miracles. Elijah and Elisha operated almost like national leaders and exerted enormous spiritual influence during an era when Israel's kings were faithless and corrupt.

But none of these guys wrote any of the books we are discussing in this chapter (and except for Moses, none wrote any of the books of the Bible).

The books covered in this chapter are the collected writings of 16 prophets who are all from the time period immediately prior to, during, and after the captivity and exile of the Jews. Each book is named for the prophet who wrote it (except the prophet Jeremiah also wrote the Book of Lamentations). Here's the list of the books of the prophets in the order they appear in the Bible.

1. Isaiah
2. Jeremiah
3. Lamentations
4. Ezekiel
5. Daniel
6. Hosea
7. Joel
8. Amos
9. Obadiah
10. Jonah
11. Micah
12. Nahum
13. Habakkuk
14. Zephaniah
15. Haggai
16. Zechariah
17. Malachi

The Prophets' Alma Mater

Most prophets received formal training. Samuel started a training program for prophets. It was perhaps the ancient world's equivalent of a vocational school, and it actually had several campuses (2 Kings 2:3,5; 4:38; 6:1). The enrollment varied from year to year, but from the time of Samuel to Malachi, the people of Israel were never prophet-less. The schools were run by a leading prophet, and the curriculum was the laws of Moses.

Not everyone who went to "Prophets College" had the God-given gift of prophecy. And not all of the prophets received formal training. Amos, for example, had not been trained at the prophets' school (Amos 7:14-15).

The books of the prophets can be categorized chronologically:

- Some were pre-exile (in the northern kingdom of Israel before the invasion by Assyria in 722 B.C., or in the southern kingdom of Judah before the invasion by the Babylonians in 586 B.C.).

- Some were during the exile (in Assyria or in Babylon).

- Some were post-exile (after the return to Jerusalem from captivity in Babylon).

The following chart arranges the prophets by time and place.

——— The Time and Place of the Prophets ———

Time Period	Date	Audience	Prophet
Pre-Exile	760–715 B.C.	Israel (the northern Kingdom)	Amos Hosea
	835–580 B.C.	Judah (the southern Kingdom)	Joel Micah Isaiah Zephaniah Jeremiah Habakkuk
	782–654 B.C.	Assyrians	Jonah Nahum
	848–841 B.C.	Edomites	Obadiah
Exile	605–535 B.C.	Jews in Babylonia	Daniel Ezekiel
Post-Exile	520–424 B.C.	Jews in Jerusalem	Haggai Zechariah Malachi

In the rest of this chapter, when we talk about "the prophets," we'll be referring to these 16 prophets who are the authors of the prophetical books of the Old Testament.

Now Hear This

The prophets are famous for making predictions that came true. But predicting the future was only a small part of what they did. Their primary job was a combination of being an investigative reporter and a preacher. In other words, they exposed moral corruption, condemned it, and demanded repentance.

The messages of the prophets took the form of either proclamation or predictions.

A Prophet Proclaims...

A prophet's primary role was to point the people to God. In doing so, the prophets proclaimed God's principles. We'll cite examples from the proclamations of Amos and Isaiah (both prophesied about 750 B.C. in the northern kingdom and southern kingdom, respectively), but these themes were echoed by other prophets as well:

- They condemned society's immorality and wickedness.

  Let me no longer see your evil deeds. Give up your wicked ways. Learn to do good. Seek justice. Help the oppressed. Defend the orphan. Fight for the rights of the widows (Isaiah 1:16-17).

- They exposed religious hypocrites who adhered to the rituals on the outside but who were spiritually dead on the inside.

  "I am sick of your sacrifices," says the LORD. "Don't bring me any more burnt offerings!...Why do you keep parading through my courts with your worthless sacrifices? The incense you bring me is a stench in my nostrils!...From now on, when you lift up your hands in prayer, I will refuse to look....For your hands are covered with the blood of your innocent victims" (Isaiah 1:11-15).

- They called people to repent from their wickedness and turn back to God.

    Now this is what the LORD says to the family of Israel: "Come back to me and live!" (Amos 5:4).

- They warned of God's wrath and judgment if the people did not repent (usually involving a foreign nation which would be used by God to punish His people).

    Come back to the LORD and live! If you don't, he will roar through Israel like a fire, devouring you completely (Amos 5:6).

But the message of the prophets was not limited to doom and gloom. They also preached of God's love.

- They spoke of God's desire to forgive and restore a relationship with mankind.

    "For the mountains may depart and the hills disappear, but even then I will remain loyal to you. My covenant of blessing will never be broken," says the LORD, who has mercy on you (Isaiah 54:10).

- They explained God's plan to redeem His people.

    In that day I will restore the fallen kingdom of David. It is now like a house in ruins, but I will rebuild its walls and restore its former glory (Amos 9:11).

A Prophet Predicts...

The prophets are most famous for what they did only occasionally—predict the future. This ability came from God, so they couldn't do it whenever they wanted to. They could only do it when God gave them the ability.

The prophets never predicted the outcome of things like sporting events or the stock market. Their predictions always related to spiritual matters. Often, the predictions focused on what would happen if the people did not repent of their sins and turn back to God.

- Micah predicted that the temple of Solomon in Jerusalem would be destroyed (Micah 3:12).

- Jeremiah predicted that the southern kingdom would be carried away into Babylonian captivity (Jeremiah 13:19).

- Hosea predicted that the northern kingdom would be carried away into Assyrian captivity (Hosea 9:3).

A Potpourri of Prophets' Prose

The prophets were not made from the same mold. Their lives and personalities were all different. So were their moods and messages:

- lyrical—*Is anyone thirsty? Come and drink* (Isaiah 55:1).

- picturesque—*Jerusalem has sinned greatly, so she has been tossed away like a filthy rag* (Lamentations 1:8).

- anguished—*I will mourn and lament. I will walk around naked and barefoot in sorrow and shame. I will howl like a jackal and wail like an ostrich. For my people's wound is far too deep to heal* (Micah 1:8-9).

- blunt—*Hate evil and love what is good* (Amos 5:15).

- angry—*So now I am filled with the LORD's fury. Yes, I am weary of holding it in!* (Jeremiah 6:11).

- comforting—*I will search for my lost ones who strayed away, and I will bring them safely home again. I will bind up the injured and strengthen the weak* (Ezekiel 34:16).

- just plain weird—*Then the third of these strange beasts appeared, and it looked like a leopard. It had four wings like birds' wings on its back, and it had four heads* (Daniel 7:6).

Major or Minor—
They're in a League of Their Own

Each of the 16 prophets is usually categorized as either a "major prophet" or a "minor prophet." The Bible doesn't refer to them this way, but most Bible scholars do.

The "major" versus "minor" distinction refers to length, not status. The major prophets are the long books, and the minor prophets are the short ones.

- Major prophets: Isaiah, Jeremiah, Ezekiel, and Daniel

- Minor prophets: all of the other 12

But not all of the predictions were depressing. Some were very encouraging. God wanted to remind the people that He would be faithful to His promises even though they were not faithful to Him.

- Jeremiah predicted that the Babylonian captivity would only last 70 years (Jeremiah 25:11; 29:10).

- Isaiah predicted that after the 70 years of captivity, the Jews would be allowed to return to rebuild Jerusalem and the temple (Isaiah 44:28).

But the most famous predictions of the prophets concern the Messiah which God promised to send. The people were anxious for the Messiah to arrive, and the prophets gave predictions that could be used to identify the genuine Messiah from the wanna-bes.

Seven Clues to the Secret Identity

The prophets gave a lot of predictions about the circumstances of the birth, life, and death of the Messiah. All of these prophecies were for one man—Jesus Christ—who was born hundreds of years after the predictions were made. Here are a few of the more famous prophecies about the Messiah:

1. He will be born in the village of Bethlehem (Micah 5:2).

2. He will be born to a virgin (Isaiah 7:14).

3. He will triumphantly enter the city of Jerusalem (Zechariah 9:9).

4. He will be rejected by His own people (Isaiah 53:1-3).

5. He will be tried in court and found guilty (Isaiah 53:8).

6. He will be beaten and spit upon (Isaiah 50:6).

7. He will die as a sacrifice for man's sins (Isaiah 53:5-12).

When Bible scholars sit around and talk about the prophets, they refer to the proclamations of the prophets as "forth-telling," and the predictions of the prophets are referred to as "foretelling."

The Major Prophets: Profiles in Neglect

Have you ever seen a shabby-looking guy on the sidewalk holding a sign which says: "The End of the World Is Near"? You ignored him as a nut-case, right? Well, that's kind of the same reaction that the prophets of the Old Testament got. You would think that people would listen to a person who was speaking for God, but that didn't happen much.

Here's a quick review of each of the books of the major prophets, up close and personal. Maybe you'll find one that particularly interests you. Because an awareness of Israel's coming Messiah is so strong in these books, we've included a few "Where's Jesus?" entries.

Isaiah: Salvation from God Alone

Isaiah is considered one of the leading Old Testament prophets. His writing style is often majestic, soaring, and highly visual. The power of Isaiah's poetry has influenced great writers and speakers from Shakespeare to Whitman to Martin Luther King, Jr.

A prophet to the southern kingdom of Judah before the Babylonian captivity, Isaiah proclaimed that the spiritual and social salvation of the Jews is available from God alone—not from alliances with other nations, not from false gods, and most certainly not from themselves.

The word *salvation* appears 26 times in Isaiah (and only seven times in all the other prophetical books). Chapters 1–39 emphasize man's need for salvation. Chapters 40–66 state that salvation is available only on the basis of God's righteousness. Our good deeds are like "filthy rags" compared to God's righteousness (Isaiah 64:6). The major theme of the Book of Isaiah is that salvation is available through trust in God alone.

> *Seek the LORD while you can find him. Call on him now while he is near. Let the people turn from their wicked deeds. Let them banish from their minds the very thought of doing wrong! Let them turn to the LORD that he may have mercy on them. Yes, turn to our God, for he will abundantly pardon* (Isaiah 55:6-7).

*W*here's Jesus?

Isaiah gives some of the best descriptions of Christ contained in the Old Testament, including details of the Messiah's life (He would be born of a virgin—7:14). But Isaiah is best known for describing the Messiah as a "suffering servant." Read chapter 53! If you've never read it before, it may still have that familiar ring—Handel used much of it in his famous oratorio, *The Messiah*.

> *He was oppressed and treated harshly, yet he never said a word. He was led as a lamb to the slaughter* (Isaiah 53:7).

Jeremiah and Lamentations: Divine Discipline

Have you ever watched someone working with clay on a potter's wheel? As the wheel spins, the potter molds the clay into the shape of a pot. If the pot starts to turn out with the wrong shape, then the potter smashes the clay and starts the molding process all over again.

That is the same illustration which God used for the prophet Jeremiah to explain the discipline which would befall the nation

Jeremiah

All of the prophets were heroic, but Jeremiah is a standout. Not because he was successful, but because he never quit during 40 years of frustrating failure. He was the last prophet to the decaying southern kingdom of Judah. He gave up friends and family, and never married, all for the sake of calling the Jews back to God. But they didn't listen. In fact, when he predicted the fall of Jerusalem, they had him jailed for being unpatriotic. He never saw the slightest hint that he was making a difference. What was the secret of his perseverance? He must have known that God didn't require him to be successful, only faithful.

of Judah for its wrong behavior. (See this great analogy in Jeremiah 18:1-11.)

The books of Jeremiah and Lamentations, both written by Jeremiah, show a man who was intensely emotional and compassionate (Jesus quoted Jeremiah more than any other prophet). Jeremiah writes candidly about his inadequacies and personal struggles (see chapters 1 and 15). For 40 years, Jeremiah warned the citizens and leaders of Judah about their blatant rejection of God's laws. Confronting people with their sin is risky, and Jeremiah suffered social and political consequences because he was faithful to preach God's warnings.

Jeremiah predicted that God would allow Judah to be invaded and that the city of Jerusalem (and the temple) would be destroyed. All of this would happen because of Judah's rejection of God. But despite this discipline, God's love for the Jews would not waiver.

"For I know the plans I have for you," says the LORD.
"They are plans for good and not for disaster, to give you
a future and a hope. In those days when you pray, I will

listen. If you look for me in earnest, you will find me when you seek me. I will be found by you," says the LORD (Jeremiah 29:11-14).

Lamentations is a book of mourning. Jeremiah wrote this extremely personal book about the siege and fall of Jerusalem by the Babylonians. He grieves for the city that he loved, and feels personally humiliated by what has happened. Yet in the midst of his pain, he declares: *"The unfailing love of the LORD never ends!...Great is his faithfulness; his mercies begin afresh each day"* (Lamentations 3:22-23).

*W*here's Jesus?

Jeremiah declares that God's discipline will not last forever. He says that God will send a new King, the "righteous Branch" from King David's family tree (Jeremiah 23:5-6). Jesus Christ, whose lineage is traced to King David (Luke 3:31), is that coming King.

Ezekiel: a Glimpse of God's Glory

Imagine that when you look into the sky, you see a huge cloud flashing with brilliant light. From fire in the center of the cloud, something emerges. It looks partially human, but it has four faces and two pair of wings. Beneath each set of wings are hands. The face in front is human, on the right a face of a lion, on the left that of an ox, and the face of an eagle in the back. This thing flies in all directions without having to turn around. Above the creature's head is a huge sapphire throne occupied by a man made of fire.

An alien being? Well, yes, but not the type you are thinking of. This is the description that the prophet Ezekiel gave (in chapter 1) when he saw the glory of God.

Ezekiel is a book filled with symbolism. While much of it is not easy to figure out, the message of Ezekiel is easily explained: Israel and the nations of the world must know God. Almost 70 times the prophet uses the phrase, "They will know that I am the Lord."

Ezekiel was part of the group taken captive and deported to Babylon. He had the unhappy job of condemning the Jews for their sinfulness *while they were suffering in exile for it!* Between the lines of chapter 2, verse 9, you can read Ezekiel's shock when he discovers what God wants him to say: "Then I looked and saw a hand reaching out ot me, and it held a scroll....Both sides were covered with funeral songs, other words of sorrow, and pronouncements of doom."

Lucky for Zeke, he also brought word of God's promise to restore the nation of Israel. In the Jews' darkest moments, God gave Ezekiel a vision of a valley full of dry bones. "These bones represent the people of Israel," God told him in Ezekiel 37:11. As Ezekiel watched, God breathed on the bones and brought them back to life. "I will put my Spirit in you, and you will live and return home to your own land," God said (Ezekiel 37:14).

Ezekiel goes farther than the other prophets in making clear that as the divine Judge of all nations, God is eager to forgive all those who repent, not just Jews.

> *Thus, I will make known my holy name among my people of Israel. I will not let it be desecrated anymore. And the nations, too, will know that I am the LORD, the Holy One of Israel* (Ezekiel 39:7).

The visions of Ezekiel make this book seem a bit bizarre. Some symbolism can be explained by reference to other Scriptures, but the rest of it may never be figured out. That shouldn't surprise us. How can we expect our limited minds to comprehend an infinite God?

---

*W*here's Jesus?

When Ezekiel called the religious leaders "bad shepherds of Israel" for permitting idolatry and immorality, he described God as a good shepherd who cares for the people who are the "sheep" of His flock (see chapter 34). In the New Testament, Jesus announces that He is the good Shepherd:

> *I am the good shepherd. The good shepherd lays down his life for the sheep (John 10:11).*

If I Dream, Am I a Prophet?

In the days of the prophets, a dream could have significant meaning (or no meaning at all):

- It could be a revelation from God about something the prophet should say.

- It could be a God-given picture of future events.

- It could be the effects of a rancid deli sandwich.

Should you interpret your dreams as prophecies from God? We say, "Keep your day job." First of all, the "visions" of the prophets weren't necessarily like dreams that occurred only when they were sleeping. The prophets could tell when the vision was from God or from indigestion. Secondly, it is doubtful that God is speaking to you in the same way that He spoke to the prophets. After all, Christians today have the complete Bible (including the teachings of Jesus) and the Holy Spirit.

Daniel: a Man of Vision

One of the things that makes the Bible believable to us is that it tells about the weaknesses of its heroes. There are a few Bible characters, however, about whom nothing negative is said. Daniel is one of them.

As young teenagers, Daniel and his friends were captured in Judah and exiled in Babylon. Because they were of royal blood and showed great promise, Daniel and his group were put into a leadership training program to instruct them in the Babylonian culture. Always at great risk, Daniel and his friends rejected the pagan culture whenever it conflicted with their commitment to God. Each time God controlled the circumstances around them so they would be protected. For example:

- The friends were once ordered to pray to a statue of the king. They refused. As their death-sentence penalty, they were thrown into a blazing furnace. God protected them, and they walked out unharmed and without their clothes even being singed (Daniel 3).

- A law prohibited prayer to anyone other than the king. Daniel wouldn't let such a law interrupt his prayers to God. He was arrested and thrown into a pit with man-eating lions. But Daniel was kept safe because God sent an angel to close the mouths of the lions (Daniel 6:22).

God gave Daniel visions about the future and the ability to interpret the dreams of others. He predicted political events of his time, events which occurred in the lifetime of Christ, and events of the end of the world, which are yet to occur. Like the predictions in Ezekiel, Daniel's predictions are clouded in symbolism, so even Daniel didn't understand the meaning of all his visions. More than the author of any other Old Testament book, Daniel gave predictions about how the world will end.

Praise the name of God forever and ever, for he alone has all wisdom and power. He determines the course of world events; he removes kings and sets others on the throne. He gives wisdom to the wise and knowledge to the scholars (Daniel 2:20-21).

Jesus Arrives

Daniel predicted that "the Anointed One" would be "cut off" exactly 483 years (173,880 days in the Hebrew calendar) after a decree to rebuild Jerusalem (Daniel 9:24-26). Such a decree was later made on March 4, 444 B.C. Exactly 173,880 days later, on March 29, A.D. 30, Jesus made his triumphal entry into the city of Jerusalem, which led to His arrest and crucifixion.

You Don't Need the Wizard of Oz When God Is on Your Side

The life of Daniel is a great example of how God can give you everything you need to make it through tough times (if you depend upon Him like Daniel did). Remember how the Wizard of Oz gave Dorothy's friends what they needed? Well, Daniel could ignore the little man behind the curtain because he depended upon the great God in heaven:

- *Courage:* God gave Daniel the courage he needed to object to the food forced upon him by the Babylonians (which was against the Jewish dietary laws). He proposed a ten-day test to prove that his choice of food was healthier. He and his friends passed the test (and probably lowered their cholesterol in the process). See Daniel 1:1-18.

- *Heart:* God placed in Daniel a desire to worship Him alone. Daniel would not share his devotion toward God with a mere mortal king. Daniel's love of God was so strong that he refused to worship idols or pray to anyone else, even if it meant being thrown to the lions for failing to do so (Daniel 6:1-22).

- *Brains:* Daniel was empowered by God to understand the dreams of King Nebuchadnezzar and the mysterious "handwriting on the wall" at King Belshazzar's banquet (chapters 2, 4, and 5).

You may not be faced with hostile kings and hungry lions like those that confronted Daniel, but we guess that you have some difficult circumstances of your own from time to time. Wouldn't it be nice if you could get help from God—the same God that helped Daniel? The Bible says you can.

The Minor Prophets: Deep Thoughts in Small Packages

Even though they are called "minor prophets," we don't want to skip over them. Remember, they are "minor" only because they are shorter in length.

---

*A*s part of the Hebrew Bible, the 12 books of the minor prophets were all contained on the same scroll.

Hosea

The marriage of Hosea and his wife, Gomer, is a beautiful picture of God's love for the Jews and the rest of mankind. Gomer was a prostitute, and during her marriage she kept returning to her occupation. Despite the humiliation and heartbreak, God instructed Hosea to show his love to his wife again "even though she loves adultery" (Hosea 3:1). In the end, their relationship was restored.

The analogy in the book is obvious. Like the northern kingdom toward whom Hosea directed his prophecies, mankind has proved to be a spiritual slut. But God remains faithful and desires to restore the original relationship through His forgiveness. No matter how many times we may reject God, He is ready to accept us back.

Against the backdrop of Hosea's painful story, God expresses His undying love in some of the Bible's loveliest language:

> "O Israel and Judah, what should I do with you?" asks the LORD. "For your love vanishes like the morning mist and disappears like dew in the sunlight" (Hosea 6:4).

> But the more I called to him, the more he rebelled....I led Israel along with my ropes of kindness and love. I lifted the yoke from his neck, and I myself stooped to feed him (Hosea 11:2,4).

> For my people are determined to desert me. They call me the Most High, but they don't truly honor me (Hosea 11:7).

Joel

The prophet Joel warns the people of the "day of the Lord," which will be punishment for their wicked ways. He predicts a future army invasion and compares it to a recent plague of crop-eating grasshoppers that devoured the land. Hope can be found in God's promise to pour out His Spirit on the people after the judgment.

> And anyone who calls on the name of the LORD will be saved (Joel 2:32).

Amos

Amos gets on the nerves of everyone around him. He's a plain-spoken farmer and sheepherder sent on a mission from God. He tells the people that because they're living in disobedience, their sacrifices stink and their songs are just noise in God's ears (5:21-23). He calls Jerusalem's upper crust lazy drunks (6:4-6). When Amaziah, the king's personal priest, asks Amos to keep his opinions to himself, Amos predicts that the priest's wife will become a prostitute.

Called to bring bad news during prosperous times, Amos condemns both the neighboring nations and the Jews for their self-centered living, particularly their oppression of the poor. Although he preaches impending doom brought by God, Amos ends this book with the assurance that God will eventually restore the nation of Israel to prosperity.

> "The time is surely coming," says the Sovereign LORD, "when I will send a famine on the land—not a famine of bread or water but of hearing the words of the LORD. People will stagger everywhere from sea to sea, searching for the word of the LORD, running here and going there, but they will not find it" (Amos 8:11-12).

Obadiah

This prophet predicts doom for Edom, a neighboring nation to Judah that invaded and ransacked Judah on several occasions and rejoiced in its hardships. Obadiah emphasizes God's judgment on those who persecute His children.

The day is near when I, the LORD, will judge the godless
nations! As you have done to Israel, so it will be done to
you. All your evil deeds will fall back on your own heads
(Obadiah 15).

Jonah

If you have ever wondered how God could forgive people who
have been cruel and hateful to you, then read Jonah's four-
chapter story. This prophet wondered the same thing. God told
Jonah to preach repentance to the wicked citizens of Nineveh.
But Jonah hated and feared those people, and he didn't want God
to give them a second chance. So he ran in the opposite direction.
Running from God leads to trouble, and Jonah ends up in the belly
of a huge fish praying for God to give him a second chance. And
God does. Jonah goes to Nineveh to preach and sparks a citywide
spiritual revival.

I knew that you were a gracious and compassionate God,
slow to get angry and filled with unfailing love. I knew how

Holy Mackerel, Jonah!
That's a Whale of a Tale!

Most fishermen we know always brag about the size
of the "one that got away." Imagine what Jonah's fish
said to his school friends when he regurgitated
Jonah after three days: "Oh, that spicy Jewish food.
I just can't keep it down!" Jonah is a short book of
only four chapters. You'll enjoy reading it.

But don't let the fish story distract you from the
main theme of the book: As shown by His interest in
the people of Nineveh, God loves all people, not
just the Jews. Think about that the next time you're
wondering what's in your fish-fillet sandwich.

easily you could cancel your plans for destroying these people (Jonah 4:2).

Micah

This prophet spoke against the prosperity of Judah before its capture by the Babylonians. He was a contemporary of the prophet Isaiah. Micah said that God would bring judgment upon Judah for oppressing the poor. Judah had allowed its riches to ruin its spiritual sensitivity. There is hope in the promise of a Messiah, who Micah prophesies will be born in the humble town of Bethlehem.

> *The LORD has already told you what is good, and this is what he requires: to do what is right, to love mercy, and to walk humbly with your God* (Micah 6:8).

Nahum

Nineveh was the capital city of Assyria. Earlier it repented in response to Jonah's preaching. About 125 years later, the nation was corrupt and immoral, and it had overthrown the northern kingdom of Israel. Nahum preached that God's destruction would fall upon Nineveh. This book teaches that God will withhold His judgment when people repent, but His justice demands consequences if they don't.

> *The LORD is good. When trouble comes, he is a strong refuge. And he knows everyone who trusts in him* (Nahum 1:7).

𝒩ot for Men Only

The role of prophet was not restricted to males. Although there are no female authors of the books of the prophets, women were also used by God as prophetesses. An example is Deborah (see Judges 4:4-9).

Habakkuk

Do you wonder why bad things happen to good people? Or, why bad things happen to God's people? The prophet Habakkuk was bold enough to ask God for an answer to these questions. He wanted to know why God would use the pagan nation of Babylon to punish Judah for offenses which weren't as bad as those committed by the Babylonians. God's answer remains true and relevant today: God will only do what is right, and even though we may not understand the situation, we should trust and rely on God's righteousness.

The righteous will live by their faith (Habakkuk 2:4).

Zephaniah

Zephaniah was one of the last prophets in Judah before the Babylonian invasion occurred. He made specific and graphic predictions about impending destruction if the Jews would not return to God. (All of this came true about 45 years later.) He predicted that Judah's refusal would result in its ruin, but a remnant

What Is the Difference Between a Prophet and a Priest?

In the Old Testament, the priest was the one who approached God as a representative of the people. The priest offered the animal sacrifices to God on behalf of all the people and asked for forgiveness of their sins.

The prophet, on the other hand, was the one who approached the people as a representative of God. The prophet spoke the message that God wanted the people to hear.

of the people would later be restored to a relationship with God.

> *Beg the LORD to save you—all you who are humble, all you who uphold justice. Walk humbly and do what is right. Perhaps even yet the LORD will protect you from his anger on that day of destruction* (Zephaniah 2:3).

Haggai

Haggai lived in Jerusalem when the exiles had returned from captivity in Babylon. The rebuilding of the temple in Jerusalem fell

Does God Like to Be Mean?

Certainly God could have prevented the invasions by the Assyrians and Babylonians. But He didn't. He allowed the Jews to be taken captive and their cities to be destroyed because of their disobedience. Since He could have chosen other methods to deal with these problems, you might wonder whether God takes sadistic pleasure in such discipline.

First of all, remember that the bad things that happened to the Jews were the result of their own disobedience. Their choices and actions removed them from God's protection, as God's prophets had warned.

Secondly, as every parent knows, sometimes you have to discipline your children because it is *best* for them. What does every parent say in the middle of discipline? "This hurts me more than it hurts you." That's exactly how it is for God. He grieves at the destruction that His children bring on themselves, but He allows it in order to bring them to repentance. Even in the middle of painful consequences, God expresses stubborn hopes for His people (see especially Jeremiah 29–32 and Hosea 14).

behind schedule as the people attended to their own personal interests. Haggai challenged them to put God first in their priorities.

> *You hoped for rich harvests, but they were poor. And when you brought your harvest home, I blew it away. Why? Because my house lies in ruins, says the LORD Almighty, while you are all busy building your own fine houses* (Haggai 1:9).

Zechariah

Haggai and Zechariah were kind of a "good guy/bad guy" prophetical tag team. Haggai was critical of the delays to rebuild the temple. Zechariah took the opposite approach: He tried to motivate the people by encouraging them to complete the temple to be ready for the coming Messiah. His message included symbolic visions about events that occurred centuries later in the life of Jesus.

> *Rejoice greatly, O people of Zion! Shout in triumph, O people of Jerusalem! Look, your king is coming to you. He is righteous and victorious, yet he is humble, riding on a donkey—even on a donkey's colt* (Zechariah 9:9).

Malachi

This is the last book in the Old Testament, and it was the last one written. The time is 430 B.C. The place is Jerusalem. The Jews had resettled, but their spiritual condition had again grown stagnant. Malachi preached a message of warning and hope. He warned of an eventual judgment for all who reject God. But his book ends with the prediction of the coming Christ (to be preceded by an advance man who turns out to be John the Baptist). Malachi even predicted that there will be a "second coming" of the Messiah.

> *The LORD Almighty says, "The day of judgment is coming, burning like a furnace. The arrogant and the wicked will be burned up like straw on that day. They will be consumed like a tree—roots and all"* (Malachi 4:1).

What's That Again?

1. Prophets were God's messengers. They spoke what He told them to say.

2. Some of the books of the prophets were written in the pre-exile period, some during the exile, and others after the Jews had returned to Jerusalem.

3. Written during the years from Israel's divided kingdom to the return from exile, the books of the prophets give great insight into the nature of God. The first five books are referred to as the books of the "major prophets," and the rest of the books are called the books of the "minor prophets."

4. The prophets condemned their society's immoral lifestyle and religious hypocrisy. They warned of God's judgment if the people refused to repent. Their predictions about the destruction of Israel and Judah came true.

5. The prophets also preached about God's forgiving nature and His plan to rescue mankind. They gave very specific clues about the identity of the promised Messiah (which would be fulfilled exactly by Jesus several hundred years later).

Dig Deeper

Here's what we recommend for studying the prophets.

If you would like to see lists of all of the prophecies from the Bible (not just the Old Testament), here is a great resource: *The Complete Book of Bible Lists* by H. L. Willmington.

For a commentary that shows how the prophetical books are applicable to your everyday life, we suggest that you read the "Be" commentary series by Warren W. Wiersbe. He has a different book for each prophet or group of prophets. For example, "Be Comforted" explains Isaiah, "Be Decisive" is about Jeremiah, and "Be Amazed" covers Hosea, Joel, Jonah, Nahum, Habakkuk, and Malachi.

If you would like to study the future predictions from Daniel, our recommendation is *God's Blueprint for Bible Prophecy* by Kay Arthur.

■ ■ ■

*Q*uestions for *R*eflection and *D*iscussion

1. What would have been the benefits and disadvantages of being an Old Testament prophet?

2. Review the six ways the prophets proclaimed God's principles *(forthtelling)*. Could someone speak as this kind of prophet to our culture today?

3. Review the one way the prophets predicted the future *(fore-telling)*. What value does this have for our culture today?

4. More than 300 Old Testament prophecies concern the earthly ministry of the Messiah, and Jesus fulfilled them all to the letter. Does that fact affect your faith? How could you use this information to tell others about Jesus?

5. What do you think the prophets were expecting when they envisioned the coming Messiah?

6. Give examples from your own life of how God has given you courage, heart, and brains to say the right thing at the right time.

7. Reread the verses we cite from each of the 12 Minor Prophets. Give a contemporary application for each one.

_____

■ ■ ■

Moving On...

If you're like us, when you finish with the prophets you are struck with this overwhelming thought: God never gives up pursuing His people. They reject Him, time and time again. But He keeps coming back. Sometimes with a warning, sometimes with a threat, sometimes with love talk or a promise of blessings. *But He keeps coming!*

In a way, that same thought is the theme of the entire Old Testament. God tries to have a relationship with mankind, but mankind rejects God. Think about it:

- God started with the Garden of Eden, but man goofed that up.

- God started over with the flood, but men went about their evil ways.

- God gave a set of laws at Mount Sinai, but the people of Israel quickly ignored them.

- And God spoke to His people through kings, prophets, and priests, but the Israelites didn't listen to them.

So after the prophets, when nobody heard from God for 400 years, you might wonder if God had given up on mankind. But those 400 years were not a period of God's inattention. They are 400 years of suspense. God was sticking with His original plan, but what was He up to? *What is God going to do next?* He *will* do something. He always does. In our lives as well...

In His continued effort to restore a relationship with mankind, God's next step was to come to earth personally (like He did in Eden); to wash away our sins (like the flood); to put a new law of love in our hearts (like at Sinai); and to give us a King, Prophet, and Priest, all in the Person of Jesus. God would replace the old covenant of laws and temporary sacrifices (made with Moses) with a new covenant of faith and permanent forgiveness (made through Jesus).

At the very time when the Babylonian army was poised to break through the gates of Jerusalem, God revealed His plan to Jeremiah (who was inside starving along with the rest of the frightened citizens). Here is what God said:

> *"The day will come," says the LORD, "when I will make a new covenant with the people of Israel and Judah. This covenant will not be like the old one I made with their ancestors when I took them by the hand and brought them out of the land of Egypt. They broke that covenant, though I loved them as a husband loves his wife," says the LORD. "But this is the new covenant I will make with the people of Israel on that day," says the LORD. "I will put my laws in their minds, and I will write them on their hearts. I will be their God, and they will be my people....For everyone, from the least to the greatest, will already know me," says the LORD. "And I will forgive their wickedness and will never again remember their sins"* (Jeremiah 31:31-34).

These verses make up the longest single quotation from the Old Testament that you'll find in the New Testament (Hebrews 8:8-12). In fact, this passage is where the word *testament* (or covenant) comes from. As you turn the page to the next chapter, you need to get ready to experience God's love for you in a whole new way. It's the biggest and best part of God's entire eternal plan, and it comes wrapped in...a diaper?

*P*art III
The New Testament

Chapter 8

The one use of the Bible is to make
us look at Jesus, that through Him
we might know His Father and
our Father, His God and our God.

George MacDonald

One of the first things you notice when you start thumbing through the New Testament is that the first four books are biographies. And all of one Person: Jesus.

Yet these aren't typical biographies. With a few exceptions, each book covers only a three-year period in Christ's life. And of that, the last week before His death is told in the greatest detail. Matthew, Mark, Luke, and John each approach Jesus from a slightly different viewpoint. But doesn't the world's first and only Perfect Person deserve that kind of examination?

That's why we say,

- To know God, you've got to understand the Bible.

- To understand the Bible, you've got to learn about Jesus.

- To learn about Jesus, you've got to read the Gospels.

It is as simple as that.

The Gospels:
The Life of Christ in Surround Sound

*I*f all the verses of the Bible were puzzle pieces, then the cover of the puzzle box would be a picture of Jesus. He is what the Bible is all about. Oh sure, there are lots of Bible stories about other people and events, but all of those individual pieces are interconnected to the predominant theme of the Bible:

- It is only through Jesus Christ that mankind can be restored to a relationship with God (John 14:6).

There is no better place to learn about Jesus than in the first four books of the New Testament: Matthew, Mark, Luke, and John. These four books, referred to as the Gospels, were written exclusively about Jesus.

Gospel is taken from an Anglo-Saxon word meaning "good news." The story of Christ—that man's relationship with God can be restored through Him—is "good news" indeed.

The Gospels record the most incredible event of history: God's visit to earth in the Person of Jesus Christ. God wanted us to see Jesus so that we could know God:

> *Jesus replied, "Philip, don't you even yet know who I am, even after all the time I have been with you? Anyone who has seen me has seen the Father!"* (John 14:9).

More than any other books in the Bible, the Gospels are written invitations. They present the truth of the "good news." Why? To get a response from readers who didn't get to meet Jesus in the flesh. The Gospels are persuasive writing in the form of history.

The truth is, you can't read through the facts of these accounts *without* making a choice. Augustine put it this way: "If you believe what you like in the Gospel and reject what you do not like, it is not the Gospel you believe, but yourself."

To read through these books without letting them bring you closer to the God who loves you would be to miss the best and most important part.

Before we talk about the life of Jesus as it is described in the Gospels, let's look at how Jesus completes the Old Testament in the New Testament.

One-Hour Cram Plan for the Life of Christ

Jesus spent 33 years on earth. You can cover some of the highlights in one hour of reading:

Luke 2—Miracle in a manger
Matthew 5–7—Sermon on the hillside
Matthew 8—Man of miracles
John 14—Final words to His friends
Mark 15—Jesus in court and on the cross
Matthew 28—Jesus rises from the dead

Messiah's Secret Identity Revealed

The Old Testament talks about the Messiah in the context of one nation: the Jews. The New Testament talks about the Messiah in the context of one Man: Jesus.

The Old Testament set the stage for the coming Messiah. Many impostors came along, but there were so many clues and predictions about the Messiah from the prophets that it was easy to spot a fraud. Then came Jesus. The Gospels boldly proclaim Jesus Christ is the one, and it can be proved because He fulfilled every one of the hundreds of predictions about the birth, life, and death of the Messiah!

Making the Connection

In a nutshell, the New Testament explains that Jesus is the Messiah who was promised in the Old Testament. Here's how it breaks down:

OLD TESTAMENT	NEW TESTAMENT
Theme: The Messiah is coming	*Theme:* Jesus is the Messiah
Partially conceals the Messiah's identity	Fully reveals Jesus as the Messiah
Explains your *need* of Jesus (you can't live up to the law's requirements)	Explains how you can *know* Jesus

A Life like No Other

The life of Jesus was spectacular. You wouldn't expect anything less than spectacular if the God of the universe were to take on the form of a human, and that's exactly who Jesus claimed to be—the Son of God. But He had facts to back up His claims. Here is a short list of what the Gospels say about His life:

1. Jesus was born of a virgin. We know it sounds inconceivable, but that's precisely what is described in Matthew 1–2 and Luke 1–2. In a nonsexual way, the Holy Spirit impregnated Mary, the mother of Jesus. Jesus grew up in Nazareth, where His earthly father, Joseph, was a carpenter. At age 12 Jesus astonished temple

The Gospels

What's in the Bible?		What's in the World?
	63 B.C.	Pompey conquers Palestine
	▼	
	44	Julius Caesar assassinated
	▼	
	37	Herod appointed to govern Palestine
	▼	
	31	Augustus Caesar becomes ruler of Roman Empire
	▼	
Jesus is born	5	
	▼	
	A.D. 4	Herod dies
	▼	
Jesus visits the temple as a boy	7	
	▼	
	14	Tiberius becomes ruler of Roman Empire
	▼	
Jesus begins his public ministry	26	
	▼	
Jesus chooses his 12 disciples	27	
	▼	
Death, resurrection, and ascension of Jesus into heaven	30	

Land of Israel During Jesus' Ministry

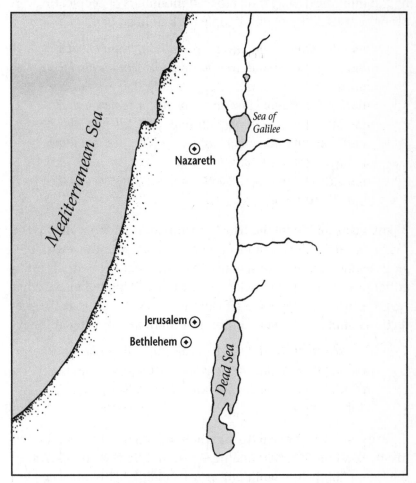

Jesus was born in Bethlehem, grew up in Nazareth, and was crucified in Jerusalem. During his three-year ministry, He didn't travel outside this area. The whole region is about the same distance as New York to Philadelphia.

scholars in Jerusalem with His learning. But we know little else about His youth.

2. Jesus performed supernatural miracles. No tricks here. Jesus actually healed people of diseases, calmed a storm by speaking to it, and multiplied a bag lunch to feed thousands of people. He even brought at least three dead people back to life.

> *John the Baptist, who was now in prison, heard about all the things the Messiah was doing. So he sent his disciples to ask Jesus, "Are you really the Messiah we've been waiting for, or should we keep looking for someone else?" Jesus told them, "Go back to John and tell him about what you have heard and seen—the blind see, the lame walk, the lepers are cured, the deaf hear, the dead are raised to life, and the Good News is being preached to the poor* (Matthew 11:2-5).

3. Jesus claimed to be the true Messiah. Jesus said that He was the "Son of God." This was not a popular message with the Jewish religious leaders because they were afraid they would lose their influential positions. Jesus criticized them for refusing to believe what was so obvious. They were refusing to acknowledge that the predictions of the Old Testament prophets pointed directly at Jesus:

> *You search the Scriptures because you believe they give you eternal life. But the Scriptures point to me! Yet you refuse to come to me so that I can give you this eternal life* (John 5:39-40).

4. Jesus was a teacher with a radical message. The Jews tried to live by the Ten Commandments, but Jesus said that they followed the "letter" of the law while ignoring its "spirit." This infuriated the hypocritical religious leaders, who prided themselves on their strict lifestyle. But Jesus said that "Thou shalt not kill" also means that you should avoid anger and hatred; "thou shalt not commit adultery" also means that your thought life should be pure. He said rules and regulations weren't what God was after. He wanted people's hearts first.

*W*hen asked, "Why do you belive in miracles?" Henry Drummond replied: "Because I see them every day in the changed lives of men and women who are saved and lifted through faith in the power of the living Christ."

Jesus was a masterful teacher. One of His favorite teaching techniques was the parable—a story lesson which conveys spiritual truth from everyday life. Two of the best-known are the parable of the good Samaritan and the parable of the prodigal son.

5. Jesus lived a sinless life. Even though Jesus was fully human, He was also fully God. He was "tempted in every way, just as we are" (Hebrews 4:15 NIV), but never sinned in thought, word, or deed. Religious "thought police" of the day were never able to trap Him in a lapse of logic or a spiritual error. Even His enemies could find nothing wrong with Him.

6. Jesus was acclaimed by the people as the Messiah. In what proved to be the fulfillment of an Old Testament prophecy, Jesus entered the city of Jerusalem in a procession where the crowds were hailing Him as the Messiah. This is known as the "triumphal entry."

7. Jesus was crucified even though He did nothing wrong. The Roman government conceded to the Jewish religious leaders and allowed them to crucify Jesus, even though the Roman authorities found Him innocent of all the trumped-up charges. Hanging on a cross was a common form of capital punishment for criminals in the Roman empire during the first century A.D.

8. Jesus came back to life after being buried for three days. On His own power, He came back to life. This was just as He had predicted. This event, referred to as "the resurrection," is the greatest proof that Jesus was the Messiah as He claimed to be.

9. Jesus floated back up to heaven. This event, known as "the ascension," occurred after the resurrection and was witnessed by many people.

Brain Twisters

Jesus was a master at speaking spiritual truth in a way that got people thinking. Here are a few samples of what He said:

- "Love your enemies" (Matthew 5:44).

- "And how do you benefit if you gain the whole world but lose your own soul in the process?" (Mark 8:36).

- "It is easier for a camel to go through the eye of a needle than for a rich person to enter the Kingdom of God!" (Matthew 19:24).

- "Many who are first now will be last then, and those who are last now will be first then" (Matthew 20:16).

- "You believe because you have seen me. Blessed are those who haven't seen me and believe anyway" (John 20:29).

God or Man...or Both

Bible scholars use the term "hypostatic union." This sounds like the mysterious force which makes your socks cling together when you take them out of the dryer. Actually, the term is used to describe the fact that Jesus was all God and all man at the same time. His deity was not reduced by His humanity, and His humanity was not overshadowed by His deity. We can't explain it, but we accept it as true because that is what the Bible teaches.

This all-God and all-man concept is important.

All God. Jesus is God the Son, the second Person in the Trinity (along with God the Father and God the Holy Spirit). Jesus is all God. Only God—by the death of Jesus on the cross—could bring salvation. He could pay the price for our sins and give us forgiveness because He was without sin Himself.

All man. Jesus is not just some alien and aloof ruler of the universe. He is a personal God who knows our struggles. He enjoyed (and suffered from) a physical body just as we do. He had a human mother.

The Gospel of John emphasizes the all-God nature of Jesus. The Gospel of Luke focuses on His all-man nature. But all four Gospels affirm that Jesus was the son of Mary *and* the Son of God.

Twelve Ordinary Men

As soon as Jesus began His public ministry on earth, He began looking for those whose hearts were committed to Him. And He found 12 ordinary men who would help change the world forever. We are talking about the disciples of Jesus, personally chosen by Jesus to learn from Him.

The word *disciple* means "learner" or "follower." From the time Jesus called the disciples after His baptism to the time three years later when He ascended into heaven, Jesus constantly taught His disciples, and slowly they learned.

Who were these 12 guys? A complete list of the disciples can be found in three of the four Gospels (Matthew 10:2-4, Mark 3:16-19, Luke 6:14-16) and in Acts 1:13. Here is a brief biography of each one:

The Inner Circle

Three of the disciples were closer to Jesus than the others. They were with Jesus at the Transfiguration (Mark 5:37), on the Mount of Olives (Mark 13:3), and in the Garden of Gethsemane (Mark 14:33).

Simon Peter. Perhaps the most famous disciple, and certainly the most outspoken, Peter was a fisherman by trade and the brother of Andrew. Peter is the guy who walked on water (Matthew 14:28-31), cut off the ear of a soldier who arrested Jesus (John 18:10-11), denied Jesus three times (John 18), later repented (Luke 22:62), and became one of the leaders of the early church. Jesus and Peter must have had a very dynamic relationship. Jesus once called him "Satan" when Peter tried to talk Him out of going to the cross (Matthew 16:23), and Jesus called Peter the "rock" upon which He would build His church (Matthew 16:18).

James. James was in a fishing partnership with his younger brother, John, and with Peter and his brother Andrew. (These four men gave up their fishing business to follow Jesus and become "fishers of men.") James must have been somewhat of a hothead. Along with John, he once wanted to order down fire from heaven to burn down a Samaritan village which had turned Jesus away (Luke 9:51-56). Jesus scolded the brothers and gave them the name "Sons of Thunder" for their little idea. James also told Jesus he would willingly "drink from the cup of sorrow" which Jesus drank, meaning he offered to die in place of Jesus. James didn't, of course, but he was the first of the disciples to be killed (Acts 12:1-2).

John. Called "the disciple Jesus loved," John was the only disciple present at the crucifixion of Jesus (John 19:26-27). Along with James, John once asked Jesus for a favor: "In your glorious Kingdom, we want to sit in places of honor next to you" (Mark 10:37). Jesus never promised the boys where they would be sitting, but John did end up seeing visions of heaven and the throne of Jesus as he wrote the Book of Revelation.

The Rest of the Gang

Not as much is known about the other nine disciples.

Andrew. An early disciple of John the Baptist, Andrew later accepted Jesus and immediately went to tell his brother, Peter, that he had found the Messiah.

Philip. Also a disciple of John the Baptist. Philip brought Nathanael to Christ. Together with Andrew, Philip introduced some curious Greeks to Jesus (John 12:20-22).

Bartholomew. Also known as Nathanael, he was the one who uttered the famous phrase concerning Jesus, "Can anything good come from [Nazareth]?" (John 1:46). Philip persuaded Bartholomew to see for himself, and Bartholomew believed, calling Jesus "the Son of God."

Matthew. Sometimes called Levi, Matthew was the despised tax collector who left his lucrative (and corrupt) profession to follow Jesus. Matthew was so taken by Jesus that he hosted a banquet in his home so that his "fellow tax collectors and other guests" could meet Him. This prompted the religious leaders to condemn Jesus for mixing with "scum," which prompted Jesus to respond, "Healthy people don't need a doctor—sick people do" (Luke 5:31).

Thomas. Famous for being the "doubter," Thomas refused to believe that Jesus was risen from the dead until he could see for himself (John 20:25). Eight days later Jesus appeared to the disciples, this time with Thomas present, and He showed Thomas the wounds in His hands and side, asking him to believe. In response, Thomas exclaimed, "My Lord and my God!" (John 20:28).

James. All we know about this guy was that he was the son of Alphaeus (whoever that was).

Thaddaeus. Also known as Judas (but not the traitor, Judas Iscariot).

Simon the Zealot. A political patriot who became a follower of Jesus and evidently kept his nationalistic zeal.

Judas Iscariot. The most infamous of all the disciples, and perhaps the most disreputable man in history. Even though Judas gave himself over to Satan early on (John 6:70), and allowed Satan to actually enter into him, Jesus knew exactly what Judas was doing, and Jesus allowed him to do it (John 13:27). Judas later betrayed Jesus for 30 pieces of silver and then hanged himself. After the ascension of Jesus, the remaining 11 disciples had a prayer meeting with about 120 other believers and chose a disciple to replace Judas. His name was Matthias (Acts 1:15-26).

What's So Special About Twelve?

Why did Jesus choose 12 disciples? Why not 10 or 20? Perhaps the number has something to do with the 12 tribes of Israel, but there may be a practical reason as well. Management experts say that 12 is an ideal number for training.

Now let's take the Gospels book by book.

Matthew's Gospel: Jesus the Messiah

The Gospel according to Matthew is the best book to start the New Testament because it begins with a direct connection to the

Old Testament. Starting with the patriarch Abraham, Matthew follows the bloodline through 42 generations of Israel's history to Jesus (Matthew 1:1-17).

While this genealogical excursion may seem tedious, it is the premise for the theme of the book: Jesus is the promised Messiah, descendant of Abraham and David, who was predicted by the Old Testament prophets.

Matthew, a Jewish tax collector, was a disciple. He wrote his Gospel to prove to his fellow Jews that Jesus was the Messiah.

> *Then he asked them, "Who do you say I am?" Simon Peter answered, "You are the Messiah, the Son of the living God." Jesus replied, "You are blessed, Simon son of John, because my Father in heaven has revealed this to you. You did not learn this from any human being"* (Matthew 16:15-17).

What's It All About?

Matthew presents events and teachings from the life of Jesus which prove that He fulfills the predictions about the Messiah:

- *He had the Messiah's virgin birth.* In addition to the Messiah's bloodline, Jesus' miraculous birth had been predicted by the prophet Isaiah. Matthew briefly tells how Mary, while still a virgin, became pregnant by God's Spirit (1:18-25). This inconceivable "virgin birth" was a true sign of the Messiah:

  > *The virgin will conceive a child! She will give birth to a son and will call him Immanuel—"God with us"* (Isaiah 7:14).

- *He had the Messiah's birthplace.* He was born in the unlikely hick town of Bethlehem (2:1), as predicted by the prophet Micah seven centuries earlier:

  > *But you, O Bethlehem Ephrathah, are only a small village in Judah. Yet a ruler of Israel will come from you* (Micah 5:2).

- *He had the Messiah's acclamation.* At the age of one or two, Jesus was visited by several astrologers from the Far East.

(These are the "wise men" who followed the star that marked the birth of Jesus, as reported in Luke's Gospel.) These men bestowed valuable gifts and worshiped the toddler, declaring Him to be the "newborn king of the Jews" (2:1-12).

- *He had the Messiah's publicity agent.* Jesus had an older cousin called "John the Baptist." John was an itinerant preacher who emphasized repentance in anticipation of the Messiah. John boldly proclaimed that Jesus was the Messiah. Matthew quotes the prophecy of Isaiah (Isaiah 40:3) that the Messiah would have a person who prepared the way for Him (3:1-12).

- *He had the Messiah's holiness.* Matthew tells how Jesus resisted the direct temptations by Satan when Jesus was alone in the wilderness. Even though He was physically weak, Jesus resisted the temptation and remained sinless—a distinction that is true of only the Messiah (4:1-11).

- *He had the Messiah's wisdom.* Matthew includes the longest recitation of the "Sermon on the Mount" (5:1–7:28). This is a famous speech given by Jesus at the beginning of His ministry. Jesus proposed a radical change in thinking. He emphasized ethics, morality, and compassion. Chapter 13 includes many parables about the "Kingdom of Heaven" which address the consequences of rejecting Jesus' message. Jesus said that the "Kingdom of Heaven" was more a condition of the heart than an adherence to religious rules and rituals.

  After Jesus finished speaking, the crowds were amazed at his teaching, for he taught as one who had real authority—quite unlike the teachers of religious law (Matthew 7:28-29).

- *He had the Messiah's power.* In chapters 8–10, Matthew relates the miracles performed by Jesus, which gave credibility to His claims of Messiahship. Curing leprosy, healing a paralyzed man, and restoring sight to the blind were all not-so-subtle clues that Jesus was the Messiah. Who else could do such things?

- *He had the Messiah's rejection.* Beginning at chapter 11, Matthew relates events with a focus on the rejection of Jesus by the religious leaders. Their positions of power were threatened by His teachings against hypocrisy. Despite all the evidence, people refused to believe in Jesus. To illustrate the fulfillment of prophecy regarding the opposition the Messiah would encounter, Matthew quotes a prophecy from Isaiah 6:

  You will hear my words, but you will not understand; you will see what I do, but you will not perceive its meaning. For the hearts of these people are hardened, and their ears cannot hear, and they have closed their eyes—so their eyes cannot see, and their ears cannot hear, and their hearts cannot understand, and they cannot turn to me and let me heal them (Matthew 13:14-15).

- *He had the Messiah's sacrificial death.* Even in the description of the arrest and crucifixion of Jesus, Matthew points to how these events fulfilled Old Testament prophecies. Such a tiny detail as entering Jerusalem on a donkey (Matthew 21:1-5) was predicted in Zechariah 9:9. The treachery of Judas, Christ's own disciple, matches the prediction in Psalm 41:9, and the 30 pieces of silver paid to Judas for his betrayal correlates with the prophetic verses of Zechariah 11:12-13 involving precisely the same amount of money (Matthew 26:14-16).

- *He had the Messiah's ultimate proof.* The Book of Matthew ends with the story of Jesus coming back to life after three days in the tomb. It was then that He gave a final challenge (called the "Great Commission") to His followers:

  I have been given complete authority in heaven and on earth. Therefore, go and make disciples of all the nations, baptizing them in the name of the Father and the Son and the Holy Spirit (Matthew 28:18-19).

Anyone could claim to have complete authority in heaven and earth. But only the real Messiah could back up that claim by coming back to life.

Matthew makes an undeniable presentation of Jesus Christ as the promised Messiah, the coming King. His death did not disrupt God's plan because God intended all along that His Son would die to provide a way of salvation for mankind. That same Son, that same Jesus the Messiah, will return in the future to establish His kingdom forever (see Matthew 24–25).

Mark's Gospel: Jesus the Servant

The author, John Mark, was too young to be one of the 12 disciples, but some of the disciples frequently met in his mother's house. He developed a strong friendship with Peter (the apostle calls Mark "my son" in 1 Peter 5:13). No doubt Peter was Mark's source of the eyewitness reports of events and lessons from the life of Jesus.

The Gospel of Mark was written to Romans. They wouldn't have been interested in the Old Testament prophecies which were so precious to the Jews. The Roman mind liked to get to the "bottom line" as quickly as possible. Consequently, Mark's Gospel is the shortest of the four. It starts abruptly and ends the same way. There's lots of action, with Jesus always on the move. The narrative continually paints a picture of Jesus as a servant.

For even I, the Son of Man, came here not to be served but to serve others, and to give my life as a ransom for many (Mark 10:45).

What's It All About?

By the events and statements of Jesus that he reports, Mark presents Jesus as a servant. Not like a butler, but as God in the Person of Jesus Christ, serving mankind by being a sacrifice for man's sin.

- *The signs of the servant.* Jesus displayed His servant nature by the compassion He showed to those in need. Mark takes every opportunity to show the miracles of Jesus. As early as chapter 1, Jesus is found healing the sick, casting out demons, curing leprosy, and making the lame to walk. When the crowds around Him are hungry, He miraculously multiplies a small lunch into enough food to feed 5000 men (Mark 6:30-44).

Are Four Gospels Necessary?

Suppose that a lawyer, a mechanic, a doctor, and a newspaper reporter are all standing on separate corners of an intersection. They all see two cars collide. Although they witness the same event, all of them might tell the story differently, depending upon what interested them the most. The doctor may describe the drivers' injuries; the mechanic will remember the details of the damage to the cars; the newspaper reporter may be interested in the reaction of bystanders; and the lawyer, well, we all know what the lawyer will be interested in.

The writers of the Gospels are like the four people standing on the street corners. They all wrote about Jesus, but they emphasized different events, lessons, and characteristics of Christ based on their own perspectives. With four viewpoints, we get a more complete description of what Jesus did and who He is.

- *The sayings of the servant.* It was a common misconception that the Messiah would be a military and political leader. Jesus wanted to teach His disciples that He would lead by being a servant. He prepared them in advance for what would happen to Him:

  Then Jesus began to tell them that he, the Son of Man, would suffer many terrible things and be rejected by the leaders, the leading priests, and the teachers of religious law. He would be killed, and three days later he would rise again (Mark 8:31).

  He also warned them that they, too, must pay the price of servanthood if they wanted to be His followers:

  "If any of you wants to be my follower," he told them, "you must put aside your selfish ambition, shoulder

your cross, and follow me. If you try to keep your life for yourself, you will lose it. But if you give up your life for my sake and for the sake of the Good News, you will find true life. And how do you benefit if you gain the whole world but lose your own soul in the process?" (Mark 8:34-36).

- *The sacrifice of the servant.* Almost half of this book covers the last eight days of the life of Christ. Mark emphasizes Christ's ultimate act of servanthood with the crucifixion. In chapters 14–16, Mark painstakingly records the humiliation and torture that Jesus endured. Although He would have preferred to avoid the pain, He was willing to do it because it was part of the heavenly Father's plan:

    "Father," he said, "everything is possible for you. Please take this cup of suffering away from me. Yet I want your will, not mine" (Mark 14:36).

By the way, since Peter was the person from whom Mark obtained his information, it's not surprising that Peter's letters (1 and 2 Peter) stress humble service. Also, when Peter was witnessing to others about Jesus, he described His caring deeds:

Jesus went around doing good and healing all who were oppressed by the Devil, for God was with him (Acts 10:38).

A servant...that is the Jesus of Mark's Gospel.

Luke's Gospel: Jesus the Son of Man

The Gospel according to Luke emphasizes the human side of Christ's nature. Luke, a trained physician, was probably a Greek. His Gospel was written to a fellow Greek, Theophilus, to provide a summary of the stories about Jesus:

Having carefully investigated all of these accounts from the beginning, I have decided to write a careful summary for you, to reassure you of the truth of all you were taught (Luke 1:3-4).

Luke's professional training and scientific mind result in a well-organized presentation. Many people consider Luke's version to be the most comprehensive Gospel. It includes all of the major events and teachings of Christ, plus a few which aren't mentioned in the other Gospels, all of which show the humanity of Jesus.

And I, the Son of Man, have come to seek and save those like him who are lost (Luke 19:10).

Do You Have Something in a Petite?

One of our favorite sermon illustrations on the "take up your cross and follow me" verse of Mark 8:34 goes like this:

A certain Christian was getting weary of carrying his cross. So he went to Jesus and asked for a smaller one. Jesus said there was a room with crosses of all sizes and that an exchange would be possible.

When they entered the room, the Christian set down his cross and started to look around. All of the crosses were huge. They were massive. Every one of them was colossal. Finally, he spotted a very tiny one.

He said to Jesus, "What about that small one over by the door? Can I have that one?"

Jesus replied, "Certainly. That is the one you came in with."

What's It All About?

Luke wanted to show that Jesus, although perfect, was completely human. As a man, Christ knew the struggles that we face in our daily lives. He was not immune to temptation, pain, and sorrow. And even though He was a heavenly King, He was not aloof. Just the opposite. He mingled with the common people, the oppressed, and the outcasts. When Jesus is referred to as "the Son of Man," this means He was one of us.

Luke's Gospel can be summarized by his themes which show that Jesus, the Son of Man, knows us, loves us, and saves us.

- *He shares our humanity.* More than any other Gospel, Luke emphasizes the humble beginning of Christ's birth and young life. Only in Luke will you find the famous "Christmas story" scene of Mary and Joseph with the baby Jesus in the stable surrounded only by local shepherd boys (2:1-20). Luke is also the only Gospel writer to include stories about Jesus as a young boy (2:21-52). Luke even underscores Christ's humanity in the description of His family tree, tracing backward all the way to Adam, the first man (3:23-38).

- *He cares for humanity.* Luke shows that Jesus was interested in people. There are stories of Jesus spending time with individuals, especially the outcasts of society: the sick, the poor, the imprisoned. In that culture, women were second-class citizens, but Jesus showed that they should be respected and treated with dignity (see the Mary and Martha story at 10:38-42).

- *He is the hope of all humanity.* Luke presents a group of parables told by Jesus that shows God's desire that everyone be saved from sin (see the story of the lost sheep, the story of the lost coin, and the story of the prodigal son in chapter 15). Luke includes this quote of Jesus, which gives the best statement of His purpose:

    And I, the Son of Man, have come to seek and save those like him who are lost (Luke 19:10).

As with the other Gospels, Luke presents the events of the trial, crucifixion, resurrection, and ascension of Christ, but he includes some details that are not in the other Gospels, particularly the personal contact Jesus had with individuals after the resurrection (see Luke 24).

John's Gospel: Jesus the Son of God

John's Gospel is completely different from the other three. John was part of the "inner circle" along with Peter and James. But

Is Jesus Too Perfect to Be Our Example?

Luke presents Jesus as the perfect man. While His lifestyle is an unattainable goal for us in our own power, God wants to equip us with the Holy Spirit. That same Spirit gave Jesus the power to live a perfect life. After accepting Christ as our Savior, we receive the Holy Spirit:

But when the Holy Spirit has come upon you, you will receive power and will tell people about me everywhere (Acts 1:8).

With the Holy Spirit in our lives, we are equipped to live more like Jesus:

But when the Holy Spirit controls our lives, he will produce this kind of fruit in us: love, joy, peace, patience, kindness, goodness, faithfulness, gentleness, and self-control (Galatians 5:22-23).

John thought of himself as Christ's favorite disciple (in his Gospel, John refers to himself as "the disciple whom Jesus loved"). So it should be no surprise that his Gospel has a more personal touch.

The Gospels of Matthew, Mark, and Luke already existed when John was writing his Gospel. For this reason, he wasn't interested in just retelling the events. Instead, he basically selected seven events and seven sayings to prove that Jesus was God. John clearly states the purpose of his book:

Jesus' disciples saw him do many other miraculous signs besides the ones recorded in this book. But these are written so that you may believe that Jesus is the Messiah, the Son of God, and that by believing in him you will have life (John 20:30-31).

What's It All About?

John wanted his readers to understand that Jesus was God so that they could trust in Him for their eternal salvation.

For God so loved the world that he gave his only Son, so that everyone who believes in him will not perish but have eternal life (John 3:16).

John wastes no time in presenting his premise that Jesus is the Son of God. In chapter 1, John refers to Jesus as "the Word" (meaning the "good news" messenger of salvation):

In the beginning the Word already existed. He was with God, and he was God (1:1).

Even in his own land and among his own people he was not accepted. But to all who believed him and accepted him, he gave the right to become children of God (1:11-12).

So the Word became human and lived here on earth among us. He was full of unfailing love and faithfulness. And we have seen his glory, the glory of the only Son of the Father (1:14).

---

*W*hat's in a Name?

Jesus is identified in the Bible by more than 100 different names and descriptions. Of all the names given to Him, He most often referred to Himself as the "Son of Man."

In addition to the events of the crucifixion and resurrection, John selects primarily seven events and seven teachings of Christ to present Jesus as God.

Seven Signs of Christ's Authority as God

1. He changed water into wine (2:1-11).
2. He healed the dying son of a government official (4:46-54).
3. He healed a lame man at the pool of Bethesda (5:1-9).
4. He fed 5000 men from a bag lunch of five biscuits and two small fish (6:1-14).
5. He walked on the water (6:16-21).
6. He gave sight to a blind man (9:1-12).

7. He brought Lazarus back to life after he had been dead and buried for three days (11:1-44).

Seven Sayings of Christ's Identity as God

1. "I am the bread of life. No one who comes to me will ever be hungry again" (6:35).

2. "I am the light of the world. If you follow me, you won't be stumbling through the darkness, because you will have the light that leads to life" (8:12).

3. "I am the gate for the sheep....Those who come in through me will be saved" (10:7,9).

Touching the Untouchables

Cultural and racial prejudice was prominent among Jews of the first century A.D. But Jesus broke all of those barriers. Despite the criticism He received from the Jewish religious leaders, Jesus spent time with the outcasts of society. Here is a partial list taken from the Gospel of Luke:

- A demon-possessed madman (Luke 4:35)
- A paralyzed man (Luke 5:17-26)
- Two hated tax collectors (Luke 5:27-31; Luke 19:1-10)
- An insane hermit (Luke 8:26-39)
- A sick woman (Luke 8:42-48)
- A dying girl (Luke 8:40-54)
- Ten men with leprosy (Luke 17:11-17)
- A blind beggar (Luke 18:35-42)

This isn't the power-lunch group, but Jesus was more interested in spending time with them than networking with the religious and political elite.

4. "I am the good shepherd. The good shepherd lays down his life for the sheep" (10:11).

5. "I am the resurrection and the life. Those who believe in me, even though they die like everyone else, will live again" (11:25).

6. "I am the way, the truth, and the life. No one can come to the Father except through me" (14:6).

7. "I am the vine; you are the branches. Those who remain in me, and I in them, will produce much fruit. For apart from me you can do nothing" (15:5).

John paints an intimate portrait of Jesus as a loving God who offered Himself as a sacrifice for us. In addition to the "I am" verses above, Jesus is declared to be the "Lamb of God." This is a very symbolic statement because a lamb was sacrificed every day in the temple, and the prophet Isaiah had compared the Messiah to a sacrificial lamb. John the Baptist said this when he saw Jesus:

Look! There is the Lamb of God who takes away the sin of the world! (John 1:29).

What's That Again?

1. The four Gospels are the historical record of the life of Jesus Christ. He is presented as the Son of God and of Mary—all God and all man at the same time. He was the only perfect, sinless man who has ever lived.

2. Each Gospel presents a unique perspective, but all agree that Jesus was the Messiah whom God had promised. The details of Jesus' life fulfilled the predictions about the Messiah, and His supernatural powers proved that He was God.

3. The political and religious leaders considered Jesus to be a threat to their power, and they plotted to kill Him.

4. The Gospels reveal that even Christ's closest disciples were slow to see that Jesus' death on the cross was all part of God's plan for the salvation of humankind. Only when Jesus proved Himself to be God by coming back to life after three days did His followers start to believe.

5. The Gospels ask every reader to learn the facts and make a decision: Jesus is alive and He is God. Only through His sacrifice for our sins can we be restored to a relationship with God.

Dig Deeper

More books have been written about Jesus Christ than any other person, so you've got a lot to choose from. Here's our short list, which will give you an idea of the different types of books which are available.

The Jesus I Never Knew by Philip Yancey. This award-winning book puts you there with Jesus when He walked the earth. You'll find Jesus to be more than a two-dimensional character; you'll meet Him face-to-face and heart-to-heart.

Bruce & Stan's Guide to God by you-know-who. In chapter 8 we examine the life of Jesus.

Tree of Life Bible Commentary on Matthew by Jon Courson. Our good friend Jon is the pastor of a large church in southern California. This two-volume set is very casual in its presentation...like listening to someone talk around the dinner table. Jon shares great insights about how the life of Christ is relevant to your life.

The Glory of Christ by R.C. Sproul. This book emphasizes that Jesus is God. It examines events from the life of Christ when His divine nature burst through and was evident to those around Him.

Bruce & Stan's Pocket Guide to Knowing Jesus is a handy reference on the life of Christ.

John: Encountering Christ in a Life-Changing Way is one of the Christianity 101 Bible Studies. We wrote this book to help readers have their own personal, life-changing encounters with Jesus.

If you would rather watch a video, then go to your local Christian bookstore and ask about the *Jesus* movie. That's the title. This is a famous movie, now available in video, that was filmed on location in Israel, and the entire dialogue is taken from Luke's Gospel. It has been shown to more than 460 million people worldwide.

■ ▨ ▧

*Q*uestions for *R*eflection and *D*iscussion

1. Describe what this statement means to you: "The truth is that you can't read through the facts of these accounts [the Gospels] without making a choice." What can you say to someone who believes that Jesus was nothing more than a prophet and a wise teacher?

2. The Jews had been anticipating the Messiah for hundreds of years, but Jesus caught them by surprise. Why?

3. What if Jesus had never claimed to be the Son of God? Can you think of another religious founder (such as Buddha, Moham- med, or Joseph Smith) who made this claim? What does that say about Jesus?

4. Read John 14:6-7. Explain how this statement from Jesus shows that He knew He was God.

5. Which of the four Gospels do you relate to best? Explain why.

6. List some of the disciples' thoughts and feelings on the evening after Jesus died. Now list some of their thoughts and feelings on the Sunday morning after they found the empty tomb.

7. Review the seven "I am" statements that Jesus made about Himself. Which one is the most meaningful to you? Why?

■ ■ ■

Moving On...

Imagine the excitement that the friends of Jesus felt when they saw Him alive again after the crucifixion. Now they knew for sure that He was God! This was a story which the whole world needed to hear.

In the next chapter we will cover the Book of Acts, which explains how the story of Jesus spread around the world. What started as a few followers of Christ in the vicinity of Jerusalem grew to be thousands of people in all parts of the world claiming that Jesus was the Messiah.

*C*hapter 9

The Church confronts the world with
a message the world craves for but resents
because it comes through the Cross of Christ.

Oswald Chambers

Critics today sometimes accuse the Christian church of being "irrelevant." And that's one of the better things they say. In the years after the resurrection, Jesus Christ's growing legion of followers were called worse:

- cannibals (they ate the body and drank the blood of Christ at communion)

- insurrectionists against Caesar (they refused to worship him)

- just plain trash (they accepted slaves and former prostitutes and criminals into their fellowships)

In one famous complaint before a city council, Christians were accused of being people who "turned the rest of the world upside down" (Acts 17:6).

If you've grown up yawning in church, you may not be prepared for what you will encounter in this chapter. Do you want renewal in your life? A stronger sense of God's presence? More of the power of God? Read on.

Do you want to know how to change *your* world? Read on.

The Book of Acts:
The Church Is Born

*C*an you recall the first time you watched the launch of a space shuttle? Remember what happened? When the countdown hit zero, the ignition set off fire and smoke and power. Megatons of thrust were exerted to lift the enormously heavy space shuttle and booster rockets against gravity and into space. For a few seconds, it didn't look like the rocket was moving, and then, slowly, it ascended, sending the astronauts to complete their mission.

We're not rocket scientists or anything, but we do know that the astronauts don't do anything in their space capsule to provide the power for the rocket. There's no one out there pushing. The space shuttle astronauts depend entirely on the engines and the fuel to move them forward.

The Rocket Ship Called the Church

The church of Jesus Christ, which was born after Jesus ascended into heaven, is like a rocket ship on an amazing journey. And if you have received the gift of salvation, you are one of its many astronauts on a mission. The Bible is your mission manual, and the Book of Acts is one of its most important sections.

Don't just read the Book of Acts as a history book. Read and study it as a manual for your Christian life.

First, a Little History

Before we get into the details of your mission, let's put the Book of Acts into context. This will help to explain why Acts is a pivotal book in the Bible, and why it is so important to your Christian heritage.

Acts was written by Luke the physician, the only non-Jewish writer in the New Testament. Acts continues the history of the Gospels (chapter 8). In fact, Acts really is a sequel to the Gospel of Luke. If you read Luke and Acts together, you get a seamless account of the story of Jesus and the story of the church.

Acts is also the basis for the epistles, or letters, of the New Testament (chapter 10). As you read Acts, you will discover that it gives the historical context for every New Testament letter except 1 and 2 Timothy and Titus.

How Did It Happen?

Acts is an amazing story of power and miracles and the explosive growth of a new movement called Christianity. How did it all happen?

How was it that a tiny band of scared-out-of-their-wits Christians (otherwise known as the apostles) were able to carry the Good News about Jesus to the ends of the known world in a mere 30 years, and do it in a way that created tremendous momentum? The answer is found in the *mission*, the *means*, the *message*, and the *method* designed and delivered by God Himself.

Cram Plan

Acts 1—God the Son leaves

Acts 2—God the Holy Spirit arrives

Acts 6–7—Stephen is stoned (Saul watches)

Acts 9—Saul is saved (Stephen watches?)

Acts 13–20—Paul goes on tour

Acts 24—Paul goes on trial

Acts 27—Paul under sail

The Mission: Go into All the World

Our last chapter ended with what is commonly referred to as the "Great Commission" (Matthew 28:19-20; Mark 16:15; Luke 24:45-48; and John 20:21). The same command given by Jesus to His disciples appears early in the Book of Acts:

> *But when the Holy Spirit has come upon you, you will receive power and will tell people about me everywhere— in Jerusalem, throughout Judea, in Samaria, and to the ends of the earth* (Acts 1:8).

Jesus was about to ascend into heaven to be at God's right hand (Hebrews 1:3). He was about to leave His followers. But before He left, He had a simple, dramatic, and extremely ambitious *mission:*

> *Tell the world about Me.*

It's not real complicated, is it? But it is incredibly profound. Start with your own community, and don't stop until you reach the world. Think about this for a moment. Most of the people who

The Book of Acts

What's in the Bible?		What's in the World?
Paul is born	5 A.D.	
	▼ 14	Tiberius becomes Roman Emperor
Death, resurrection, and ascension of Jesus into heaven	▼ 30	
Day of Pentecost	▼ 30	
Paul's conversion on the road to Damascus	▼ 35	
	▼ 37	Caligula succeeds Tiberius as Roman Emperor
	▼ 40	Herod Agrippa becomes king of Judea
	▼ 41	Claudius succeeds Caligula
	▼ 43	London is founded
Paul's first missionary journey	▼ 46	
Jerusalem Council	▼ 50	
	▼ 54	Nero succeeds Claudius
Paul sails to Rome and is put under house arrest	▼ 59	
Paul is released from prison	▼ 62	
	▼ 64	Fire almost destroys Rome (Nero blames Christians)
Paul is martyred	▼ 66	

Paul's Missionary Journeys

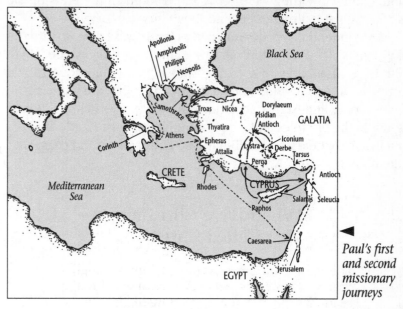

Paul's first and second missionary journeys

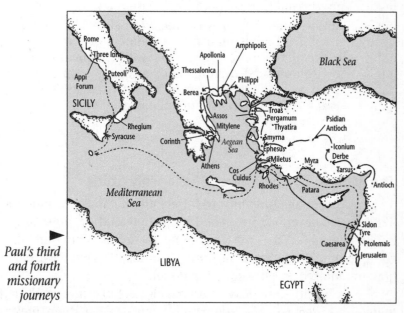

Paul's third and fourth missionary journeys

The apostle Paul took four missionary trips, spreading the story of Jesus to the then-known world.

walked with Jesus had never traveled more than a few miles from home, and now they were being asked to go to the ends of the earth. It must have been beyond their comprehension.

No wonder the apostles watched as Jesus "was taken up into the sky" (Acts 1:9). We don't know how long they stood there "straining their eyes to see him," but it was long enough for a couple of angels to come over and ask, "So, what are you waiting for?" (Bruce and Stan translation). It's almost as if Jesus looked down as the disciples looked up, mouths open, and said to two of the heavenly host nearby, "Fellas, you better go remind them that the mission starts now."

When Were Christians First Called Christians?

The name *Christian* is the most common designation of anyone who believes in salvation through Jesus Christ, yet it only appears three times in the Bible. The first is Acts 11:26: "It was there at Antioch that the believers were first called Christians" (the other references are Acts 26:28 and 1 Peter 4:16). In our culture today, the name has lost some of its meaning since so many people claim to be Christians when in fact they don't qualify (that's why we sometimes use the term "Christ follower").

The Means: by the Power of the Holy Spirit

Keep this image in your mind: Here are the apostles, all alone. Jesus, their Master, is gone. And He's just given them a seemingly impossible job. What are they going to do, and how are they going to do it? It all has to do with the *means* (the wherewithal or how-to required to get something done).

Not only did Jesus leave the apostles a *mission*, but He left them the *means* to carry the mission out. He left them fuel to burn in the rocket ship. He left them the Holy Spirit. Here again is Acts 1:8:

But when the Holy Spirit has come upon you, you will receive power and will tell people about me everywhere.

Acts is sometimes called the "Acts of the Apostles," but it could also have been called the "Acts of the Holy Spirit" because it tells about the acts of the risen Christ by the Holy Spirit through the apostles. Jesus had promised the Holy Spirit at the end of His life on earth (Luke 24:49). And here as He left the earth to return to heaven, Jesus made good on His promise. Seven weeks after Jesus returned to heaven, the Holy Spirit came upon the believers on a day known as "the day of Pentecost."

---

*H*ow Literally Do You Take the Great Commission?

To "commission" someone is to give them the authority and the power to do something. When it comes to the Great Commission, the authority to go out and tell others about Jesus has been given by Jesus Himself, and the power comes from the Holy Spirit (more about that later). The commission given to the apostles applies to us today. We have the same authority, the same power, and the same mission as they did.

The Holy Spirit in the Life of the Believer

God the Holy Spirit is the third Person in the Trinity, which also includes God the Father and God the Son. Just as God was present on earth 2000 years ago in the bodily form of His Son, Jesus, God is present today through the Holy Spirit. In this way, God is not just *near* us. He is *inside* us—forever (John 14:16-17).

The Holy Spirit is the fuel you need for your life as you do your part to complete your mission in the rocket ship called the church.

Wherever and whenever God has acted, the Holy Spirit has been present. He was there at Creation (Genesis 1:2). He enabled men to write God's Word (2 Peter 1:21). He brought about the birth of Jesus (Luke 1:35). The Holy Spirit was with Jesus during His earthly ministry (Luke 3:21-22). And He is the "first installment" of everything God is going to give us (2 Corinthians 1:21-22).

*W*ithout the power of the Holy Spirit, all human efforts, methods, and plans are as futile as attempting to propel a boat by puffing at the sails with our own breath.

D. M. Dawson

Since the day of Pentecost, the Holy Spirit has given Christians power to spread the message of Jesus around the world. When He arrived, the Holy Spirit changed the disciples' lives immediately and dramatically, and He can do the same for you:

- *Power.* The Holy Spirit gave the disciples the power to perform miracles, cast out demons, and speak in other languages (Acts 2–5). The Holy Spirit will give you power to do what God asks you to do.

- *Understanding.* The Holy Spirit helped the disciples to understand what Jesus had taught them. He will give you the same understanding as you communicate with God through prayer and Bible study (John 14:26).

- *Comfort.* The Holy Spirit (also known as "the Comforter") brought divine encouragement to the early Christians, who experienced extreme persecution. You will also receive comfort from the Holy Spirit during your trials.

- *Guidance.* The Holy Spirit provided guidance and direction for the first-century Christians (Acts 13:4). He will guide you as you seek the Lord in your decisions both large and small.

- *Inspiration.* The Holy Spirit "breathed into" the writers of the Bible, including several early church apostles. The Holy Spirit will help you express yourself and tell others about what God has done for you, whether you give a speech, write a letter, compose a song, or talk to your neighbor.

The Message: Anyone Who Calls on the Name of the Lord Will Be Saved

When the Holy Spirit came upon the believers on the day of Pentecost, there was a huge commotion. Some of those watching in the crowd said, "What can this mean?" (Acts 2:12). Others thought the believers were drunk. Just when it seemed things might get out of control, Peter stepped forward with the 11 other disciples next to him and preached the most powerful *message* of his life.

How Will They Know Unless They Have a Preacher?

The sermon Peter preached wasn't just any sermon. It was the first sermon proclaiming the Good News *message*.

Anyone who calls on the name of the Lord will be saved (Acts 2:21).

Peter

From a human perspective, Peter was probably the most unlikely candidate to step up as a leader of this new movement. A rough and impulsive man, Peter had been inconsistent in his life. He would make great claims (such as when he told Jesus he would never deny Him), and then stumble badly (he denied Jesus three times). Another time Jesus severely rebuked him (Mark 8:33). Yet Jesus also saw Peter's heart. When Jesus asked His disciples, "Who do you say I am?" Peter replied, "You are the Messiah, the Son of the living God" (Matthew 16:16). This prompted Jesus to bless Peter and to declare that he was the rock upon which He would build His church (Matthew 16:18). Peter became the first leader of the new church and its most powerful preacher.

New Testament scholar Merrill Tenney says that this sermon (Acts 2:14-36), as well as the preaching during this early period of the church, showed three characteristics:

1. The preaching was centered on the life and Person of Jesus Christ.

2. The preaching was apologetic in nature.

3. The preaching was very biblical in content.

Tenney concludes that both the *doctrine* and the *history* of Scripture were a part of the apostles' messages.

You may or may not have an occasion to preach in the formal sense in front of a group of people. But you will be asked, perhaps by one person, to talk about your faith. Be ready to explain what your faith in Jesus is all about from a perspective that is both personal ("Here's what Jesus did for me") and historical ("Here's how Jesus has worked in the lives of other people").

Don't Say You're Sorry

We're using some words we need to talk about for a minute. Not only are they important to understanding the Book of Acts and the activities of faithful men like Peter and Paul, but they are also practical to know today.

Apologetics. Not the same as "excusing yourself for something." An *apologist* is one who knows how to answer questions about the Christian faith. Here's how Peter said it: "If you are asked about your Christian hope, always be ready to explain it" (1 Peter 3:15).

Theology. The study of God (the Greek word for God is *theos*). A *theologian* is one who has thoroughly studied Bible *doctrines*, which are the beliefs and principles presented in the Bible.

The Method: the Church

At the conclusion of his sermon, Peter had an "altar call." In other words, he invited the people listening to receive Jesus into their lives.

> *Peter replied, "Each of you must turn from your sins and turn to God, and be baptized in the name of Jesus Christ for the forgiveness of your sins. Then you will receive the gift of the Holy Spirit!"* (Acts 2:38).

The Holy Spirit was a very real presence in that meeting. The Bible says that "about three thousand in all" were added to the church because they "believed what Peter said" (Acts 2:41).

What a spectacular beginning! Going back to our rocket analogy for a moment, think of the church, also known as the body of Christ, as the rocket ship itself. God had already supplied...

- *The Mission:* Go into all the world.
- *The Means:* By the power of the Holy Spirit
- *The Message:* Anyone who calls on the name of the Lord will be saved.

All of this provided tremendous thrust. Now God was initiating a *method*—the vehicle to carry the message to the ends of the earth. His method was—and still is—the church.

> *They joined with the other believers and devoted themselves to the apostles' teaching and fellowship, sharing in the Lord's Supper and in prayer* (Acts 2:42).

The church was born on the day of Pentecost, and its membership jumped from a few people to more than 3000 in a single day. The rocket ship was off the launching pad!

---

*P*rofessor A.T. Robertson used to say that one proof of the inspiration of the Bible is that it has withstood so much poor preaching. Likewise one proof that the church is God's instrument is that it has not blown apart with all of us in it.

Duke McCall

The Church Is a Body

We tend to think of the church as a *place,* such as the First Baptist Church on Third and Main. The true church, however, is made up of believers who share the common experience of receiving the gift of salvation and the gift of the Holy Spirit. Here's how the apostle Paul explained it to the Corinthian church:

> *The human body has many parts, but the many parts make up only one body. So it is with the body of Christ. Some of us are Jews, some are Gentiles, some are slaves, and some are free. But we have all been baptized into Christ's body by one Spirit, and we have all received the same Spirit* (1 Corinthians 12:12-13).

To be baptized by the Holy Spirit into this body means you are *identified* with Christ. This is a different baptism than water baptism, which is a public demonstration that you have identified with Christ by receiving Him into your life. Spirit baptism is the way God brings you into the body of Christ, or the church. You don't need to ask for it.

Acts 2:42 says that believers who were saved and baptized began meeting together in groups and devoted themselves to teaching, fellowship, the Lord's Supper, and prayer.

When you become a part of a local church, God uses you and your unique spiritual gifts to help spread His message. Never mind that you aren't perfect. None of us are! Max Anders writes, "The gospel is carried *to* imperfect people *by* imperfect people. Then those imperfect people are to band together to help one another grow to spiritual maturity."

The World's Greatest Missionary

Before he became the world's greatest missionary, the apostle Paul was the church's greatest enemy. After describing the growth of the church in the first six chapters, the Book of Acts turns its attention to Paul, first known as Saul.

Saul hated the Christians and their message of faith in Jesus. Along with some of the Jewish officials who had put Jesus on trial, Saul did everything he could to make life miserable for the Chris-

What Are Spiritual Gifts?

A spiritual gift is just that: a gift given to each of us by the Holy Spirit. The Bible talks about "the special abilities the Holy Spirit gives to each of us" (1 Corinthians 12:1). Each Christian has one or more of these abilities, or gifts, in order to minister to the needs of the body of Christ, or the church. The Bible describes more than 15 different types of spiritual gifts (they are listed in 1 Corinthians 12, Romans 12, and Ephesians 4), including the gifts of serving, teaching, administration, evangelism, wisdom, mercy, and encouragement.

In this way, the body of Christ really is like a living organism, with many different parts each serving an important function. Paul writes that "all of you together are Christ's body, and each one of you is a separate and necessary part of it" (1 Corinthians 12:27).

tians. But it wasn't until the Jewish leaders arrested Stephen, one of the most powerful preachers of the early church, that things turned really ugly.

They trumped up charges against Stephen, who answered his accusers in a magnificent speech (Acts 7). He told them that Jesus, whom they had killed, was at the right hand of God! Enraged, the Jewish leaders dragged the young missionary out of the city and stoned him to death. Saul was a witness at Stephen's execution (Acts 7:60).

Stephen became the church's first *martyr*, which is the name given to anyone put to death for professing his or her faith. After Stephen's death, the persecution of Christians became fierce.

The Least-Likely Candidate

Leave it to Jesus to choose the least-likely candidates to carry out His message. Acts 9 tells the dramatic story of Saul's conversion on the road to Damascus, where Saul was going to arrest more Christians. In something that reads like it could belong in a science fiction novel (except that this is true!), Saul was knocked to the ground by a "brilliant light from heaven," and a voice called out: "Saul! Saul! Why are you persecuting me?"

When Saul asked who it was, the voice replied, "I am Jesus, the one you are persecuting." Saul didn't need any more convincing. In an instant, Saul was transformed from the greatest persecutor of Jesus and His followers into Paul, the greatest advocate the church would ever have. While Peter continued to preach to the Jews, Paul prepared himself to preach to the Gentiles.

Paul was God's choice to reach the Gentiles. Here's what Paul wrote to the Roman church:

> *For I am, by God's grace, a special messenger from Christ Jesus to you Gentiles. I bring you the Good News and offer you up as a fragrant sacrifice to God so that you might be pure and pleasing to him by the Holy Spirit* (Romans 15:15-16).

What's the Difference Between Jews and Gentiles?

A Jew is a Hebrew, a descendant of Abraham (Genesis 12:3). God promised Abraham that his descendants would be a great nation (not a nation in the traditional sense with borders and such, but a nation of people). God also promised to bless His chosen people and to bless the world through them. Christian theologians agree that this blessing came through the Person of Jesus Christ, who came to the nation of Israel as the promised Messiah (Isaiah 53). When Jesus was rejected by the Jews, salvation came to all people, including non-Jews, or Gentiles (John 1:11-12). God still has a covenant (or agreement) with Israel, but now both Jews and Gentiles alike can receive the gift of salvation and become a part of the family of God.

$\mathcal{A}$cts = Peter + Paul (the Human Story)

Acts 1–12 focuses on the apostle Peter and the church in Jerusalem. The main thrust of this church was to reach the Jews in *Judea* and *Samaria*. Acts 13–28 focuses on the apostle Paul and the church in Antioch. Paul carried the Good News to the *ends of the earth* to the Gentiles.

Paul's conversion was all part of God's sovereign plan to take His message from the Jewish-centered church of Jerusalem to the Gentile church of the Roman world, which was just about everywhere else.

To the Ends of the Earth

Even though Paul was highly educated in Jewish laws and tradition, he studied and prepared to be a missionary of the Good News of Jesus for three years. And he developed a missionary style which is best characterized by 1 Corinthians 9:22:

> *Yes, I try to find common ground with everyone so that I might bring them to Christ.*

This doesn't mean that Paul tried be like the people he was trying to witness to. Rather, it meant that he cared about others and constantly attempted to find out what made them tick so that he could relate Christ to them.

Paul also did his best to take the Good News to places where it had never been heard before. In about 30 years, Paul personally established dozens of churches and took the message about Jesus to every corner of the Roman world.

Missionary Journey #1—Asia Minor

Paul's home base was Antioch of Syria, where the believers were first called Christians (Acts 11:26). Antioch was the third-largest city in the Roman empire and an ideal starting point for traveling by sea or land. The Gentile church there was large and had a number of teachers who were sensitive to the leading of the Holy Spirit (Acts 13:1-2). Paul teamed up with a man named Barnabas for his first missionary journey, which began in A.D. 45, and

Paul: A Fool for Christ

The apostle Paul was the greatest missionary the world has ever seen. Aside from Jesus Himself, Paul is the most influential person in the history of Christianity. Not only did he carry the Good News about Jesus to "the ends of the earth" in his lifetime, but his letters (called *epistles*) to first-century churches and individuals helped to shape the foundations of the Christian belief system.

Paul was not married (and encouraged other singles to follow his example). Then again, maybe he didn't have any opportunities. He was described by a second-century believer as "a man of little stature, partly bald, with crooked legs, a vigorous physique, with eyes set close together and nose somewhat hooked." (Wonder how his enemies described him?)

However Paul looked, it's clear that this apostle was opinionated, honest, fiery, fearless, and smarter than Bruce plus Stan. But for all of his gifts, Paul often referred to himself as "the least" of the apostles and a "fool for Christ."

Paul (his Roman name) was born Saul (his Jewish name) in Tarsus, an important commercial city that embraced Greek culture and traditions. Saul was thoroughly trained in Jewish theology and customs (Acts 22:3). In fact, his teacher, Gamaliel, was a grandson of the founder of the Pharisaic school, whose teachings influence Judaism to this day. To say that Saul was thoroughly Jewish would be an understatement. Yet he also spoke Greek fluently and was a Roman citizen—qualities that would be crucial to his later success.

took him to the island of Cyprus and to a region in Asia Minor known as Galatia (in what is now Turkey). Paul's first letter, Galatians, was sent to the churches in this region. When Paul and Barnabas returned to Antioch, they gave a full report to the Christians, "telling all that God had done and how he had opened the door of faith to the Gentiles, too" (Acts 14:27).

Missionary Journey #2—Europe

Paul and Barnabas parted company before Paul embarked on his most ambitious missionary journey— one that would carry him to Europe. The time was approximately A.D. 50. Paul built a new

The Church Is for Everyone

The idea that "the door of faith" was now open to the Gentiles didn't sit well with some of the Jewish Christians in Judea who believed that the new believers had to keep the ancient Jewish customs, most importantly the practice of circumcision (ouch!). Big arguments broke out, and the two sides—the Jewish Christians, otherwise known as "Judaizers," and the Gentile Christians— decided to meet in Jerusalem in what has since become known as the Council at Jerusalem (Acts 15). All the big boys were there: Paul, Barnabas, Peter, and James. Speaking as a Jew, Peter said that "God, who knows people's hearts, confirmed that he accepts Gentiles by giving them the Holy Spirit, just he gave him to us. He made no distinction between us and them, for he also cleansed their hearts through faith" (Acts 15:8-9).

Of course, the Gentile Christian men were pretty excited because Peter let them off the hook on that circumcision deal. More importantly, it meant that in the church there was to be no distinction between Jew or Gentile, male or female, slave or free, rich or poor.

team that included Silas, Luke (the biographer), and Timothy, who became Paul's secretary and helper. Together the missionary team went into Asia Minor and on to cities such as Philippi, Thessalonica, Berea, Corinth, and Athens (in what is now Turkey, Bulgaria, and Greece).

Missionary Journey #3—Turkey

Paul's third tour took him to Ephesus in present-day Turkey, where he spent three years. Because of Paul's influence, the entire province (called "Asia" by the Romans) was evangelized, and it remained a stronghold for Christianity in the Mediterranean world for centuries. Paul then traveled through Greece once again before sailing to Jerusalem, where he reported to the Jerusalem church (Acts 21). Then things took a turn for the worse. Some Jews who were opposed to Christianity saw Paul in the Temple and organized a mob against him. A riot broke out, and the Roman authorities that presided over Jerusalem decided to arrest the rabble-rouser (this actually protected Paul because the mob wanted to kill him).

Preaching Under Pressure

Paul's testimonies are recorded in great detail in the Book of Acts. They were usually given while he was on trial or in chains. Read these testimonies and see for yourself how powerful God's Word can be when it's lived out through a life given over to Jesus:

- in Jerusalem (Acts 22)
- before Governor Felix (Acts 24)
- before King Agrippa (Acts 26)
- in Rome (Acts 28; see also Philippians 4:22)

Paul was eventually transferred to Caesarea (it took nearly 500 Roman soldiers to escort him safely). There Paul appeared before Governor Felix, his successor, Festus, and eventually King Agrippa, who ruled over Palestine. Paul once gave his powerful testimony to all of these officials, always preaching God's love and the forgiveness of sins through Jesus.

*T*he Bible records that the first European to accept the message of the Good News was a Greek woman by the name of Lydia. She was a prominent and wealthy businesswoman who opened her heart and her home to the gospel (Acts 16:13-15).

On to Rome and Caesar

The end of Acts reads like a modern-day novel. Because Paul appealed to his Roman citizenship and to Caesar, the most powerful ruler on earth, the officials in Palestine had no choice but to send him to Rome in A.D. 59. While in Rome, Paul spent two years under "house arrest," waiting for his appeal to be heard, which meant that other Christians could get in contact with him even though he wasn't free to move around. In fact, the Bible records that Paul "welcomed all who visited him, proclaiming the Kingdom of God with all boldness and teaching about the Lord Jesus Christ. And no one tried to stop him" (Acts 28:30).

The Bible doesn't tell us if Paul ever had the opportunity to witness before Caesar because the story of Acts ends before Paul's appeal was heard. We have a feeling (and this is only a Bruce and Stan gut instinct) that Paul got his day in Caesar's court. Wouldn't that have been something to see! But whether he did or didn't, Paul's influence in the Roman world for the cause of Christ was immeasurable.

*P*eople do not reject the Bible because it contradicts itself. They reject it because it contradicts them.

Anonymous

History Lesson: "What Happened to Rome?"

When Paul arrived in Rome in A.D. 59, it was the largest and most important city in the world. Estimates of the population range from 1 to 4 million. Rome was famous for its roads, magnificent buildings, pagan religious temples, and system of government. It's hard to separate the history of Rome from the early church. It was the Caesar Augustus who decreed the census which

Some Will, Some Won't

One of the reasons Christians are so timid about sharing the Good News with people is that we think people will reject the message and in doing so reject us. Paul gave his testimony and talked about Jesus regardless of who would listen. He cared for people, but he wasn't really concerned with who accepted the message and who didn't. The Bible says that when Paul spoke to a large number of people, "some believed and some didn't" (Acts 28:24).

Only God can bring people to a point of belief through the Holy Spirit. Remember, Jesus didn't say, "Go into all the world and talk people into accepting me." He simply told us to "tell people about me everywhere" (Acts 1:8).

brought Mary and Joseph to Bethlehem (Luke 2:1). Jesus died on a Roman cross, and His tomb was guarded by Roman soldiers (Matthew 27:65). And Paul spent two years in the custody of Roman guards. The Caesar to whom Paul appealed (Acts 26:32) was actually Nero (it was during Nero's reign that Rome burned).

Christianity was outlawed by the Romans because its belief in God went against the Roman emperor cult (emperors were considered gods). But Christianity eventually "defeated" the Roman empire. After Emperor Constantine converted to Christianity in the fourth century, Christianity became a legal religion. In fact, the emperor went so far as to replace the Roman eagle on his soldiers' shields with another symbol—the Christian cross.

The Legacy of Acts and the Early Church

Despite the intense persecution of the early Christians (or perhaps *because* of it), the early church grew and thrived. Thanks to great and fearless men and women of God who obeyed Jesus' Great Commission and followed in the footsteps of the apostles, the Good News continued to reach the ends of the earth. Here are just a few of the key figures who helped spread God's message in the first centuries after the early church:

Justin Martyr (100–165) was the earliest Christian *apologist,* and took to heart what Peter wrote: "If you are asked about your Christian hope, always be ready to explain it."

How They Died

All of Jesus' disciples except for John were killed by the Romans, religious leaders, or mobs. Here's a short list from *Foxe's Book of Martyrs* of how some of the disciples and the apostle Paul died:

- *James*— Executed in A.D. 44 by the order of King Herod Agrippa I

- *Matthew*—Beheaded in Ethiopia about A.D. 60

- *Andrew*—Crucified on an X-shaped cross, which came to be known as St. Andrew's Cross

- *Mark*—Dragged to death by a mob in Alexandria

- *Peter*—Executed by the order of Nero. Tradition holds that Peter requested that he be crucified upside down because he did not consider himself worthy of being crucified in the same way Jesus was.

- *Paul*—Beheaded in Rome in A.D. 66.

- *Thomas*—Tortured and burned to death by a mob in India

- *Luke*—Hanged from an olive tree in Athens in A.D. 93

Irenaeus (130–200) refuted Gnosticism, which was a strong movement combining concepts from Judaism, Greek philosophy, pagan religion, and Christianity (sound familiar?). He eloquently explained the fundamental Christian doctrines of God, Christ, man, and salvation.

Origen (185–254) defended the Christian faith against the heretics and the Roman authorities.

Jerome (331–420) translated the Bible into Latin (called the Vulgate).

Augustine of Hippo (354–430), also known as St. Augustine, was the greatest thinker between the early church and the Reformation. His ideas helped shape Christian doctrine in the areas of faith and reason, the problem of evil, divine grace, and the Trinity.

What's That Again?

1. The Acts of the Apostles is a history of the birth of the church. It records the ascension of Christ, the coming of the Holy Spirit at Pentecost, and the amazing spread of Christianity.

2. Like a rocket ship, the early church needed tremendous thrust to get it off the ground. One way to understand what happened is by four words: *mission, means, message,* and *method.*

3. The church's *mission* was to tell all people everywhere about Jesus.

4. The church's *means,* or fuel, was the Holy Spirit. Acts has often been called the Acts of the Holy Spirit.

5. The church's *message* was that anyone who called on the name of Jesus would be saved.

6. The church's *method* to bring believers together in a flourishing community was the church itself—"the body of Christ." Every believer, regardless of race, gender, or political status, became an equally valued part of this body.

7. The first half of Acts focuses on the church's spread in Palestine; Peter is the main character. The second half focuses on the church's spread in the rest of the Roman empire; Paul is the main character.

8. The book ends abruptly. The story of Jesus' followers is still being told today.

Dig Deeper

You may not like history, but you will enjoy these books on the early church.

> *Acts: the Church Afire* by R. Kent Hughes. It's for anyone who wants an accurate, heartfelt treatment of Acts with a contemporary application.
>
> *The Biblical Times* by Derek Williams. A truly remarkable book for all you history buffs. This book recreates newspaper-style "front-page" headlines and articles from all the great biblical events—including everything in Acts—and blends them with other world events.
>
> *Foxe's Book of Martyrs* by John Foxe (rewritten and updated by Harold Chadwick). An Englishman who lived in the sixteenth century, John Foxe wrote this amazing and inspiring book to document the persecution against the church. The book has been revised and updated countless times. We recommend this edition because it includes an account of present-day persecution and contemporary martyrs.
>
> *The Works of Josephus.* The first-century Jewish historian, Josephus, wrote a complete history of the Jews through the destruction of Jerusalem in A.D. 70. He is the most reliable extrabiblical historian to write about the people and places in existence around the time of Christ. The best way to buy this book is in the single-volume edition.

■ ■ ■

*Q*uestions for *R*eflection and *D*iscussion

1. Jesus told His followers to go into all the world nearly 2000 years ago. Has the church fulfilled the Great Commission, or

has it not yet reached some people? List three places where you think unreached people might live.

2. List some ways you can "go into all the world" without ever leaving home. Is anything preventing you from doing these things right now?

3. Take a look at the list of five things that the Holy Spirit promises to every Christian. Which of these do you have right now? Do you need any others?

4. Review the three characteristics of the preaching of the early church. Does the preaching in your church follow this pattern? If not, what's missing?

5. Read 1 Peter 3:15. Are you ready to explain your Christian hope? Outline a plan to get you more "ready." What are some practical ways to get better at answering questions about your faith?

6. How would your witnessing change if you weren't so concerned about how people responded? How would your witnessing change if you lived in a culture where believing in Christ was illegal?

7. The early Christians suffered for their faith. Even though you may not be suffering in the same way, give three reasons why Christians worldwide might be persecuted now more than ever before.

■ ■ ■

Moving On...

If you are a Christian, you could correctly say that your spiritual heritage began the moment you became a part of the family of God. But you are also a part of a human heritage which includes the men and women we've talked about in this chapter, as well as millions who have lived and died through the centuries until today.

Have you ever wondered how the *message* of Jesus Christ has remained the same since the time when Jesus and the apostles walked the earth? Well, it's God's message, and He has preserved it through His Word. Do you see now why the Bible is so important, and why God cares so much that you read and study it? The Bible contains the truth about God and His message. It also tells us how to live our lives every day in light of that truth.

The next chapter concerns the most practical part of the Bible—the *letters*—written to the Christians in the young churches you just read about. The letters are personal and fresh. They will help you live your life in a way that will please God and bring glory to Jesus.

Chapter 10

Shakespeare could take a sheet of paper,
write a play on it, and make people laugh
and cry—that is talent. Bill Gates can take a
sheet of paper, sign his name on it, and
make it worth millions of dollars—that is
wealth. God can take a sheet of paper, place
His holy words on it, and change the course
of humanity—that is the Bible.

Bruce Bickel and Stan Jantz

After the four Gospels and the Book of Acts, the New Testament contains 21 books which are really letters written to churches or individuals. In this chapter, we'll look at those 21 letters, called "epistles." (The last book of the New Testament, Revelation, is the subject of chapter 11.)

These letters were written to Christians in the first century. Christianity was new for them, and they were anxious to hear and learn how God, through the Holy Spirit, could help them in their relationships and circumstances. Fashion styles and technologies may be different today, but you'll notice that the fears and problems early Christians struggled with are pretty much the same as ours. The epistles share God's secrets for growing Christians, and you can learn those secrets by reading these letters!

On a personal note, we admit that we probably spend the majority of our individual Bible-reading time in the epistles. These books help us be better husbands, fathers, and friends.

The Epistles:
The Bible Mailbag

*W*hat's *A*head

- [ ] What's an Epistle?
- [ ] Lots of Learning Going On
- [ ] Paul Writes to the Churches
- [ ] Paul Gets Personal
- [ ] General Correspondence

*D*o you go to your mailbox each day with at least a little sense of anticipation? We do. Doesn't everybody hope to get a letter from a friend?

Imagine life in the first century, before e-mail and phone service. Letters were the only way to communicate from a distance. Every letter was received with great excitement.

The 21 books of the New Testament which we cover in this chapter are first-century letters. These letters, called "epistles," are not biographies of Jesus like the Gospels, and they are not a historical account of the growth of Christianity as is found in Acts. Instead, they are personal letters written to churches and individuals in cities throughout the Mediterranean region.

One-Hour Cram Plan: A Chain Letter to You from the First Century

- Romans 6; 12—You (yes, even you) can win over sin.

- 1 Corinthians 12–13—Celebrate special gifts from the Holy Spirit...

- Ephesians 4–6—...and shine for Christ at church, home, and work!

- Philippians 1–4—Get this: You can experience joy, no matter what happens...

- Colossians 3—...if you let Christ be Lord of every part of your life.

- Hebrews 11–12—Fact is, you've been chosen to be a hero of faith—no kidding!

- James 1–3—But (here's the tough part) you'll have to practice matching what you do with what you preach.

What's an Epistle?

In chapter 9, we reviewed the Book of Acts, which describes how Christianity spread throughout the cities of the Roman empire. Paul started many churches in these cities on his missionary journeys. Imagine the friendships he developed. For these new Christians, he was their teacher and spiritual big brother. It must have been difficult for everyone when he had to leave a city. They would miss his teaching, and he would be curious to know how they were doing.

To stay in touch with these fledgling churches, Paul wrote letters to them. These letters weren't intended to be purely social (he never asks about the weather). Instead, Paul used his letters as a chance to give further instruction about God and godly living. So some of these letters are a little like written sermons. As a matter of fact, that is the meaning of the word *epistle*.

Remember that these new Christian churches didn't have Bibles. Oh sure, they had the Old Testament Scriptures (but it wasn't called the "Old Testament" then because there wasn't yet a "New Testament"). But the Old Testament didn't present the teachings of Christ, and it certainly didn't explain the differences between Christianity and their heritage of Judaism. So when a church received a letter from Paul, it was a big deal. The letter would be read to the entire church; it would be studied by the church leaders; it would be discussed by the new Christians in their homes; it would be read and read and read again. Then the letter would be passed to another church so all of the Christians could benefit from Paul's instruction.

$\mathcal{T}$ake a Letter

All of the epistles were handwritten, but not necessarily by the author. Sometimes the author would dictate the letter to another person who would transcribe it (a first-century type of voice-recognition word processor).

The letters were hand-delivered, and the messenger would often report back to the author about how the letter was received and how things were going in the church.

Paul wasn't the only author of the epistles. Other letters were written by Peter, James, John, and Jude. Here are some clues for remembering who wrote what:

- Paul wrote 13 of the 21 epistles. The ones he wrote are named for the groups of people to whom he was writing (such as "Romans" to the Christians in Rome, or "Corinthians" to the Christians in the city of Corinth), or for an individual recipient (such as "Timothy" and "Titus").

- Seven of the other epistles are named after the authors (James, Peter, John, and Jude).

The Epistles

What's in the Bible?		What's in the World?
Death, resurrection, and ascension of Jesus into heaven	30 A.D.	
	▼	
Day of Pentecost	30	
	▼	
Paul's conversion on the road to Damascus	35	
	▼	
Paul's first missionary journey	46	
	▼	
James (the brother of Jesus) martyred	62	
	▼	
Peter and Paul martyred	66	
	▼	
	70	Jerusalem destroyed
	▼	
	73	Mass suicide by Jews at Masada to avoid Roman capture
	▼	
	79	Mt. Vesuvius erupts in Italy
	▼	
John dies	98	

The Background of the New Testament

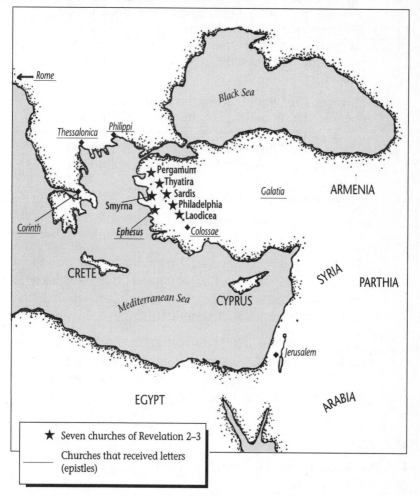

The Background of the New Testament

Letters proved to be the best way for Paul and the other epistle writers to keep in touch with Christians across the Mediterranean region.

Impostor or Apostle?

Disciple means "follower," and *apostle* means "messenger." After the death and resurrection of Christ, the 12 disciples were referred to as apostles because they had the special assignment of spreading the message of Jesus Christ to the world.

Because Paul wasn't one of the 12 disciples, some people questioned his authority as an apostle. Paul qualified as an apostle, however, because the resurrected Christ revealed Himself to Paul, so Paul had an opportunity to walk and talk with Jesus (Acts 9:3-18). In 2 Corinthians 10–13, Paul defends his credentials as an apostle.

- Hebrews is the only epistle written by an unknown author. We know it isn't a guy named "Hebrews" because the epistle is named for the group of people to whom it was written—the Hebrew (Jewish) Christians.

- If more than one letter was written to the same audience or by the same author, then they are numbered in order (for example, the three letters written by John are referred to as 1 John, 2 John, and 3 John).

Mail Slots

It is possible to place the epistles in three groups based on their predominant themes.

1. **Romans through Galatians:** *"Christ in You."* Christians are different from the rest of the world because God lives in them through the Holy Spirit. Their Christianity should affect the things that they think, say, and do.

2. **Ephesians through Philemon:** *"You in Christ."* Every Christian belongs to God and is part of the "body of

Christ" (the family of all Christians). Christians have the responsibility and privilege of caring for and ministering to each other.

3. **Hebrews through Jude:** *"Walking by Faith."* Faith is more than just theory. It translates into power, which equips Christians to handle all of the circumstances of life.

Lots of Learning Going On

Paul and the other epistle writers wrote not only about theory (i.e., how faith in Jesus frees you from sin), but also about the practical reality of being a Christian (i.e., how the Holy Spirit in your life can change you from the inside out).

Here are Bruce and Stan's "Top Six Epistle Topics."

TOP TOPIC #1: How to Be a Christian

Remember that the epistles were written primarily to new Christians. They didn't have years of Sunday school classes, Christian radio programs, or interactive computer Bible software programs. Most of their learning came from the teaching of the apostles, and the gaps in their training were filled in by the epistles.

This is good news for you because you can read the same mail if you are interested in finding how this whole Christianity thing works. All of the basics are explained.

Sin. You can learn about the snare of sin.

> *These evil desires lead to evil actions, and evil actions lead to death* (James 1:15).

Salvation. The death of Jesus on the cross provides the way for us to be saved from sin's death penalty.

> *For you know that God paid a ransom to save you from the empty life you inherited from your ancestors. And the ransom he paid was not mere gold or silver. He paid for you with the precious lifeblood of Christ, the sinless, spotless Lamb of God* (1 Peter 1:18-19).

Faith. What does it mean to believe in Jesus? How do you get faith, and how do you know if you've got it?

> *So we are made right with God through faith and not by obeying the law* (Romans 3:28).

> *What is faith? It is the confident assurance that what we hope for is going to happen. It is the evidence of things we cannot yet see* (Hebrews 11:1).

Holy Spirit. How does the Holy Spirit "happen"? What can you expect to happen in your life when God is living in it?

> *The Spirit of God, who raised Jesus from the dead, lives in you. And just as he raised Christ from the dead, he will give life to your mortal body by this same Spirit living within you* (Romans 8:11).

> *But we know these things because God has revealed them to us by his Spirit, and his Spirit searches out everything and shows us even God's deep secrets* (1 Corinthians 2:10).

The Return of Jesus. Jesus is coming back...but *how* and *when?*

> *The Lord isn't really being slow about his promise to return, as some people think. No, he is being patient for your sake. He does not want anyone to perish, so he is giving more time for everyone to repent. But the day of the Lord will come as unexpectedly as a thief. Then the heavens will pass away with a terrible noise, and everything in them will disappear in fire, and the earth and everything on it will be exposed to judgment* (2 Peter 3:9-10).

A Christian is not one who is seeking God's favor and forgiveness—he is one who has found them.

T. Roland Philips

A Gift for You from the Holy Spirit

The epistles explain that every believer has special gifts from the Holy Spirit which empower that person, in a special way, to serve others. These are referred to as "spiritual gifts." Now, Paul didn't know you personally, so you won't find your name on a gift list in the epistles. But there are several lists of the different gifts (see Romans 12:3-8 and 1 Corinthians 12:4-11).

TOP TOPIC #2: If You Wanna Live Right, You Gotta Think Right

Do you want to know how to live correctly? The epistles teach that you must think correctly. How do you make sure that you are thinking correctly? Well, the epistles lay out this strategy:

- Right living comes from right thinking.
- Right thinking comes from understanding and obeying the Scriptures.

Understanding and obeying the Word of God requires both an offensive and defensive response.

Offensive. Promote and pursue sound doctrine (biblical truth).

> *Hold on to the pattern of right teaching you learned from me. And remember to live in the faith and love that you have in Christ Jesus* (2 Timothy 1:13).

Defensive. Guard against false teachers.

> *He must have a strong and steadfast belief in the trustworthy message he was taught; then he will be able to encourage others with right teaching and show those who oppose it where they are wrong* (Titus 1:9).

TOP TOPIC #3: You Can Experience Inner Peace

As difficult as your life may be, you probably don't have it as tough as the first-century Christians. They were turned into lion food for Nero's perverted entertainment. So you can be sure the epistles contain some powerful advice for learning to hold your life together when your world is falling apart.

Contentment. *I have learned the secret of living in every situation, whether it is with a full stomach or empty, with plenty or little. For I can do everything with the help of Christ who gives me the strength I need* (Philippians 4:12-13).

Hope. *So I pray that God, who gives you hope, will keep you happy and full of peace as you believe in him. May you overflow with hope through the power of the Holy Spirit* (Romans 15:13).

Comfort. *He comforts us in all our troubles so that we can comfort others* (2 Corinthians 1:4).

Tranquillity. *Give all your worries and cares to God, for he cares about what happens to you* (1 Peter 5:7).

Peace. *Don't worry about anything; instead, pray about everything. Tell God what you need, and thank him for all he has done. If you do this, you will experience God's peace, which is far more wonderful than the human mind can understand* (Philippians 4:6-7).

TOP TOPIC #4: Secrets to Lasting Friendships

The epistles teach that Christians belong together. We weren't designed to be disconnected and independent from each other. The epistles tell us how to be a friend.

Sympathy. *When others are happy, be happy with them. If they are sad, share their sorrow* (Romans 12:15).

Forgiveness. *Get rid of all bitterness, rage, anger, harsh words, and slander, as well as all types of malicious behavior. Instead, be kind to each other, tenderhearted, forgiving one another, just as God through Christ has forgiven you* (Ephesians 4:31-32).

Acceptance. *You must make allowance for each other's faults and forgive the person who offends you* (Colossians 3:13).

Love. Love is patient and kind. Love is not jealous or boastful or proud or rude. Love does not demand its own way. Love is not irritable, and it keeps no record of when it has been wronged. It is never glad about injustice but rejoices whenever the truth wins out. Love never gives up, never loses faith, is always hopeful, and endures through every circumstance (1 Corinthians 13:4-7).

$\mathscr{F}$orget the Prozac

Paul says that the only source for real inner peace is the Holy Spirit, who produces "spiritual fruit" in your life.

But when the Holy Spirit controls our lives, he will produce this kind of fruit in us: love, joy, peace, patience, kindness, goodness, faithfulness, gentleness, and self-control (Galatians 5:22-23).

TOP TOPIC #5: All in the Family

Paul and the other epistle writers made it clear that Christianity works at home just as well as it does in the church. In fact, it's probably more important at home. After all, at church you are on your best behavior. But at home, well, we know that's usually a different story.

How to have a successful marriage.

So again I say, each man must love his wife as he loves himself, and the wife must respect her husband (Ephesians 5:33).

In the same way, you wives must accept the authority of your husbands, even those who refuse to accept the Good News....In the same way, you husbands must give honor to your wives. Treat her with understanding as you live together (1 Peter 3:1,7).

How to raise good kids.

And now a word to you fathers. Don't make your children angry by the way you treat them. Rather, bring them up with the discipline and instruction approved by the Lord (Ephesians 6:4).

You children must always obey your parents, for this is what pleases the Lord (Colossians 3:20).

A Bible that's falling apart often belongs to a person who isn't.

TOP TOPIC #6: How to Build a Church

We're not talking here about steel beams and stained glass windows. When the epistle writers talk about "the church," they are referring to a local collection of Christians (although sometimes they are referring to all Christians everywhere).

The Church is like a body. *Now all of you together are Christ's body, and each one of you is a separate and necessary part of it* (1 Corinthians 12:27).

The Church is a family of Christians. *See how very much our heavenly Father loves us, for he allows us to be called his children, and we really are! But the people who belong to this world don't know God, so they don't understand that we are his children* (1 John 3:1).

We hope this overview shows you that the epistles are the place to turn when you want to know about the "hows" and "whys" of being a Christian. Now we'll cover each letter one by one.

Paul Writes to the Churches

The first nine letters of the New Testament were written by Paul to groups of Christians in various cities.

ROMANS: Christian Faith in a Nutshell

During the first century, Rome was the capital city of the world. Expecting that he would visit the growing church in Rome at some time in the future, Paul wrote this letter as an introduction.

What a Church Leader Looks Like

Because the church is so important, the epistle writers gave specific instructions about the criteria required of church leaders. Here are a few of the character traits, taken from 1 Timothy 3, that a church leader must have:

- He must have a good reputation both inside and outside the church.
- He must be faithful to his wife.
- He must exhibit self-control.
- He must be hospitable.
- He must not be greedy.
- He must manage his household well, and his children must obey and respect him.
- He must not be a new Christian.

He wanted to make sure that these Christians were well-grounded in the fundamentals of their faith.

The Gospels examined the *life* of Christ. In Romans, Paul examines how a Christian is changed by the *death* of Christ.

- *We were spiritually dead.* Paul doesn't mince words in declaring our need for salvation. He boldly states that everyone has sinned (Romans 3:23) and that sin has an eternal death penalty (Romans 6:23).

- *Christ made us spiritually alive.* Paul next explains how the death of Christ provides the solution. Salvation comes from belief in Christ. We don't deserve it. There is nothing we can do to earn it. It is a free gift of eternal life (Romans 6:23).

- *The struggle between dead and alive.* Paul gets very practical when he explains that being a Christian isn't easy. Our old nature will still conflict with our new nature in Christ:

*I don't understand myself at all, for I really want to do
what is right, but I don't do it. Instead, I do the very thing
I hate* (Romans 7:15).

Paul emphasizes in Romans that being a Christian is a continual process of choosing to follow your new Christlike nature instead of your old sinful nature. In the last chapters, Paul gives practical tips on what it means to live the Christian life.

Jesus can transform our nature from sinful to holy. With Him in our lives, we are empowered to resist the behavior of our former nature and live in a way that is pleasing to God.

*So now there is no condemnation for those who belong to
Christ Jesus. For the power of the life-giving Spirit has
freed you through Christ Jesus from the power of sin that
leads to death* (Romans 8:1-2).

*C*hurch—First-Century Style

When we say the word *church*, what comes to your mind? You might think of a building—a place where people meet on Sunday to worship God.

The Christians of Paul's time knew nothing of buildings. For them, the "church" was the group of Christians who met in homes. It stayed that way until Emperor Constantine ended the persecution of Christians 200 years later.

1 and 2 CORINTHIANS: Instructions to Immature Christians

On his second missionary journey, Paul started a church in Corinth. After he had been gone awhile, he heard about problems in the church and wrote his first letter. His second letter was sent a few months later when he heard that the church had corrected some of the problems.

- The church in Corinth was filled with immature Christians. Paul gently chews them out for arguing with each other. He wasn't so gentle when he blasted them for ignoring blatant sexual immorality among Christians.

- Paul explains how the Holy Spirit equips each Christian with abilities to minister to others (1 Corinthians 12).

- One of the most famous chapters of the entire Bible is 1 Corinthians 13 (the "love" chapter). This type of self-lessness is only possible if Christ is living in you.

Whether in the church or in society, the lifestyle of a Christian should reflect the traits of Christ.

Or don't you know that your body is the temple of the Holy Spirit, who lives in you and was given to you by God? You do not belong to yourself, for God bought you with a high price. So you must honor God with your body (1 Corinthians 6:19-20).

I have decided to stick with love. Hate is too great a burden to bear.

Martin Luther King, Jr.

GALATIANS: Born (Again) to Be Free

Galatia was a region in the Roman empire in what is now Turkey. There were several churches in this area, and Paul got ticked off at every one of them. He had spent considerable time in Galatia teaching the fundamental concepts of Christianity. After he had left, a religious sect called the Judaizers came into town. They preached a phony gospel that required Christians to obey all of the Jewish traditions (such as celebrating the feasts and male circumcision).

Paul expresses his shock that the Galatians were so easily misled by the Judaizers. He reminds them that Christianity is all about freedom from rules. The Book of Galatians is a Christian's declaration of independence. Paul explains a Christian's freedom from religious rules and freedom from the grasp of sin.

- *Freedom from religious rules.* Paul reminds the Galatian Christians that they were saved by faith in Jesus Christ (see Galatians 3:26). They didn't earn their salvation by keeping the Ten Commandments or by doing anything else.

- *Freedom from the power of sin.* Although there are no rules constraining a Christian, the privilege of freedom should not be abused by an immoral lifestyle. Instead, Christians should allow the power of the Holy Spirit to produce Christlike characteristics (which are described as the "fruit of the Spirit" in Galatians 5:22).

Christianity is not a bunch of do's and don'ts. Instead of being governed by rules and regulations, a Christian's behavior is the result of love for Jesus.

> *So Christ has really set us free. Now make sure that you stay free, and don't get tied up again in slavery to the law* (Galatians 5:1).

EPHESIANS: A Part of the Body

In his letter to the Christians in the church at Ephesus, Paul reminds them about the great treasure they have in Christ Jesus.

- Paul devotes almost the entire first half of this letter to reminding Christians of God's limitless love for them:

  > *And may you have power to understand, as all God's people should, how wide, how long, how high, and how deep his love really is. May you experience the love of Christ, though it is so great you will never fully understand it* (Ephesians 3:18-19).

- As different parts of "the body of Christ," Christians may each have various roles, but they should act in unity, with Christ in control as the "head."

- Our faith in Christ should affect our lifestyle, particularly our relationships at home and at work (see Ephesians 5:21–6:9).

The incomprehensible love of Christ belongs to the Christian. The Christian's life and relationships should reflect that fact.

I, a prisoner for serving the Lord, beg you to lead a life worthy of your calling, for you have been called by God (Ephesians 4:1).

PHILIPPIANS: A Cause for Rejoicing

This little letter is a combination thank-you note and an "attaboy" slap on the back. Paul had a real soft spot in his heart for the Philippian church. He was instrumental in starting the church, and he had many close friends there who were going through tough times. Paul emphasizes the joy that a Christian has despite difficult circumstances. (We guess he knew what he was talking about because he wrote this letter while he was chained in prison in Rome.) Paul gives some excellent advice on how a Christian can rejoice despite difficult circumstances.

*P*hilippians would be a great book to read if things are going wrong in your life. It will help you put things into perspective.

Consider suffering for Christ as a privilege. Christians are really citizens of heaven and are just temporarily on earth (Philippians 1:20-29).

Be humble. Look at the example of Jesus. He left heaven to come to earth (Philippians 2:1-11).

Recognize what is important. Compared to knowing Christ, nothing else is important (Philippians 3:7-11).

Difficult circumstances become less significant (and easier to endure) when compared to knowing and experiencing the love of Christ.

> *Everything else is worthless when compared with the priceless gain of knowing Christ Jesus my Lord. I have discarded everything else, counting it all as garbage, so that I may have Christ and become one with him* (Philippians 3:8-9).

*P*aul had been in jail in Philippi. In an earthshaking conversion, his prison guard became a Christian (Acts 16). This jailer became part of the Philippian church.

COLOSSIANS: Back to Basics

Paul had taught the Christians in the church at Colosse that salvation was a free gift. When he was gone, however, the Christians in that church were being influenced by false teachers who said that basic Christianity wasn't sophisticated enough. They taught that intellectualism was the way to reach higher levels of spiritual understanding.

Paul wrote the letter to the Colossians to tell them to cut through all of the garbage because Jesus is all that matters (only Paul said it a little more tactfully).

Paul reminds them about Christ's preeminent role in Creation, in salvation, and in the life of Christians. Moving from doctrine to a practical application, Paul then explains how a Christian should reflect the influence of Christ at home, at work, and in the church.

All that is needed for salvation is found in Christ. It is as simple as that.

> *Don't let anyone lead you astray with empty philosophy and high-sounding nonsense that come from human thinking and from the evil powers of this world, and not from Christ. For in Christ the fullness of God lives in a human body, and you are complete through your union with Christ. He is the Lord over every ruler and authority in the universe* (Colossians 2:8-10).

1 and 2 THESSALONIANS: Hang in There

Paul had started a church in the Greek city of Thessalonica. This was a tough city for new Christians. The society was sexually promiscuous, and the culture was hostile toward anyone who lived (let alone preached) a moral lifestyle.

In his first letter, Paul gives the Christians there encouragement and comfort. He commends them for their growing faith, and he explains that they should not despair over the death of their Christian friends, who will be resurrected to life when Jesus returns.

Have you ever written a letter and had the reader take it the wrong way? Well, that's what happened to Paul. Apparently, some people in the Thessalonica church misinterpreted some comments in his first letter. Since Paul had said Christ was returning, they quit their jobs and mooched off other Christians. Paul's second letter is emphatic about the return of Jesus, but he says that no one knows the time. Consequently, he tells the Christians to keep working diligently in their jobs and ministries until it happens.

Stand firm in the Christian faith even if you suffer persecution. Meanwhile, look forward with expectancy to the return of Christ.

> *Now may the God of peace make you holy in every way, and may your whole spirit and soul and body be kept blameless until that day when our Lord Jesus Christ comes again* (1 Thessalonians 5:23).

Paul Gets Personal

These next four letters of the New Testament were also written by Paul, but they were written to specific individuals instead of churches.

1 and 2 TIMOTHY: Pursue a Godly Life

Timothy was one of Paul's closest friends. Paul was the mentor, and Timothy was his protégé. Paul entrusted Timothy with forming the leadership in the church at Ephesus. He wrote two letters to instruct Timothy on a variety of topics critical to effective leadership and godly living.

In 1 Timothy, Paul covers the subjects of:

- Worship (chapter 2)
- Criteria for church leaders (chapter 3)
- Warnings against false doctrine (chapter 4)

$\mathcal{B}$e a Paul...Be a Timothy

Many churches have a program called "Operation Timothy." The idea is for a more mature, experienced Christian to disciple a younger, inexperienced Christian in the same way that Paul discipled Timothy. A disciple is literally one who learns certain biblical principles from another and is held accountable to maintain them.

If you are young in the Christian faith, you should find someone who can be your spiritual mentor. If you are mature in the Christian faith, you should consider discipling someone else.

By the time he wrote his second letter to Timothy, Paul was in prison. Rome had declared Christianity illegal, and Paul's enemies used the decree to lock him up for good. He knew it was only a matter of time before persecution would come to the growing church in Ephesus, and the theme of this letter is encouragement for Timothy to "remain faithful to the things you have been taught" (2 Timothy 3:14).

Be a good student of God's Word so you are not misled by false teaching.

> *Don't let anyone think less of you because you are young. Be an example to all believers in what you teach, in the way you live, in your love, your faith, and your purity* (1 Timothy 4:12).

$\mathcal{P}$aul Writes His Own Epitaph

Second Timothy was the last letter which Paul wrote before his execution. Writing from his jail cell, perhaps Paul had his epitaph in mind when he wrote:

As for me, my life has already been poured out as an offering to God. The time of my death is near. I have fought a good fight, I have finished the race, and I have remained faithful (2 Timothy 4:6-7).

TITUS: Doing Right Is the Result of Thinking Right

Like Timothy, Titus was a young pastor and a disciple of Paul. His assignment was the Mediterranean island of Crete and its collection of small churches. The Cretans were a pretty immoral bunch, and Paul knew that the young Titus needed instructions in how to live and teach others in this environment.

The letter to Titus is Paul's clear instruction for Christian leaders to teach others the truth of God. The themes of this letter include:

- Character counts (chapter 1).
- Follow sound teaching; avoid false doctrines (chapter 2).
- Submit to civil authorities (chapter 3).

Real Christianity is revealed by proper belief and proper behavior.

> *And we are instructed to turn from godless living and sinful pleasures. We should live in this evil world with self-control, right conduct, and devotion to God, while we look forward to that wonderful event when the glory of our great God and Savior, Jesus Christ, will be revealed* (Titus 2:12-13).

PHILEMON: Freedom in Christ

This letter is more like a New Testament postcard. It was written to Philemon, a prominent member of the Colossian church (which met in Philemon's house). Philemon was a slave owner, which was common in those days, even for Christians. In fact, the subject of this letter is one of Philemon's slaves, Onesimus.

Evidently, Onesimus had escaped from his master and traveled to Rome, where he met Paul. (Since Paul was then in prison, perhaps Onesimus had been arrested as a runaway slave.) It should come as no surprise that Paul introduced Onesimus to the Christian faith. (Paul loved a captive audience.) Now Paul is sending Onesimus back to Philemon with this letter.

Why Did Christians Own Slaves?

The economic structure of the first-century Roman empire was dependent upon slave labor, and slavery was a predominate part of society. The treatment of slaves was inhumane and evil. Yet, Christians certainly didn't have the political clout to mount a crusade for the abolishment of slavery. Instead, Christianity introduced into society the radical concept of relationships between all people based on respect for each other. Christian love replaced the slave's antagonism toward his master, and it persuaded the master that human beings could not be treated as mere property.

Making an analogy to Christianity, Paul encourages Philemon to gracefully and forgivingly accept Onesimus back:

- Slaves had no rights or hope for the future. Before becoming a Christian, a person is a slave to sin with no rights or hope.

- When a person becomes a believer, his dignity as a human being is restored and his future is secured. In the same way, Philemon should recognize the dignity of Onesimus and forgivingly restore the relationship with him.

Forgiveness should be a natural occurrence in relationships between Christians.

Perhaps you could think of it this way: Onesimus ran away for a little while so you could have him back forever. He is no longer just a slave; he is a beloved brother, especially to me. Now he will mean much more to you, both as a slave and as a brother in the Lord (Philemon 15-16).

General Correspondence

Don't get the idea that Paul was the only literate apostle. It's just that he was the most prolific. The Bible contains epistles written by other devoted followers of Christ. This last set of New Testament letters is an eclectic group, covering subjects from deep theology to practical living.

HEBREWS: A Bible in the Bible

The letter of Hebrews was written to Jewish Christians who were perhaps drifting away from the truth they had heard.

The letter of Hebrews is like a Reader's Digest condensed version of the entire Bible. If you look at Hebrews by itself, it presents everything you need to know about how God has chosen to operate in this world, from eternity past to eternity future. Not only that, but most of the major themes and major Old Testament people of the Bible are included in this amazing letter.

In Old Testament times, God spoke through the prophets, and the priests offered sacrifices for sins. But Jesus, God's own Son, came to earth and is a far superior Priest and Prophet because it is through Him that the penalty for our sins is paid forever.

> *Under the old covenant, the priest stands before the altar day after day, offering sacrifices that can never take away sins. But our High Priest offered himself to God as one sacrifice for sins, good for all time. Then he sat down at the place of highest honor at God's right hand* (Hebrews 10:11-12).

Author Unknown

One of the great unsolved mysteries of the Bible is the identity of the author of Hebrews. Some say it is Paul; some say it is Luke. Others say it could have been Barnabas or Apollos or Silas or Philip. Only God knows, and He's not telling.

JAMES: Real Faith

James wrote to Jewish Christians who were living in the regions outside of Palestine. Although his letter was written

James

James had something in common with Jesus: their mother, Mary. James and Jesus were half brothers. Why only half? Because Joseph was the father of James, but not the father of Jesus. (Remember that Jesus was born of a virgin. See Matthew 1:18,22-23.)

The Bible tells us that for a long time James didn't believe that Jesus was the Messiah. Talk about a case of sibling rivalry. Imagine having a brother who claimed to be God. When Jesus came back to life after being crucified, however, James had all the proof he needed (see 1 Corinthians 15:7). After that, James grew in his faith and understanding of Jesus, and he later became one of the leaders of the Christian church in Jerusalem.

before Hebrews, it follows logically afterward, taking the theme of faith to the next step. James emphasizes that real faith produces good deeds (often referred to as "good works"). Good deeds are not the source of salvation, but James says that they are proof of salvation.

James gets very practical in what he writes. His letter describes:

- How to get wisdom (1:5-8)
- How to control what you say (3:1-12)
- How to keep from judging others (4:11-12)
- How to keep money in perspective (5:1-6)

If you really believe in God, people will see the proof of your faith in your actions.

So you see, it isn't enough just to have faith. Faith that doesn't show itself by good deeds is no faith at all—it is dead and useless (James 2:17).

$\mathcal{R}$eading Between the Lines

Peter knew what he was talking about on the subject of persecution. When he wrote his letters, he was probably in Rome when the Christians were undergoing horrible torture. When he wrote 2 Peter, he knew that his days were numbered. He was right because he was executed for his faith in Jesus. Tradition says that he was crucified upside down.

1 and 2 PETER: Life Is Tough

Peter wrote two letters to Jewish Christians who had been scattered because of persecution for their faith. For these followers of Christ, life was tough—really tough. In an attempt to bolster their faith, Peter tackles some difficult questions:

- How should you live when the trials of life overwhelm you?
- What should you do during terrible times?
- How should you respond when you suffer for doing right?

Peter explains that Christ in your life can give you the power and perspective to endure tough times. He also says that if you follow the Word of God, you won't be misled by false teachings.

Through God's power, you can make it through the difficulties of life. In fact, God can use those circumstances to improve you.

As we know Jesus better, his divine power gives us everything we need for living a godly life. He has called us to receive his own glory and goodness! And by that same mighty power, he has given us all of his rich and wonderful promises (2 Peter 1:3-4).

$\mathcal{S}$uffering is a misfortune, as viewed from the one side, and a discipline as viewed from the other.

Samuel Smiles

1, 2, and 3 JOHN: Love Letters

Love. It's a word that best characterized John the apostle, who wrote these three letters (plus the Gospel of John and Revelation).

- He called himself "the disciple Jesus loved" (John 21:20).
- He was inspired to write the Bible's most famous verse, John 3:16, which is about the essence of God's love.
- He wrote more about Christians loving each other than any other Bible author.

First, Second, and Third John are three letters that follow John's trademark of love. They talk about loving God, loving God's Word, and showing love to others.

The more you get to know God, the more you love Him. Knowledge of God's Word will lead to loving God, and loving God will lead to loving others as Christ did.

> *Love means doing what God has commanded us, and he has commanded us to love one another, just as you heard from the beginning* (2 John 6).

$\mathcal{B}$ible Postcards

Some of the epistles are so short they almost could have been written on postcards. Each of these epistles is only one chapter in length: Philemon (25 verses), 2 John (13 verses), 3 John (15 verses), and Jude (25 verses).

JUDE: Defend the Truth

Jude, like James, was a half brother of Jesus. He wrote this short letter to Jewish Christians to motivate them to protect the pure truth of the Christian faith. Jude doesn't take false teaching lightly. He says that Christians should aggressively defend their faith against those who seek to pervert or pollute it. In particular, he objected to false teachers who used God's grace and forgiveness as a loophole to live any way they pleased, in defiance of God's standards.

Christians need to grow in their spiritual maturity so that they can protect their faith from people who try to twist the Word for their own purposes and ideas.

Dearly loved friends, I had been eagerly planning to write to you about the salvation we all share. But now I find that I must write about something else, urging you to defend the truth of the Good News (Jude 3).

What's That Again?

1. The epistles were written during the first century A.D. after Christ's resurrection and return to heaven. These were letters written by Paul, Peter, John, and others to local churches, individuals, or Christians in general.

2. The epistles give instructions to new believers on a variety of topics important to the Christian faith. These letters cover:

   - the steps to become a Christian
   - instructions for maturing as a Christian
   - explanations of the Holy Spirit's presence and power in every Christian's life
   - God's design for the organization and operation of the local church
   - the relationship and ministry of Christians to each other
   - practical tips for marriages, families, friendships, employment, and finances
   - relying on God's strength to get through tough times
   - the importance of knowing, understanding, and obeying God's Word and rejecting false and inaccurate interpretations

3. The tone and themes of the letters differ, depending upon the author and the audience. Some are intended to encourage the readers who were suffering persecution. Others were written to reprimand the readers who were ignoring the truth they had been taught.

Dig Deeper

Here are some of our favorite books on the epistles and the subjects they cover:

> For a good commentary series, look at the *MacArthur New Testament Commentary*. John MacArthur gives an excellent explanation of Scripture in a passage-by-passage format.

> The epistles are all about how to live the Christian life. We cover that subject in chapter 12 of *Bruce & Stan's Guide to God*.

> For more about the Holy Spirit, we suggest *The Holy Spirit* by Billy Graham.

> If you are interested in church organization and leadership, read *Biblical Eldership* by Alexander Strauch. His book explains all of the passages of the New Testament that deal with church leadership.

> Salvation by grace alone is a predominant theme in the epistles, especially those written by Paul. We recommend that you read *What's So Amazing About Grace* by Philip Yancey.

> *Ephesians: Finding Your Identity in Christ* is one of the Christianity 101 Bible Studies. It gets straight to the heart of a believer's identity in Christ.

■ ■ ■

*Q*uestions for *R*eflection and *D*iscussion

1. Imagine yourself as a new Christian in one of the churches started by Paul. Describe how you would feel and what would

happen when a the church received a handwritten letter from Paul.

2. Read the lists of spiritual gifts found in Romans 12:3-8 and 1 Corinthians 12:4-11. Do you know which of these gifts the Holy Spirit has given you? How are you using your gifts? If you don't know what spiritual gifts you have, how can you discover them?

3. Why does right living come from right thinking, which comes from understanding and obeying the Scriptures? Why doesn't this process work in reverse? Why must belief always precede behavior?

4. Christianity is not a bunch of do's and don'ts, rules and regulations that govern followers of Christ. How does this set Christianity apart from other religions and belief systems?

5. Paul uses the analogy of a human body to describe how Christians relate to each other in the church. Why does he make that comparison?

6. Give three reasons why it is advisable to have a spiritual mentor. How would you go about finding a mentor? How would you go about finding someone to disciple, or should you wait for your potential protégé to approach you? Why or why not?

7. The epistles are full of lessons about how a Christian grows into a deeper relationship with God. Explain one or two lessons that you have learned from the epistles about God or yourself.

8. In what ways do your actions evidence your salvation? Can a professing Christian never produce good works? See Ephesians 2:10 and James 2:17.

■ ■ ■

Moving On...

Several of the epistles were written to Christians who were being persecuted because of their faith in Jesus. Why would they cling to a belief that caused them so much pain and hardship? Well, as explained in 1 Peter, Christians not only experience the love of Christ during their lifetimes, but they also have the hope of eternal life when Jesus comes back to earth a second time. Peter wrote:

> All honor to the God and Father of our Lord Jesus Christ, for it is by his boundless mercy that God has given us the privilege of being born again. Now we live with a wonderful expectation because Jesus Christ rose again from the dead. For God has reserved a priceless inheritance for his children. It is kept in heaven for you, pure and undefiled, beyond the reach of change and decay. And God, in his mighty power, will protect you until you receive this salvation, because you are trusting him. It will be revealed on the last day for all to see (1 Peter 1:3-5).

We turn now to the last book in the Bible, Revelation. What an appropriate way to end the Bible. It begins with a description of the events of Creation from eternity past, and it ends with the events preceding eternity future. In between it addresses questions that have fascinated people for generations: How and when does it all end? What happens to the Christians? What happens to the people who rejected a belief in Jesus? What about heaven? What about hell?

Strap on your seat belt. You're about to take a wild ride into the future.

*C*hapter 11

Everybody wants to go to heaven,
but nobody wants to die.

Loretta Lynn

No book of the Bible has been more puzzled over than the Book of Revelation. For many people it holds the key to the future of the world. For others it is a curiosity, a fairy tale full of strange symbols and creatures. The truth is that Revelation is the final statement, closing argument, and last scene of the Bible.

If you listen carefully in the pages of this book, you'll hear the clock of time clicking...and the clock is definitely winding down. When the events described here are done, the clock will stop. Time will end. And an unbroken eternity will stretch into the future.

Ready for some time travel? Destination: eternity future.

The Book of Revelation:
How It's Going to End

*I*f you have a particularly high IQ, you might be starting *Knowing the Bible 101* with this chapter. You want to know how the Bible ends before you start. Like the great poet T.S. Eliot, you have realized, "In my end is my beginning." You're certainly smarter than the guy who ended up under a tombstone that reads, "I expected this, but not just yet."

But the Bible has a surprise for you. The beginning and the end of this amazing book of God actually have a lot in common. "Revelation is a wonderful way to finish the story which began in Genesis," wrote Henrietta Mears. "All that was begun in the book of beginnings is consummated in Revelation."

In *Genesis*, the creation of heaven and earth are described.
In *Revelation,* the new heaven and new earth are described.

In *Genesis*, God says, "Let there be light."
In *Revelation*, Jesus is the light of the new heaven.

In *Genesis*, sin is born.
In *Revelation*, sin is destroyed.

In *Genesis*, Satan makes his entrance.
In *Revelation*, Satan makes his exit.

In *Genesis*, death comes to humankind.
In *Revelation*, death dies.

In Revelation, as in the Bible, Jesus is the theme. He brings together the last strands of the "scarlet thread of redemption" which runs throughout the Scriptures. The message of the scarlet thread?

- God created you.
- God loves you.
- God sent Jesus to die for you.
- God is going to send Jesus again to bring you back to Him.

Revelation presents Jesus as the Beginning and the End of all things here on earth. He was involved in making the earth, and He will return to remake it. And in between He wants very much for you to know Him and receive His free gift of life.

Cram Plan

Revelation 1—a blessing for those who read this book
Revelation 2–3—a message for the church
Revelation 4–5—a glimpse of heaven
Revelation 6—the seven seals and the four horsemen
Revelation 13—the beast emerges
Revelation 19— Christ the Conqueror
Revelation 21—the holy city
Revelation 22— Jesus is coming

I am the Alpha and the Omega—the Beginning and the End. To all who are thirsty I will give the springs of the water of life without charge (Revelation 21:6).

A Revealing Overview

This book is sometimes called "the Revelation (or Apocalypse) of John," because John the apostle is the author (he also wrote the Gospel and the three epistles that bear his name). A more accurate title for the book is "the Revelation of Jesus Christ." Notice how it opens:

This is a revelation from Jesus Christ, which God gave him concerning the events that will happen soon (Revelation 1:1).

Most scholars date this book from about A.D. 95, making it—as you would expect—the last book written in the Bible. John recorded his amazing visions on the island of Patmos, where he had been exiled by the Roman government for his missionary activities. The apostle was an old man by this time, probably the last of Jesus' chosen still living.

His book starts out as a series of letters to seven churches in present-day Turkey. Then it proceeds to relate a series of dramatic and often-frightening visions of the end times. Jesus told John to "write down what you have seen—both the things that are now happening and the things that will happen later" (Revelation 1:19). As Jesus' instructions imply, the book falls into two parts:

Part 1: Things that are now happening (Revelation 1:1–3:22). Letters to churches. All this material focuses on events happening in John's time and up through our own, the "age of the church."

The Last Disciple

John was the only disciple of Jesus who was not martyred. The emperor Domitian did try to boil him in oil, but John was not harmed. As a result, he was released and banished to the Isle of Patmos, where Jesus showed him the visions of Revelation.

The Book of Revelation

What's in the Bible?		What's in the World?
	69 A.D.	*Vespasian becomes Roman Emperor*
	▼	
	70	*Jerusalem destroyed*
	▼	
	81	*Domitian becomes Emperor*
	▼	
The apostle John banished to the Isle of Patmos	**90**	
	▼	
John writes Revelation	**95**	
	▼	
John dies	**98**	

Part 2: Things that will happen later (Revelation 4:1–22:21). Visions and symbols. These chapters show what will happen in the future when God brings the story of our world to a close.

Apocalypse Now or Star Wars?

Is the Book of Revelation *apocalyptic* or *prophetic?* Well, in a manner of speaking, it's both. Actually, *apocalypse* means "revelation." *Apocalyptic literature* is a specific type of Jewish writing which has its roots in Old Testament *prophecy.* In the Old Testament, a prophet was a spokesman for God. He was given insight into the mind of God and, literally, the message of God. So when a true prophet spoke or wrote, he was declaring the message of God to the people. After the prophets, God no longer spoke to Israel directly. The hope of God's kingdom, promised by the prophets, began to fade.

That's when apocalyptic literature developed. From 200 B.C. to A.D. 100, this form of writing attempted to explain present evil in the world through symbols and to give the assurance that God's kingdom would soon come. Of these works, only Revelation carries the authority of inspiration.

One thing the book isn't, and that's *science fiction.* Even though Revelation uses dreams, visions, and symbols, it's not make-believe. It's the way Jesus chose to reveal the truth to us.

Jesus Explains the Signs of the Times

In Matthew 24, the disciples asked Jesus, "Will there be any sign ahead of time to signal your return and the end of the world?" (Matthew 24:3). His answer helps us understand Revelation. Jesus said He would return after three things had occurred:

- Jerusalem will be destroyed (Matthew 24:2).
- Trouble and tribulation will abound (Matthew 24:4-28).
- The gospel will be preached throughout the world (Matthew 24:14).

Even though these three signs were in the future at the time Jesus gave them, they no longer are:

- Jerusalem was destroyed in A.D. 70.

- Trouble and tribulation began for Christians shortly after Jesus left the earth and haven't let up since.

- The gospel has been preached throughout the world in every generation since Paul and other evangelists fanned out across the known world.

Nothing more *has* to happen to trigger the return of Jesus Christ to earth. The second coming of Jesus could happen anytime. That's what is meant by the *imminent* return of Christ.

Just like Candid Camera

Remember the slogan for the TV show "Candid Camera"? *"Somewhere, someday, when you least expect it, someone's going to come up to you and say..."* That's exactly what Jesus said:

> *You also must be ready all the time. For the Son of Man will come when least expected* (Matthew 24:44).

Down through the ages, people have been just as curious as the disciples to know when Jesus is coming back. People in every generation have thought they were at the "end of the age." Not just the weird guys wearing the "Repent for the End Is Near" sandwich boards either. Martin Luther believed that the big upheavals which triggered the Reformation in the sixteenth century were a sure sign of the imminent return of Jesus.

We've Got a Prediction, Too

Okay, we're ready to stick our necks out. We're about to become a part of the grand tradition of people (great and small, weird and normal—you decide where we fit in) who have set the

---

*G*od's people should plan for a voyage of a thousand years, but be prepared to abandon ship tonight.

Joe Bayly

date for the Lord's return. Are you ready? Here it is (drumroll please):

Jesus is coming in your lifetime.

How do we know that? What basis are we using for this prognostication? Simple. Either Jesus will return before you die or you will be confronted by Him at the moment of your death.

We're not trying to play word games here. We just want to encourage you to respond to Jesus today. Don't put it off because you don't know when you're going to go.

The Hope of His Coming

In the Bible the return of Christ is called the *parousia,* which is Greek for the "appearing" or the "coming" of Jesus in glory at the end of the age. The hope of Christ's appearing was a powerful comfort to Christians facing persecution (see Colossians 3:4; Titus 2:13; and 1 Peter 1:7).

The Future Can Wait (Revelation, Part 1)

Before describing "things which will happen later," Jesus told John to write down "things that are happening now." Jesus was very specific when He told John to send His message in the form of a letter to "the seven churches: Ephesus, Smyrna, Pergamum, Thyatira, Sardis, Philadelphia, and Laodicea" (Revelation 1:11). The letters to each one are recorded in Revelation 2 and 3.

1. Ephesus—"Look how far you have fallen from your first love!" (2:1-7). The Ephesian church had lost their affection for the Lord. They were doing a lot of things right, and the Lord commended them. But their *love* for Jesus had been buried beneath their *service* for Jesus.

2. Smyrna—"I know about your suffering and your poverty" (2:8-11). Jesus offered tremendous encouragement to the suffering and persecuted church. He told them to not be afraid and to "remain faithful even when facing death." He told them that He would give them the crown of life.

3. Pergamum—"You have remained loyal to me...and yet I have a few complaints against you" (2:12-17). Jesus appreciated the good things the people at Pergamum were doing, but His "complaints" centered on their accommodation to the world. They had become too tolerant of those who enticed them to sin.

4. Thyatira—"I will give to each of you whatever you deserve" (2:18-29). Like the Christians in Pergamum, the people of the church at Thyatira loved Jesus and were willing to serve Him. Jesus said they would be rewarded. But He encouraged them to throw out false teachers they had allowed among them.

5. Sardis—"You are dead. Now wake up!" (3:1-6). No one knew doctrine better than the people in Sardis, but their knowledge and spirituality didn't show itself in their lives. Jesus described them as lifeless and "far from right in the sight of God." Jesus said, "Go back to what you heard and believed at first."

6. Philadelphia—"I know all the things you do, and I have opened a door for you that no one can shut" (3:7-13). Jesus was especially fond of the church in Philadelphia. They had a true heart for missions, even when they were persecuted severely. Because they had persevered, Jesus promised to protect them.

7. Laodicea—"Since you are like lukewarm water, I will spit you out of my mouth!" (3:14-22). The Laodiceans were wealthy and complacent. They weren't doing anything terribly wrong, but they weren't on fire for Jesus either. They were "neither hot nor cold." Jesus even said, "I wish you were one or the other."

---

*S*in will keep you from this Book, or this Book will keep you from sin.

John Bunyan

The Future Is Coming Soon (Revelation, Part 2)

The remainder of the Book of Revelation centers on what Jesus showed John. You'll notice recurring phrases like

- "And I saw..." (5:1)
- "Then I looked up. . ." (8:13)
- "Then I saw..." (14:14)

We can almost imagine the white-haired apostle sitting in his personal theater, watching the most amazing epic movie of all time.

Another element that keeps popping up is the number *seven*. Here are what scholar Merrill Unger calls the "Seven Sevens of the Apocalypse":

1. The seven churches (Revelation 2:1–3:22)
2. The seven seals (6:1–8:1)
3. The seven trumpets (8:2–11:19)
4. The seven personages (12:1–13:18)
5. The seven bowls (15:1–16:21)
6. The seven dooms (17:1–20:15)
7. The seven new things (21:1–22:21)

Did the number key just get stuck, you wonder, or does the number seven mean something? Scholars believe that the answer is pretty simple: Revelation is about the completion of things, the big wrap-up. Jesus reveals the symbols in patterns of seven as if to make the message crystal-clear: *"Don't wait for the sequel, boys and girls. This is all she wrote!"*

Now we want to help you make sense out of the major topics in the remainder of Revelation. So here we go with...

Countdown to Heaven: Seven Last Things

1. The Last Bad Guy: the Antichrist. The worst human being the world has ever known will be the Antichrist. You could take Stalin and Hitler and Genghis Khan all rolled into one guy, put him into

What About the Bible Code and All Those Numbers?

You might have heard of *numerology,* the study of the significance of numbers in the Bible. The Jews used numbers and patterns to show meaning or relationship. And then there's the so-called "Bible Code," a secret code hidden in the letters of the Hebrew Bible which supposedly gives details about people and events in the past, present, and future. What's that all about? Recently people have plugged the "codes" into computers. The best we can say about Bible codes is that they can provide endless hours of harmless entertainment. Just don't get distracted from the Bible's real message—and that's written in *words* for all to read and understand.

What About 666?

Revelation 13:18 says that the number of the beast is 666. But what does it mean? Numerologists say that the number *six* represents man's imperfection (just as the number *seven* represents completion or perfection). Three sixes could mean complete imperfection, or it could refer to the unholy trinity of Satan, the beast, and the false prophet. Whatever 666 represents, it isn't good.

a World Wrestling Federation ring with the Antichrist, and it would be no contest. In Revelation, the Antichrist is called the beast, and perhaps the reason he will be so evil is that Satan (the dragon) will give him "his own power and throne and great authority" (Revelation 13:2).

2. The Last, Big Test: the Tribulation. A tribulation can be any kind of trial faced by Christians (John 16:33). When it comes to the Great Tribulation, the reference is to the tremendous increase in evil in this world as the "last days" approach. Jesus talked about "a time

Who is the Antichrist?

We don't know, and the Bible doesn't tell us. We do know that he will lead the rebellion against Jesus and His work on earth. The crazy thing is that for a while the world will "[follow] the beast in awe" (Revelation 13:3). That's why many people believe the Antichrist will be a great world leader. Whoever he is, the Antichrist will eventually turn on God and demand that everyone worship him instead.

of greater horror than anything the world has ever seen" (Matthew 24:20).

Revelation describes a time when Satan goes all out, bringing terror to the earth like never before: "For the Devil has come down to you in great anger, and he knows that he has little time" (Revelation 12:12).

Scholars seem to agree that this refers to the Great Tribulation. Some Bible teachers take their cue from Daniel 9:27 and confine this time of calamity to seven years. Generally, they fall into three camps on this event:

- *Pretribulation.* Christ will return for His followers before the tribulation.

- *Midtribulation.* Christ will return in the middle of the seven-year period before things really get bad.

- *Posttribulation.* Christ returns when the tribulation is over.

3. The Last Disappearing Act: the Rapture and the Second Coming. You won't find the word *rapture* in the Bible, but Bible scholars have used the word to describe the following great event:

For the Lord himself will come down from heaven with a commanding shout, with the call of the archangel, and with the trumpet call of God. First, all the Christians who have died will rise from their graves. Then, together with

them, we who are still alive and remain on the earth will
be caught up in the clouds to meet the Lord in the air and
remain with him forever. So comfort and encourage each
other with these words (1 Thessalonians 4:16-18).

The traditional view of the rapture is that its purpose is to allow Christians, dead or alive, to literally meet Jesus in the air and join His heavenly procession as He arrives "on the clouds of heaven with power and great glory" (Matthew 24:30). In the last hundred years or so, some scholars have separated the rapture of the church from the second coming of Christ. By this view, Christ will remove His followers from the earth so that they won't have to experience the Great Tribulation.

Where Does Israel Fit In?

Israel is and always has been God's chosen nation (Genesis 12:3). When Israel rejected the promised Messiah (John 1:11), God's plan of salvation through Jesus extended to the Gentiles, so that all people could be saved through faith (Acts 15:9).

Some Christians believe that God will someday restore Israel as a nation and a people (Romans 11:31). Certainly when the nation of Israel was reborn politically in 1948 (the first time exiled Jews had gathered in Palestine since the destruction of Jerusalem in A.D. 70), the signs seemed to point to Israel playing a major role in end-time events.

4. The Last Roundup: Satan Finally Gets His. Our world seems fascinated by Satan (which is exactly the way he wants it). What a shame. Satan isn't some cute guy in a red suit with a pitchfork. Don't mess with him, and don't associate with people who do. Satan is the enemy of God and your greatest enemy, prowling around "like a roaring lion, looking for some victim to devour" (1 Peter 5:8).

Armageddon—Earth's Biggest Battle

Because of its strategic location in northern Israel (near present-day Haifa), the plain of Megiddo, or Armageddon, has been the site of many fierce battles through the centuries. The fiercest battle in history will be fought at Armageddon as the demonic forces of the beast do battle against the Lord and His people (Revelation 16:13-16). But with the armies of heaven at His side, Jesus will be victorious (Revelation 19:11-16).

Satan hates Jesus (Revelation 12:13), and he hates Christians (Revelation 12:17). He is your accuser before God (Zechariah 3:1). And before he is finally defeated, he will wage a war against heaven and earth unlike anything ever seen from eternity past to eternity future.

The good news is that God will eventually throw Satan and his superhuman puppet, the Antichrist, into the lake of fire, where "they will be tormented day and night forever and ever" (Revelation 20:10).

What About the Millennium?

The word *millennium* refers to a thousand-year period of time when Jesus Christ will reign on earth with the saints (Revelation 20). Sometimes the terms *kingdom* and *millennium* are used interchangeably. There are three major viewpoints on when the millennium will take place:

Postmillennialism. The church will bring about peace on earth. Then Jesus will return.

Amillennialism. The thousand-year period of peace is symbolic of Christ reigning in the hearts of believers.

Premillennialism. A literal thousand-year event is sandwiched between the return of Jesus to earth and final judgment.

5. The Last Verdict: the Final Judgment. According to the Bible, there appear to be two separate judgments coming for all humankind, dead or alive. The first will be for Christians. Paul wrote that Christians "must all stand before Christ to be judged. We will each receive whatever we deserve for the good or evil we have done in our bodies" (2 Corinthians 5:10). Paul also used the analogy of a builder to describe this Believer's Award Ceremony:

> *Everyone's work will be put through the fire to see whether or not it keeps its value. If the work survives the fire, that builder will receive a reward. But if the work is burned up, the builder will suffer great loss. The builders themselves will be saved, but like someone escaping through a wall of flames* (1 Corinthians 3:13-15).

Revelation refers to the second judgment—the final judgment—as the "great white throne" judgment (Revelation 20:11-15). This little passage isn't a whole lot of fun to read. It's worse than any horror movie you can imagine. And here's the most chilling verse of all:

> *And anyone whose name was not found recorded in the Book of Life was thrown into the lake of fire* (Revelation 20:15).

Everyone—believers and unbelievers, the living and the dead—will be judged by God Himself. As the writer of Hebrews put it, "It is destined that each person dies only once and after that comes judgment" (Hebrews 9:27).

Forget about that cute little image of everyone waiting in line telling jokes. One day we will stand before Almighty God to give an accounting for our life and our decisions. And you can bet that the first question God is going to ask is this one: "What did you do with My Son?"

*W*hy should anyone be shattered by the thought of hell? It is not compulsory for anyone to go there.

Thomas Merton

6. The Last, Worst Place: Hell. Few people seem to take hell seriously. But hell is real and worse than you can imagine. Jesus said that someday He will send His angels to "remove from my Kingdom everything that causes sin and all who do evil, and they will throw them into the furnace and burn them. There will be weeping and gnashing of teeth" (Matthew 13:41-42). Clearly, Jesus taught that hell is a place of eternal torment and punishment waiting for those who reject His message.

But I Thought God Was a God of Love

Rather than think of hell as cruel and unusual punishment, we should remember that it's impossible for God to be cruel. He is completely just and fair:

> *But you are a God of forgiveness, gracious and merciful, slow to become angry, and full of unfailing love and mercy* (Nehemiah 9:17).

No innocent person will suffer at His hand. No one will receive a punishment he does not deserve. Peter wrote that God "does not want anyone to perish, so he is giving more time for everyone to repent" (2 Peter 3:9). Jesus didn't come to save the innocent, but the lost (Luke 19:10). We all know what John 3:16 says, but do you remember the verse that follows?

> *God did not send his Son into the world to condemn it, but to save it* (John 3:17).

Some scholars believe that hell will be so awful because in it people will be separated from God forever. R.C. Sproul takes a little different view. He writes that the problem of the ungodly "will not be separation from God, it will be the presence of God that will torment them."

If you have accepted the free gift of salvation through God's Son, Jesus, you will enjoy an incredible existence far beyond anything you could ever imagine or deserve. It's called heaven.

---

*T*he New Jerusalem described in Revelation 21 is not heaven. Larry Richards writes that the New Jerusalem is "the capital city of an entirely new universe created by God as the home of a redeemed humanity." Some scholars believe that the saints will live and rule in the New Jerusalem during the millennium.

---

7. The Last, Best Place: Heaven. Heaven isn't imaginary. It isn't fairy-tale stuff. Heaven is a real place. Jesus talked about going to prepare a *place* for those who have put their trust in Him (John 14:1-4). Heaven is also called "glory" (Hebrews 2:10) and our "home" (2 Corinthians 5:1).

Heaven is the place where God lives. Heaven is where Jesus came from, where He lives now, and from where He will return someday (Acts 1:11). When a Christian dies, he or she immediately goes to heaven to be in the presence of Jesus (Luke 23:43; Philippians 1:23). Hebrews 12:23 suggests that Christians who have died are in heaven without their resurrected bodies, waiting for a time when the body and soul will be reunited in a glorified state.

In Revelation, we have a description of what it will be like to be in heaven:

> *"Look, the home of God is now among his people! He will live with them, and they will be his people. God himself will be with them. He will remove all of their sorrows, and there will be no more death or sorrow or crying or pain. For the old world and its evils are gone forever." And the one sitting on the throne said, "Look, I am making all things new!"* (Revelation 21:3-5).

This is a Christian's "blessed hope." We will be in God's presence. We will someday see God in Jesus face-to-face. The first moment we begin to enjoy and worship Jesus will be the first time we feel completely fulfilled and—finally—*home!*

Heaven is our true home. And we will live there forever.

*T*he Death of Death

Death will be the last enemy to be defeated (1 Corinthians 15:26). Jesus conquered death spiritually and physically on our behalf when He was crucified and resurrected. In heaven, when Jesus reigns in glory, there will be no death of any kind for us (Revelation 21:4). Death will finally die.

Heaven will be eternally significant because of what will be absent: tears, sorrow, crying, pain, and death. But most significant will be what heaven will include: Jesus Christ. Jesus promised His disciples that He was going to prepare a place in heaven to share with them.

What's That Again?

1. The theme of the Bible and the theme of Revelation is that Jesus is God's gift of hope to the world.

2. Revelation describes current conditions (things that are happening now) and future events (things that will happen later).

3. Nothing has to happen in our world for Jesus to return. The second coming of Jesus is *imminent*—it could happen at any time. Bruce and Stan predict that Jesus is coming in your lifetime.

4. The warnings and lessons in the letters Jesus dictated to the seven churches in Asia apply to us today.

5. Although we don't know *when* the seven future events in Revelation will take place, we know that they *will* take place.

6. God does not want to condemn anyone. He is completely just and fair. No innocent person will suffer the consequences of judgment.

7. Those who have accepted the free gift of salvation will be welcomed into heaven to spend eternity with Jesus.

Dig Deeper

Read these books before the world comes to an end!

Revelation: Four Views edited by Steve Gregg. This impressive volume presents the four traditional interpretations of Revelation—historicist, preterist, futurist, and spiritual—in a parallel commentary fashion so you can draw your own conclusions.

Bruce & Stan's Guide to Bible Prophecy. A clear, correct, and casual guide to all Bible prophecy, not just Revelation.

Now, That's a Good Question! by R.C. Sproul. Our favorite theologian answers the kinds of questions Christians ask about their life and their faith. Some great answers to questions about the end times.

Fast Facts on Bible Prophecy by Thomas Ice and Timothy Demy. More than 175 in-depth definitions and explanations of Old and New Testament prophecy passages and concepts.

Escape the Coming Night by David Jeremiah. A dramatic narrative of Revelation that relates today's headlines to what the Bible says.

Revelation: Unlocking the Mysteries of the End Times is one of the Christianity 101 Bible Studies. This study will help you understand why—when God is involved—the end of the world can be something to look forward to.

■ ▨ ■

*Q*uestions for *R*eflection and *D*iscussion

1. Give your take on this statement: Nothing more has to happen to trigger the return of Jesus Christ to earth.

2. Do you believe Jesus is coming in your lifetime? In what way might that change the way you live?

3. Read 2 Peter 3:8-10. How do these verses fit with the words of Jesus in Matthew 24:44?

4. Which of the seven churches of Revelation is most like your church? What could you do to help your church get back on the right track (unless your church is like the church in Philadelphia)?

5. The pretribulational view that all Christians will be raptured before the events of the Great Tribulation has been around for the last hundred years or so. Before that, the view that Christians will go through the Tribulation was the prevailing view. Why this recent change in emphasis?

6. How will the judgment of believers differ from the judgment of unbelievers?

7. Your best friend, who doesn't believe in heaven or hell, is going to die tomorrow, and only you know it. How do you convince your friend that hell is real, that heaven is an option, and that the choice is up to him or her?

■ ▨ ■

Moving On...

There is a great verse in the Book of Hebrews which talks about faith in terms of *hope:*

> *What is faith? It is the confident assurance that what we hope for is going to happen. It is the evidence of things we cannot yet see* (Hebrews 11:1).

If this last chapter has taught you anything, we hope it has taught you that Jesus is your *hope.* If you know Jesus, you can have the confident assurance that Jesus is coming back for you. Because of what Jesus did for you in the *past,* you can live in the *present* in His power, and you can know that you have a *future* with Jesus in heaven. This is your hope.

Part IV

Taking God at His Word

Chapter 12

Kierkegaard said that most of us read the Bible the way a mouse tries to remove the cheese from the trap without getting caught. Some of us have mastered that. We read the story as though it were about someone else along time ago; that way we don't get caught. But if we see the Bible as the story of the triumph of God's grace, the story of God searching for *us*, then look out. The story will come alive. God will find us and we will know that we are found.

Maxie Dunnam

If you have read straight through this book from the beginning, then you've got our congratulations. (If you skipped ahead to this chapter, then we'll congratulate you after you go back and read the parts you missed.) But reaching the end of this book is really just a starting point for you.

We hope we have been able to help you get a better understanding of what the Bible is all about. Now you've got enough information to jump in and start studying the Bible to discover for yourself what it says about God and His plan to connect with you in a personal way. The next step is up to you.

Don't make the mistake of thinking that knowing *about* the Bible is enough. You need to check it out for yourself. Your time won't be wasted. The Bible promises that it can improve your life, and in this final chapter we'll examine those claims so you can decide if you're interested in what it promises to deliver.

The Bible Is for You

*W*hat's *A*head

- [ ] What You Need to Remember
- [ ] What the Bible Can Do for You
- [ ] What's Next for You?

*Y*ou've come a long way from Genesis through Revelation. You've traveled through the centuries and covered lots of people and places. You've learned dates and doctrine. You've studied prophets and predictions. Now it's time to take a deep breath and let your mind rest for a while. You could pop a cranial corpuscle attempting to remember everything...so don't even try.

What You Need to Remember

As you finish reading this book, we'll be pleased if you remember only two facts about the Bible. That won't be too tough. Here they are:

Fact #1: The Bible is all about Jesus. *Halley's Bible Handbook* summarizes the Bible this way:

> The Old Testament is an account of a Nation. The
> New Testament is an account of a Man. The Nation

315

was founded and nurtured by God to bring the Man into the world. His appearance on the earth is the central event of all history. The Old Testament sets the stage for it. The New Testament describes it.

Since the Old Testament tells why God needed a plan to restore a relationship with the human race, and since the New Testament explains that Jesus was the plan, the point of the whole Bible can be summed up in one verse:

> *For God so loved the world that he gave his only Son, so that everyone who believes in him will not perish but have eternal life* (John 3:16).

Fact #2: The Bible was written for you. The Bible was not written as a bland historical textbook to be placed on the shelf as a reference book for Trivial Pursuit questions. It was never intended as a boring coffee-table book to read only at Christmas or to serve as a coaster for beverage glasses. No, the Bible is God's intensely personal correspondence to *you*. It is God's written verification that His Son, Jesus, is the way God desires to save *your* life.

> *But these are written so that you may believe that Jesus is the Messiah, the Son of God, and that by believing in him you will have life* (John 20:31).

You may forget the dates and places, but if you remember these two facts, you will always be reading the Bible in the right context and from the correct perspective.

---

*G*od Doesn't Play Hide-and-Seek

Are you interested in meeting God? The Bible is the place where that will happen. Are you skeptical? That's okay. As long as you are sincere in your search, God promises that He will reveal Himself to you. Here's His written guarantee:

> *"If you look for me in earnest, you will find me when you seek me. I will be found by you,"* says the LORD (Jeremiah 29:13-14).

What the Bible Can Do for You

We wrote this book to encourage you to explore the Bible in greater detail and with more intensity. However, in case we didn't accomplish our purpose—at least not yet—don't stick your Bible back on the shelf.

The Bible is worthy of your time and effort. And not just because we say so. Here is God's own promise of what the Bible can do for you:

> *All Scripture is inspired by God and is useful to teach us what is true and to make us realize what is wrong in our lives. It straightens us out and teaches us to do what is right. It is God's way of preparing us in every way, fully equipped for every good thing God wants us to do* (2 Timothy 3:16-17).

Let's take a moment to analyze that verse because it gives seven ways you can personally benefit from reading the Bible.

Bible Reading Benefit #1: Motivation

All Scripture is inspired by God....

If you need motivation to read the Bible, here it is. The words of the Bible are the words of God. "Inspired" means "God-breathed." Through the Holy Spirit, God gave His words to the various authors. Their writings are God's message to us.

Notice that "all Scripture" is from God. Not just parts of the Bible, not just some of the verses, but all of it. Wherever you turn in the Bible, you will find God speaking to you.

When the Almighty Creator of the universe speaks, all of us ought to listen. Reading novels or instructional manuals is optional, but reading the words of God is mandatory, especially if you want your life to count for eternity. Besides, God wouldn't have gone to so much trouble to give us His message if He didn't think it was important.

The Bible finds us where we are and, with our permission, takes us where we ought to go.

Bible Reading Benefit #2: Instruction

*All Scripture is inspired by God **and is useful to teach us
what is true....***

The Bible will instruct you about the truths of God. Do you
want to know more about God? Do you want to understand His
plan for your life? What He requires of you? There are a lot of opinions floating around, but you can use the Bible as the standard for
testing everything else that claims to be true.

How to Get Personal with God

Of all the instruction you will find in the Bible, the most
important concept is God's plan for starting a personal relationship
with you. This is the ultimate truth! It is called "God's Plan of Salvation," and here is how it works:

- We are all sinners and will never satisfy God's perfect
  standards.

    *For all have sinned; all fall short of God's glorious stan-
    dard* (Romans 3:23).

- The penalty for our sins is eternal death.

    For the wages of sin is death (Romans 6:23).

- God still loves us, so Jesus died to pay the penalty for our
  sins.

    *But God showed his great love for us by sending Christ to
    die for us while we were still sinners* (Romans 5:8).

- We can be saved from our sins by turning away from
  them and accepting Jesus as the Lord and Savior of our life.

    *For if you confess with your mouth that Jesus is Lord and
    believe in your heart that God raised him from the dead,
    you will be saved. For it is by believing in your heart that
    you are made right with God, and it is by confessing
    with your mouth that you are saved* (Romans 10:9-10)

- If we accept Jesus into our lives, we will have eternal life.

    *So whoever has God's Son has life; whoever does not
    have his Son does not have life* (1 John 5:12).

- Jesus is the only way to get right with God.

> *Jesus told him, "I am the way, the truth, and the life. No one can come to the Father except through me"* (John 14:6).

You haven't really studied the Bible until you have met the Author.

Bible Reading Benefit #3: Detection

> *All Scripture is inspired by God and is useful to teach us what is true **and to make us realize what is wrong in our lives.**...*

The Bible can serve as a warning device for your life, helping you detect the thoughts and actions which are harmful to you.

Bible Reading Benefit #4: Correction

> *All Scripture is inspired by God and is useful to teach us what is true and to make us realize what is wrong in our lives. **It straightens us out.**...*

When a ship gets off course, the captain needs to make a correction. When your life is out of whack, the Bible can give you the help to make the necessary corrections.

If you are shooting for the moon and you are off by only a fraction of a degree, you will miss the target by miles. So it is with life. A small error, left uncorrected, can lead to huge problems later on.

> *And God has actually given us his Spirit (not the world's spirit) so we can know the wonderful things God has freely given us* (1 Corinthians 2:12).

---

*A*re you worried that you won't be able to understand the Bible? Don't be. If you are a Christian, the Holy Spirit is inside you. Part of His job is to help you understand the Word of God.

Bible Reading Benefit #5: Direction

> *All Scripture is inspired by God and is useful to teach us what is true and to make us realize what is wrong in our lives. It straightens us out **and teaches us to do what is right.**...*

The Bible can give direction to your life. You won't have to wonder about the ever-changing moral compass of society. The Bible draws clear lines about what is right and wrong. From the Ten Commandments in the Old Testament, to "love your neighbor as yourself" in the New Testament, the Bible gives practical advice for life.

Other books were given to us for information, but the Bible was given to us for transformation.

Bible Reading Benefit #6: Preparation

> *All Scripture is inspired by God and is useful to teach us what is true and to make us realize what is wrong in our lives. It straightens us out and teaches us to do what is right. **It is God's way of preparing us in every way.**...*

God wants to prepare you to be capable and ready to meet all the demands of life. His Word, the Bible, gives you the information and inspiration that are part of the preparation process. This doesn't mean that you will be sinless, but you will be mature and ready for whatever God wants to do through your life—and all that He allows to happen in your life.

Bible Reading Benefit #7: Realization

> *All Scripture is inspired by God and is useful to teach us what is true and to make us realize what is wrong in our lives. It straightens us out and teaches us to do what is right. It is God's way of preparing us in every way, **fully equipped for every good thing God wants us to do.***

Most people are wandering around aimlessly in life, looking for purpose and meaning. If you read the Bible, you will realize God's purpose for your life. He wants to equip you so that you can minister to others and worship Him. In our zeal for the truth of Scripture, we must never forget one of its purposes: to equip us to do good.

The realization of your place in God's plan will change your life. You won't be studying God's Word simply to increase your knowledge or to prepare you to win arguments. You will be reading the Bible knowing that God's Word will strengthen your faith and lead you to do good.

What's Next for You?

Are you ready to start reading the Bible on your own? Of course you are! Here are a few helpful hints before we say good-bye:

Get started right away. Don't put it off. God is anxious to communicate with you.

Read the Bible every day. Make it part of your daily routine.

Begin with prayer. Ask God to give you understanding of what you read.

Do it systematically. If you need a reading plan, we have included several in the appendix.

When you read the Bible, ask yourself these questions:

> *What does it say?* This is called "observation." Don't forget to check out the context of what is written.
>
> *What does it mean?* This is called "interpretation." Look for the single most important meaning in the passage.
>
> *What does it mean for me?* This is called "application." How is your life going to change based upon what you read?

---

*T*he Bible, God's inerrant Word, is forever true whether or not anyone reads or believes it; but it becomes of value to you when you get hold of it for yourself. Never leave a passage of Scripture until it has said something to you.

Robert A. Cook

Go where it is taught. If you aren't already attending a church that teaches directly from the Bible, you should find one. You'll be excited to hear other people's insights from the Word of God. If you're just getting started in regular Bible reading, ask if the church has a Bible study group you can attend.

Warning: When you spend time in God's Word on a daily basis, you will notice changes in your life. You won't be the same, and you'll be pleased with the changes.

What's That Again?

1. The Bible is all about Jesus. The Bible was written for you.

2. The Bible is the truthful and reliable words of God. It can improve your life through its motivation, instruction, detection, correction, direction, preparation, and realization.

3. The Holy Spirit assists every Christian with understanding the Bible.

Dig Deeper

Don't substitute any other book for the Bible, but you may wish to use a study guide to help you as you read your Bible daily. Here are a few "devotional guides" which may be of help to you:

> *My Utmost for His Highest* by Oswald Chambers. This is a classic. Be sure to get the updated edition.

> *The Daily Bible.* Here is the entire Bible arranged chronologically and divided into 365 segments. Includes historical transition notes by F. LaGard Smith.

> *Your Daily Walk* from Walk Thru the Bible Ministries. Provides a one-year overview of the entire Bible in 365 page-a-day segments. Each page gives you easy-to-

read commentary on the Bible passage with practical application.

Josh McDowell's One Year Book of Family Devotions by Bob Hostetler. Each day includes a suggested Bible reading, a real-life story, a suggested activity, and a prayer. An excellent tool for discussing biblical values in your family.

Tabletalk from Ligonier Ministries. This monthly publication from R.C. Sproul goes into select Bible passages in detail. There are also many related articles written by Dr. Sproul and others. You can order *Tabletalk* from Ligonier Ministries in Orlando, Florida (www.ligonier.org).

■ ■ ■

Questions for Reflection and Discussion

1. Discuss these two statements: (1) The Bible is all about Jesus, and (2) the Bible is all about you.

2. In what ways can reading the Bible personally benefit you?

3. How often do you read the Bible now? (Be honest.) If reading the Bible benefits you, do you need to read the Bible more? What would motivate you to do that?

4. Must *all* Scripture—not just some of it or 90 percent of it—be inspired by God? Why or why not? Does your understanding of inspiration affect the way you read the Bible?

5. How could you use the verses listed under "How to Get Personal with God" to lead someone to Christ?

6. Has reading the Bible ever helped you realize something was wrong in your life? Describe that experience. What would have happened if you had stayed on your incorrect course?

7. What suggestions would you make to someone who was sincerely interested in learning more about the Bible? Be specific.

_____

▣ ▣ ▣

Moving On

We've come to the end of this guide through the Bible. We hope you have at least gotten a glimpse of all that God has in store for you in the pages of His Holy Word. The next step is up to you.

You can be sure we are praying that you will realize the Bible is your direct connection to God. We know that once you get started, you will be amazed as God comes alive to you. The Bible is truly the Word of God—filled with God's words about you, for you, and to you.

$\mathcal{A}$ppendix

We're excited that you are interested in reading the Bible, so we have put a few things in our appendix that you might find helpful.

- Bible Reading Plans
- Famous Passages of the Bible
- What the Bible Says About...
  - Topics for Family Life
  - Topics for Life in General
  - Topics Relating to Living Your Life with God
  - What to Read When You're Feeling...

Bible Reading Plans

In the Dig Deeper section of chapter 12, we mention some books that are designed to help you read systematically. But you don't necessarily need a special book for that purpose. Here are a few ways that you can handle reading the Bible on a daily basis:

Plan #1: The "Three-Week Introductory" Plan. If you have never read the Bible before, or if you're looking for a good way to get started again, read the Gospel of John. There are 21 chapters. So if you read one chapter each day, you'll be done in three weeks.

Plan #2: The "Becoming Wise in a Month" Plan. Every day, read a chapter from the Book of Proverbs. There are 31 chapters, so read the one which corresponds to the day's date (i.e., if it is the eighth of the month, read chapter 8).

Plan #3: The "30 Days to Knowing More About Jesus" Plan. Follow this month-long chronological biography of Jesus that we have compiled from the Gospels:

Day 1	What Jesus is all about	John 1:1-18
Day 2	Heavenly messenger to Mary and Joseph	Luke 1:26-38 Matthew 1:18-25
Day 3	Birth and childhood of Jesus	Luke 2
Day 4	Jesus is baptized by John	Luke 3:1-22
Day 5	Jesus is tempted by Satan and starts his ministry	Luke 4
Day 6	Jesus chats with Nicodemus	John 3:1-21
Day 7	Fishermen become followers	Luke 5:1-11; Matthew 4:18-22
Day 8	Famous sermon—Part I	Matthew 5

Day 9	Famous sermon—Part II	Matthew 6
Day 10	Famous sermon—Part III	Matthew 7
Day 11	Speaking in parables	Mark 4:1-34
Day 12	A typical day on the job	Matthew 14
Day 13	Resentful religious leaders	John 7
Day 14	Moses and Elijah make a guest appearance with Jesus	Matthew 17:1-13 Mark 9:2-13
Day 15	Jesus talks about attitudes	Matthew 18
Day 16	Encounters with Jesus	John 8
Day 17	Jesus praying and saying	Luke 11
Day 18	Lazarus is raised from the dead	John 11
Day 19	A triumphal entry into Jerusalem	Matthew 21:1-9 Luke 19:28-44
Day 20	Blasting the hypocrisy of the religious leaders	Matthew 23
Day 21	Jesus talks about the future	Matthew 24
Day 22	A last supper with the disciples	John 13
Day 23	Jesus prays about what is to come	John 17
Day 24	Betrayed, arrested, and tried	John 18
Day 25	Death on a cross	Mark 15
Day 26	He has risen from the dead	Matthew 28:1-10; Luke 24:1-11
Day 27	Postresurrection appearances	Luke 24:12-43; John 20:11-31
Day 28	A final fish fry with the disciples	John 21
Day 29	One more thing before I go	Matthew 28:16-20; Luke 24:44-53
Day 30	Peter explains it all	Acts 2

Plan #4: The "New Testament in a Year" Plan. Ten minutes a day will get you through the entire New Testament in a year. To keep on schedule, read one chapter a day, Monday through Friday, for 52 weeks. (Don't be surprised if you get excited and read more than one chapter in a day or find yourself wanting to read on the weekends.)

Famous Passages of the Bible

All parts of the Bible are worthwhile, but some passages are more popular than others. Here are some of the all-time favorites.

Old Testament

Creation and Adam and Eve	Genesis 1–3
Noah and the flood	Genesis 6–8
Abraham prepares to sacrifice Isaac	Genesis 22:1-19
Joseph and his dreams	Genesis 37–49
Moses—baby in the bulrushes	Exodus 1–2
Moses—crossing the Red Sea	Exodus 14
The Ten Commandments	Exodus 20:1-17; Deuteronomy 5:6-21
Samson	Judges 14–16
David and Goliath	1 Samuel 17
"The Lord is my shepherd" psalm	Psalm 23
Daniel in the lion's den	Daniel 6
Jonah and the great fish	Jonah 1-4

New Testament

(For events from Jesus' life, see Bible Reading Plan #3.)

Beatitudes	Matthew 5:3-12; Luke 6:20-23
Sermon on the Mount	Matthew 5–7
Lord's prayer	Matthew 6:9-15; Luke 11:1-13
Golden rule	Matthew 7:12; Luke 6:31
Christians get the Holy Spirit	Acts 2
Paul's conversion	Acts 9
Spiritual gifts	Romans 12:6-8; 1 Corinthians 1:2–14; Ephesians 4:11-12; 1 Peter 4:10
Lord's supper	1 Corinthians 11:17-34
The love chapter	1 Corinthians 13
Fruit of the Spirit	Galatians 5:22-23
Spiritual armor	Ephesians 6:11-18
The faith "Hall of Fame"	Hebrews 11

What the Bible Says About...

You can usually find a more extensive "concordance" in the back of most Bibles, but here is a short one to get you started.

Topics for Family Life

Children	Deuteronomy 6:6-7; Psalm 127:3-5; Proverbs 13:24; 22:6; 23:13-14; 29:15,17; Ephesians 6:4; Colossians 3:21
Husbands	Genesis 18:19; 1 Corinthians 7:3-4; Ephesians 5:21,23-29,33; 6:4; Colossians 3:19; 1 Peter 3:7

Marriage	Genesis 2:18-24; Proverbs 5:15-19; Song of Songs 8:6-7; 1 Corinthians 7:2-3,7-9; Ephesians 5:21-33; Hebrews 13:4
Parents	Exodus 20:12; Proverbs 22:6,15; 23:22; Ephesians 6:1-3; Colossians 3:20
Wives	Genesis 2:18; Proverbs 12:4; 14:1; 19:14; 31:10-31; 1 Corinthians 7:3-4; Ephesians 5:21-24,33; Colossians 3:18; 1 Timothy 3:11; Titus 2:3-5; 1 Peter 3:1-6

Topics for Life in General

Abortion	Exodus 21:22-23; Job 10:8-12; Psalm 127:3-5; 139:13-16; Isaiah 44:2
Choosing a career	Proverbs 31:10-31; Matthew 19:4-6; Ephesians 5:22-33; Jude 24-25
Contentment	Proverbs 15:15; 23:17; Philippians 4:11-13; 1 Timothy 6:6-10; Hebrews 13:5
Danger	Psalm 23:4; 32:7; 34:7,17,19; 91:1-2,11; 121:1-8; Isaiah 43:2; Romans 14:8
Death	Job 19:25-27; Psalm 23:4; 116:15; 139:16; Isaiah 25:8; Matthew 22:30; John 11:25-27; 14:1-7; Romans 8:31-39; 14:7-9; 1 Corinthians 15:51-55; 2 Corinthians 5:1,6-8; Philippians 1:21; 1 Thessalonians 4:13-18; 5:9-10; 2 Timothy 4:7-8; Hebrews 9:27; Revelation 21:4
Difficulties	Romans 8:28; 2 Corinthians 4:17; Hebrews 5:8; 12:7,11; Revelation 3:19
Finances	Psalm 24:1; 37:25; 50:10,14-15; Proverbs 22:7; Matthew 6:19-34; 1 Corinthians 4:2; Philippians 4:19; 1 Timothy 6:9-10
Friendship	Proverbs 17:17; 18:24; Luke 10:25-37; John 13:35; 15:11-17; Romans 16:1-2; Galatians 6:1,10
Homosexuality	Leviticus 18:22; 20:13; Romans 1:26-27; 1 Corinthians 6:9-10
Honesty	Romans 13:13; 1 Thessalonians 4:11-12; Hebrews 13:18; 1 Peter 2:11-12
Leadership	Isaiah 11:1-9; 32:1-8; 1 Timothy 3:1-7; 2 Timothy 2:14-16; Titus 1:5-9
Love	Matthew 22:34-40; John 14:15-21; 15:9-17; 1 Corinthians 13; Galatians 5:22-23; Ephesians 5:1-2; Colossians 3:12-14; 1 John 2:5-17; 3:7-24

Money	Psalm 37:16; 49:10-13,20; Ecclesiastes 5:10-15; 1 Timothy 6:10,17-19
Occult	Leviticus 20:27; Deuteronomy 18:9-12; 1 Samuel 28:7-12; 2 Kings 21:6; Isaiah 8:19; 19:3; 47:13-14; Acts 19:18-20; James 4:7
Peer pressure	Joshua 1:9; Psalm 37:5; Proverbs 1:7-19; Romans 8:28; 12:1-2; 2 Corinthians 12:9; Galatians 6:1-5; Ephesians 5:1-20; 1 Peter 5:7; 1 John 5:4-5
Priorities	Matthew 4:1-11; 6:25-34; Mark 8:34-38; Luke 10:25-37; 12:13-34; Romans 12:1-2; 1 Corinthians 1:20-31; 1 Timothy 6:3-10; 1 John 2:15-17
Retirement	Numbers 6:24-26; Psalm 145; Matthew 25:31-46; Romans 12:1-2; Philippians 3:12,21; 2 Peter 1:2
Self-image	1 Samuel 16:7; Psalm 138:8; 139:14-16; Philippians 1:6; Hebrews 12:2
Sexual morality	Matthew 5:27-32; 15:19; Romans 1:18-32; 13:12-14; 1 Corinthians 5–7; Galatians 5:19-26; Colossians 3:1-17; 1 Thessalonians 4:3-8; Revelation 21:8
Sickness	Psalm 23; Mark 1:29-34; 6:53-56; James 5:14-16
Temptation	Proverbs 2:10-12; 1 Corinthians 10:12-13; Hebrews 2:14-18; James 1:2-15
Time management	Proverbs 12:11; 28:19; Mark 13:32-37; Luke 21:34-36; 1 Timothy 4:11-16; Titus 3:8-14
Truth	Psalm 119:153-60; John 8:31-47; 14:6-14; 16:4-15; 1 Timothy 2:1-7

Topics Relating to Living Your Life with God

Assurance of salvation	Matthew 24:35; John 5:24; 6:37; 10:27-30; 20:31; Romans 8:16,31,35-39; Hebrews 13:5; 1 John 5:11-13
Confessing sin	Psalm 32:1-6; Proverbs 28:13; Romans 14:11-12; 1 John 1:9
Eternal life	Luke 20:37-38; John 11:25-26; 1 Corinthians 15:19-22; 1 John 5:11-14
Faith	Matthew 17:20; Romans 4:3; 5:1-3; 10:17; Ephesians 2:8-9; Colossians 2:6-7; Hebrews 11:1,6; 12:2; James 1:3-6; 1 Peter 1:7;1 John 5:4
Fellowship	Psalm 122:1,9; Matthew 18:20; John 13:34; Acts 2:42,46; 1 Corinthians 1:9; Hebrews 10:24-25; 1 John 1:3,7
Forgiveness	Psalm 32:1-11; 51:1-17; Matthew 5:7, 39-48; 6:14-15; Romans 3:21-26; 8:31-39;

	10:5-13; Ephesians 4:31-32; Colossians 3:13; 1 John 1:5-10
God's will	Psalm 15; Micah 6:6-8; Matthew 5:14-16; Luke 9:21-27; Romans 13:8-14; 2 Peter 1:3-9; 1 John 4:7-21
Heaven	1 Kings 8:27; Matthew 6:19-21; John 14:1-3; 2 Corinthians 4:18–5:19; Ephesians 1:3; Colossians 3:1-2; 1 Peter 1:3-4; Revelation 4:1-11; 21:22–22:5
Hell	Matthew 10:28; 13:42,50; 18:8-9; 25:41,46; Luke 16:23-24; 2 Thessalonians 1:8-9; Revelation 20:10-15
Holy Spirit	Acts 5:3-4; 1 Corinthians 3:16; 6:19; 12:4-6; 2 Corinthians 13:14; 1 Peter 1:2
New life	Matthew 20:20-28; Romans 6:1-14; 12:1-21; Galatians 5:16-26; Ephesians 4:17-32; 1 John 4:7-21
Overcoming sin	2 Corinthians 5:17; Ephesians 4:22-24; Colossians 3:9-10; Titus 3:5-6
Salvation	John 3:1-21; Romans 1:16-17; 3:21-31; 5:1-11; 10:5-13; Ephesians 1:3-14; 2:1-10
Satan	Isaiah 14:12-15; Ezekiel 28:12-19; James 4:7; 1 John 4:4
Second coming of Christ	Luke 21:34-36; Acts 1:11; 1 Thessalonians 4:13-18; Titus 2:13; 2 Peter 3:8-14; 1 John 3:2-3
Sin	Isaiah 53:5-6; 59:1-2; John 8:34; Romans 3:23; 6:23; Galatians 6:7-8
Spiritual Growth	Romans 8:12-13; Galatians 5:16-23; Ephesians 3:17-19; 5:18; Colossians 1:9-11; 3:16; 1 Timothy 4:15; 2 Timothy 2:15; 1 Peter 2:2; 2 Peter 1:5-8; 3:18
What would Jesus do?	John 13:15; Romans 12:2; 1 Corinthians 2:16; Ephesians 5:1-2; Philippians 2:5,9; 1 John 2:6
Worship	Psalm 2:11; Psalm 96:8; Isaiah 12:5-6; John 4:21-24; Hebrews 12:28-29

What to Read When You're Feeling...

Addicted	Psalm 40:1-5,11-17; 116:1-7; Proverbs 23:29-35; 2 Corinthians 5:16-21; Ephesians 4:22-24
Afraid	Psalm 27:1,14; 56:11; 91:1-2; 121:1-8; Proverbs 3:25; 29:25; Isaiah 41:5-13; 51:12; Mark 4:35-41; John 14:27; Romans 8:28-29,31,35-39; Philippians

4:19; 2 Timothy 1:7; Hebrews 13:5-6;
1 John 4:13-18; Jude 24-25

Angry
Proverbs 14:17,29; 15:1,18; 19:11;
29:22; Ecclesiastes 7:9; Matthew 5:21-
24; Romans 12:17-21; Galatians 5:16-
26; Ephesians 4:25-32; James 1:19-21

Anxious
Psalm 25; Matthew 6:24-34; 10:26-31;
1 Peter 1:3-5; 5:7

Depressed
Psalm 16; 43; 130; Isaiah 61:1-4;
Jeremiah 15:10-21; Lamentations
3:55-57; John 3:14-17; Ephesians 3:14-21

Disappointed
Psalm 42:5,11; 43:5; 55:22; 126:6;
John 14:27; Romans 8:28;
2 Corinthians 4:8-10,16-18; 1 Peter 5:7

Discouraged
Joshua 1:9; Psalm 27:14; 34; 43:5;
Isaiah 12:1-6; John 14:1-3,27; 16:33;
19:25-27; Romans 15:13;
2 Corinthians 4:16-18; Philippians
4:10-13; Colossians 1:5,9-14; Hebrews
4:16; 6:9-12; 1 Peter 1:3-9; 1 John
5:14; Revelation 22:1-4

Frustrated
Job 21:1-16; 24:1-17; 36:1-26;
Matthew 7:13-14

Guilty
Psalm 32:1-2; Romans 8:1;
2 Corinthians 5:21; Ephesians 1:7;
Colossians 2:9-17; Titus 3:5

Impatient
Psalm 13; 37:1-7; 40:1-5; Ecclesiastes
3:1-15; Lamentations 3:25-33;
Hebrews 6:13-20; James 5:7-11

Indecisive
Joshua 24:15; 1 Kings 3; Esther 4-7;
Psalm 139; Daniel 2:14-23;
1 Corinthians 10:31; Colossians 3:12-
17; Hebrews 12:1-2; James 1:5

Insecure
Deuteronomy 31:1-8; Psalm 73:21-26;
108; Philippians 4:10-20; 1 John 3:19-24

Jealous
Proverbs 14:30; 24:19-20; Romans
1:29; 1 Corinthians 13:4; 1 Timothy
6:4; James 3:14-16

Lonely
Psalm 22; 42; John 14:15-31;
1 Corinthians 7:25-38; 12:1-31

Persecuted
Psalm 109; 119:153-60; Matthew 5:3-
12; John 15:18–16:4; Romans 8:18-30;
2 Corinthians 4:1-15; Hebrews 12:1-
11; 1 Peter 4:12-19

Prejudice
Matthew 7:1-5; Acts 10:34-36;
Galatians 3:26-29; Ephesians 2:11-22;
Colossians 3:5-11; James 2:1-13

Proud
Psalm 131; Mark 9:33-37; Luke 14:7-
11; 18:9-14; 22:24-27; Romans 12:14-
16; 1 Corinthians 1:18-31;
2 Corinthians 12:1-10

Rejected	Psalm 38; Isaiah 52:13–53:12; Matthew 9:9-13; Luke 4:16-30; John 15:18–16:4; Ephesians 1:3-14; 1 Peter 2:1-10
Resentful	Leviticus 19:17-18; Matthew 5:23-26; Luke 6:27-36; Ephesians 4:25-32
Stressed	Isaiah 55:1-9; Matthew 11:25-30; John 4:1-30; 2 Corinthians 6:3-10; Revelation 22:17
Suicidal	Exodus 20:13; Deuteronomy 31:6; Psalm 50:15; 77:7-15; 98:1-2; Jeremiah 33:3; Lamentations 3:22-24; Nahum 1:7; Matthew 11:28; John 10:10; 1 Peter 5:8-10
Tempted	Psalm 19:12-14; 141; Luke 4:1-13; Hebrews 2:11-18; 4:14-16; James 1:12-18
Tired	Psalm 3:5-6; 4:4-8; Isaiah 35:1-10; Matthew 11:25-30; 2 Thessalonians 3:16; Hebrews 4:1-11
Worried	Proverbs 11:7; Ecclesiastes 5:10-20; Matthew 6:24-34; Luke 12:13-21; 1 Timothy 6:6-10
Worthless	Isaiah 6:1-8; Jeremiah 1:4-10; Galatians 1:11-24; Ephesians 4:1-16; 1 Peter 2:4-10

Index

We've included this Index to help you find a particular person, place, or Bible word. It doesn't include everything...just our favorite stuff. If you can't find it here, try looking at the Contents or reading the Introduction for other helpful tips.

Download a Deeper Experience

Bruce Bickel and Stan Jantz are part of a faith-based online community called ConversantLife.com. At this website, people engage their faith in entertainment, creative arts, science and technology, global concerns, and other culturally relevant topics. While you're reading this book, or after you have finished reading, go to www.conversantlife.com/brucebickel and www.conversantlife.com/stanjantz and use these icons to read and download additional material from Bruce and Stan that is related to the book.

 Resources: Download study guide materials for personal devotions or a small-group Bible study.

 Videos: Click on this icon for interviews with Bruce and Stan and video clips on various topics.

 Blogs: Read through Bruce and Stan's blogs and articles and comment on them.

 Podcasts: Stream ConversantLife.com podcasts and audio clips from Bruce and Stan.

conversant **life** .com

engage your faith

The authors would enjoy hearing from you.
The best ways to contact them are
Twelve Two Media
P.O. Box 25997
Fresno, CA 93729

E-mail
info@christianity101online.com

Web site
www.twelvetwomedia.com

Exclusive Online Feature
Here's a study feature you're really going to like!
Simply go online at

www.christianity101online.com

There you will find a website designed exclusively for readers of *Knowing the Bible 101* and other books and Bible studies in the Christianity 101® series. When you log on to the site, just click on the book you are studying, and you will discover additional information, resources and helps, including

- *Background Material*—We can't put everything in this book, so this online section includes more material, such as historical, geographical, theological, and biographical information.

- *More Questions*—Do you need more questions for your group study? Here are additional questions for each chapter. Bible study leaders will find this especially helpful.

- *Answers to Your Questions*—Do you have a question about something you read in this book? Post your question and an "online scholar" will respond.

- *FAQs*—In this section are answers to some of the most frequently asked questions about the topic you are studying.

What are you waiting for? Go online and become a part of the Christianity 101® community!

Christianity 101® Bible Studies

Genesis: Discovering God's Answers to Life's Ultimate Questions

"In the beginning" says it all. Genesis sets the stage for the drama of human history. This guide gives you a good start and makes sure you don't get lost along the way.

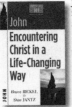

John: Encountering Christ in a Life-Changing Way

This study reveals who Jesus is by demonstrating the dramatic changes He made in the lives of the people He met, including Nicodemus, the woman at the well, Lazarus, and John, "the disciple whom Jesus loved."

Acts: Living in the Power of the Holy Spirit

Bruce and Stan offer a straightforward look at the ongoing ministry of Jesus through the church. They highlight the drama of the early Christians' triumph over darkness and their explosive growth from a band of 120 fearful followers to a thriving, worldwide church.

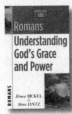

Romans: Understanding God's Grace and Power

Paul's letter to the church in Rome is his clearest explanation and application of the good news. This fresh study of Romans assures you that the Gospel is God's answer to every human need.

1 & 2 Corinthians: Finding Your Unique Place in God's Plan

This enlightening study explores the apostle Paul's helpful responses to issues that churches continue to face today: maintaining unity in the church, exercising spiritual gifts, and identifying authentic Christian ministry.

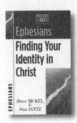

Ephesians: Finding Your Identity in Christ

Verse for verse, the book of Ephesians is one of the most profound, powerful, and practical books in the Bible. This guide reveals the heart of Paul's teaching on who believers are in Christ.

Philippians/Colossians: Experiencing the Joy of Knowing Christ

This new 13-week study of two of Paul's most intimate letters will inspire you to know Christ more intimately and maintain your passion and vision. Filled with helpful background information, up-to-date applications, and penetrating, open-ended questions.

Galatians: Walking in God's Grace

The apostle Paul blows the lid off fake, "rules-added" Christianity and describes life in God's Spirit, through His grace—which is still God's way of freeing you to live out your full potential as His child.

James: Working Out Your Faith

James is bursting with no-nonsense guidance to help you grow in practical ways, including perceiving God's will, maintaining a proper perspective on wealth and poverty, and demonstrating true wisdom in your speech and actions.

Revelation: Unlocking the Mysteries of the End Times

Have you ever read the final chapters of the Scriptures, only to finish with more questions than answers? Bruce and Stan help you understand Revelation's encouraging message and apply it to your life today.